GIVE AND TAKE

GIVE AND TAKE

THE COMPLETE GUIDE TO NEGOTIATING STRATEGIES AND TACTICS

Revised Edition

CHESTER L. KARRASS

HarperBusiness
A Division of HarperCollins*Publishers*

A hardcover edition of this book was published in 1993 by HarperBusiness, a division of HarperCollins Publishers.

First paperback edition published 1995.

Designed by George J. McKeon

The Library of Congress has catalogued the hardcover edition as follows:

Karrass, Chester Louis.
Give and take : the complete guide to negotiating strategies and tactics / Chester L. Karrass. — Rev. ed.
p. cm.
Includes index.
ISBN 0-88730-606-3 (cloth)
1. Negotiation. I. Title.
BF637.N4K27 1993
658.4—dc20 92-54749

ISBN 0-88730-743-4 (pbk.)

95 96 97 98 99 ❖/RRD 10 9 8 7 6 5 4 3 2 1

This book is dedicated to my wife, Virginia, and children, Lynn and Gary, and dear George and Elie who were always there. With all it's been a loving kind of give and take.

ACKNOWLEDGMENTS

Serious work on a subject as complex as negotiation cannot be accomplished without help. I wish to acknowledge the far-sighted research support provided by the Hughes organization and its executives, Theodore Kotsovolos and the late William A. VanAllen, a bright star that dimmed all too soon.

In addition help was graciously provided by Gary and Lynn Karrass with whom I exchanged many words and ideas. For the assistance and good judgment that it takes to change a manuscript into a finished product I owe much to the talented efforts of my editor, Cynthia Vartan.

CONTENTS

INTRODUCTION

The two hundred strategies and tactics in this book have been organized in an easy-to-use fashion to help people put them to work. They have been successfully applied for thousands of years by people who learned them by intuition or from generation to generation. Now, in the light of modern psychology and business, we have the tools to understand the subtleties of negotiation as never before. With this guide to negotiation, anyone can apply the ideas in their business and personal transactions.

This is the first book written as a complete guide to practical negotiating strategies, tactics, and countermeasures. If this appears to be too bold a statement, it isn't. I have run into nothing like it in ten years of research and specialization in negotiation.

For the past twenty years, as Director of Karrass Seminars, I have been presenting negotiating seminars to thousands of business executives all over the world. Like everyone, they want to know what works at the table, why it works, and what to do to defend themselves. This book was written in response to a real need: the desire of practical people to conduct their negotiations more effectively.

GIVE AND TAKE

ACCEPTANCE TIME

The idea of acceptance time is so simple that it is often overlooked. Yet, when understood, it has the power to make each of us more effective.

People need time to accept anything new or different. Both parties walk into a negotiating session with somewhat unrealistic goals. They start with all kinds of misconceptions and assumptions. Being human, they hope against hope that their goals will, for a change, be easily met. The process of negotiating is usually a rude awakening. The low price hoped for by the buyer begins to look impossible. The easy sale that the seller longs for eludes him or her. Wishes are converted into reality through the cold water of bargaining.

Can we expect the buyer or seller to adjust to these new and undesired realities immediately? Of course not. Resistance to change is universal. It takes time to get used to ideas that are foreign or unpleasant. We can even get used to the idea of death given a long enough period to do so. Acceptance time is as important in negotiation as it is in life.

The buyers need time to accept the thought that they will have to pay a higher price than planned. The sellers are not ready to retreat from their price in the first few minutes of negotiation. *Both they and their organizations need adequate acceptance time.* That is why the perceptive seller tells the buyer of a possible price increase long before it happens. It gives the buyer and his or her people time to reconcile themselves to the idea.

When you ask people to change new ideas for old, you are asking that they discard old friends. Right or wrong, they have grown accustomed and committed to them. Put yourself in their position. Isn't it logical that they will be more receptive to your viewpoint, given the time to adjust? The Asians say, "Time brings things by slow degrees." Leave room in your planning for the concept of acceptance time.

ACHIEVEMENT AND ASPIRATION LEVEL: IS WHAT YOU GET RELATED TO WHAT YOU WANT?

At one time or another, most of us have told our children, "If you aim higher, you'll come out better." We tend to subscribe to that idea in our daily lives. The crucial business question is, "If you aim higher in negotiation do you come out better?"

Two professors tried an experiment. They built a barricade between bargainers so that neither could see or hear the other. Demands and offers were passed under the table. Instructions to both were identical, with one exception: One was told he or she was expected to achieve a $7.50 settlement; the other a $2.50 settlement. The experiment was designed to favor neither party—that is, both had an equal chance to get $5. What happened in test after test? People who expected $7.50 got around $7.50, while those told to expect $2.50 got close to $2.50.

I tried a similar experiment, but the conditions were different. Where the professors' subjects were students, mine were professionals; where they limited communication, I created face-to-face encounters on a one-to-one or team-to-team basis. Where they induced an artificial level of aspiration, I let each person decide individually. My experiment verified that people with higher expectations got higher settlements. Those expecting less were willing to settle for less.

How people set and revise goals in life provides an insight into how they do so in negotiation. People fix targets for themselves even when they are unaware they are doing so. When we choose a neighborhood to live in, a fraternity, or even a church, we say something about our status goals. Business executives describe their goals by the people they mingle with and the kinds of people they hire as assistants. We are continually setting objectives in life, getting feedback, and revising goals up or down.

An individual's level of aspiration represents the *intended* performance goal. It is a reflection of how much he or she wants; that is, a standard that they set for themselves. *It is not a wish, but a firm intention to perform that involves the individual's self-image.* Failure to perform results in loss of self-respect. When people are asked, "What score would you *like* to get next time?" they are more unrealistic in setting goals than those who are asked, "What score do you *expect* to get next time?" In one case, self-image is involved; in the other, it is not. In the first case, there is less commitment to the score than in the second.

Aspiration level, risk taking, and success are related. In choosing goals, individuals are like gamblers laying a bet. They balance a need for success with its tangible and intangible rewards against the probability of failure and its possible costs. People cannot make this computation consciously. Instead, they do so unconsciously, based on their past history of success and failure in similar situations.

Aspirations rise and fall with the tide of success. Level of aspiration is the yardstick by which people take bets on their own performance. It is a roulette wheel in which an individual's biggest bankroll is at stake: self-respect. Goals are set in accordance with the risk a person is willing to take. People set targets in negotiation as they do in life. They change them as success or failure is experienced.

A negotiation is a full-circle feedback system. Goals are set by the buyer and seller. Then comes the feedback. Every demand, concession, threat, delay, fact, deadline, authority limit, and good-guy/bad-guy remark has an effect on each party's expectations. The "price" goes up and down in their heads with each word and new development.

In negotiation, people who set a higher target and commit themselves to it will do better than those willing to settle for less. There is a risk. People who aspire to more get more, but they also deadlock more. The trade-off is one that can be evaluated only by good judgment. Despite the risk, *Up your aspiration level.*

ADVANCE PAYMENTS: WATCH OUT

No matter how much a subcontractor cries that he or she needs advance payments, I don't give any unless:

1. There are measurable guarantees that the funds will be used precisely for the purposes indicated.
2. There are firm and measurable performance milestones tied to the payments.
3. There are sufficient and measurable reserves held back at each milestone to assure that the next milestone and the total job will be performed.

Sometimes, despite my attitude against advance payments, I fail to follow my own rules. More often than not, when that happens, I get taken. But then, even at my age, there are at least a few dumb mistakes in me yet.

AGENDA

Those who control the agenda formulate the questions and time the decisions. In business as in diplomacy, the agenda represents an opportunity to gain and hold the initiative. It is the first test of purpose in a negotiation and sets the stage for what follows.

Diplomats fuss about the agenda. Not so businesspeople. They rarely give it much thought and thereby forfeit a good opportunity. I have seen multimillion-dollar negotiations in which the agenda discussions took only fifteen minutes. Neither party attached value to the matter, nor understood its significance.

It is a lot easier for buyers to control the agenda than sellers. Occasionally, a good salesperson can take the reins if the buyer is indifferent. Both should be aware of what an agenda can do to shape the outcome of a negotiation.

A good agenda can clarify or hide motives. It can establish rules that are fair to both or biased in one direction. It can keep talks on track or permit digressions. It can coordinate the discussion of an issue with moves away from the table. It can force a quick decision or permit a patient exploration of facts. The person who controls the agenda *controls what will be said and, perhaps more important, what will not be said.*

Always try to negotiate an agenda before talks begin. It will help you keep the initiative. The following guidelines are pertinent:

1. Don't accept the other person's agenda without thinking through the consequences.
2. Consider where and how issues can best be introduced.
3. Schedule the discussion of issues to give yourself time to think.

4. Study your opponents' proposed agenda for what it deliberately leaves out.
5. Be careful not to imply that your "must" demands are negotiable. You can show your resolve early by not permitting such items into the discussion.

An agenda is a plan for discussion. It is not a contract. If either party doesn't like the format after talks begin, they must have the courage to change it. Neither can afford to treat the matter lightly.

AGREEMENTS, UNDERSTANDINGS, AND PROCEDURES: A BIG DIFFERENCE

President Bush found himself whipped about in dealing with the Iraqis before, during, and after Desert Storm, the Iraq war. Every time he thought he had an agreement, he was told it was only an understanding. When he thought he had an understanding, the Iraqis, under Saddam Hussein, said it was a simple procedural problem. If you don't understand the difference between agreements, understandings, and procedures in negotiation, you may find yourself in worse shape than Bush.

It is worthwhile to develop a uniform way of looking at these three words. For practical purposes, we may consider a procedure as a way of doing something, an understanding as an expression of a mutual viewpoint and attitude on an issue, and an agreement as a conclusive commitment to mutually acceptable terms.

You are probably wondering what difference all this makes. After all, isn't a deal a deal? My contention is that it is not enough merely to reach an agreement. Even when two parties have the best of intentions, agreements break down for a variety of reasons. Breakdowns occur because those responsible for implementing the agreement often do not understand the common viewpoints, attitudes, and backgrounds that brought about the agreement. Sometimes the breakdown occurs because neither party knows how to make the agreement work or how to prove that it is or is not working.

Assume that you are a landscape contractor and I am the owner of a home and lot. We agree that you will do certain specific work and that I will pay you $20,000 for that work. But before signing the agreement, we reach an understanding as to what quality is expected and the general kinds of plants and bricks to be used. We also agree that any later changes will be made at cost.

A good agreement should not only spell out the work and dollars involved, but also the understanding behind the written words and a procedure for measuring cost in the event that additions or deletions of work occur. A poor contract would leave us bickering about whether the quality level achieved met our verbal understanding and whether costs were being accumulated fairly.

The next time you are in a negotiation, better say to yourself, "It is not enough just to reach agreement on terms. Are there any understandings and procedures that ought to be laid out in detail right now?"

ANSWERING QUESTIONS: TIPS FOR BETTER ANSWERS

The seventeenth-century English philosopher Sir Francis Bacon said that negotiation was a process of discovery. Questions are raised and answers given, statements made and rebuttals offered. Great pressure falls on us to provide quick statements and sensible answers to hard questions. The trouble is that few of us are good at thinking on our feet. We get our best answers in the car going home.

Better answers are possible. It is surprising what a few simple precautions will do to improve your ability to handle questions. Perhaps the most important thing is to write down in advance the questions most likely to arise. An associate acting in the role of devil's advocate can raise a host of hard questions prior to negotiation. The more time you have to think about them, the better your answers will be.

The suggestions that follow work in any question-and-answer situation. Those who have faced a barrage of questions from probing buyers, skeptical auditors, or the Internal Revenue Service will recognize their value.

1. Give yourself time to think.
2. Never answer until you clearly understand the question.
3. Recognize that some questions do not deserve answers.
4. Answers can be given that satisfy part of a question rather than all of it.
5. One way to evade a question is to answer one that was not asked.
6. Some answers can be postponed on the basis of incomplete knowledge or not remembering.
7. Make the other party work for answers. Get him or her to clarify the question.
8. When the other person interrupts, let him or her.
9. Correct answers in negotiation are not necessarily good answers. They may be foolish. Don't elaborate.

I will never forget one witness at the Iran-Contra hearings. For almost two days, he sat before the senators and was asked a barrage of questions about where and to whom the money went. Hardly one was answered. The witness never quite understood the question, so he kept answering questions that were never asked. He smiled a lot, never got angry, and remained confused to the end. It was the committee that finally gave up.

The art of answering questions lies in knowing what to say and what not to say. It does not lie in being right or wrong. A negotiation is not a classroom. There are few yes-or-no answers.

ANSWERS THAT DON'T ANSWER

People who want to be very careful about their answers use certain pet expressions. The next time you listen to a politician, a witness, or an opposing negotiator trying to field hard questions, watch for these responses:

1. Please repeat the question.
2. I don't quite understand the question.
3. That depends on . . .
4. That's quite another subject.
5. You've got to understand the history. It really began . . .
6. Before I answer that you've got to understand the detailed procedure.
7. It appears to me . . .
8. As I recall it . . .
9. I don't recall.
10. I have no firsthand experience with that but have heard . . .
11. It varies because . . .
12. Sometimes it does work that way.
13. That depends on . . .
14. It's not a question of yes or no. It's a question of degree (more or less).
15. Your question is just splitting hairs. You're like a professor playing with words.
16. You must understand the reason. It was not just one thing that caused it, but many. For example . . .
17. Let's get specific (in response to a general question).
18. It generally works this way (in response to a specific question).
19. Please break the question down into its parts.
20. No, it's not quite the way you said.
21. I can't talk about that because . . .

22. It's a matter of how you look at it.
23. I don't mean to quibble with you, but . . .
24. I can't agree with the statement part of your question.

ASSOCIATES YOU DON'T NEED

There is a theory in psychology which says that if I like Joe and you like Joe, we are likely to find other things we both like. This theory is called "cognitive balance." The principle applies to the attitudes of people toward other persons, objects, or ideas. It also works in reverse. If I like Joe and you don't, we will have trouble getting together on other issues. I will either persuade you to like Joe, or you will begin to move away from me and my ideas.

I recall a recent situation in which this theory was operative. A defense contractor formed a team with a conglomerate to bid on a large government job. The contractor learned later in off-the-record conversations that he had lost the job because the conglomerate associate had a bad reputation for taking advantage of the government.

Common sense says that a person should disassociate from those who make it harder to reach an agreement. Legitimate businesspeople look down on those who associate with deadbeats, con men, or fast talkers. Those who traffic with shady underworld characters make poor partners. In the business world, as elsewhere, it is presumed that "birds of a feather flock together."

The tactics of disassociation are as important as those of association. Good planning requires that a person search for the right partners. It also requires that a negotiator ask, "Will any of my associates make it harder for me to reach a favorable settlement with the other party?" If so, do something about it.

ASSUMPTIONS ARE NOT TO BE TRUSTED

Never trust your assumptions. They are as likely to be wrong as right. I had a professor who used to start his class every term by writing the word "assume" on the blackboard. "ASS–U–ME," he said, "can make an ass of you and me."

Salespeople make a lot of dumb assumptions, such as "She'll never pay that much"; or "There's lots of competition"; or "He doesn't have enough money"; or "They don't want to do business with us after the last screw-up"; or "I'm sure we're not the low bidder." Such assumptions can defeat the salesperson before he or she starts and may, in fact, be dead wrong.

Assumptions are potential hurdles that can move us in the wrong direction. They can lead buyers to make high offers when low ones are called for. They can cause sellers to make low demands and quick concessions when opposite actions are warranted. Assumptions can seduce us into believing deadlines when patience is by far the better course.

The reality of negotiation is that we must and should make assumptions about our opponents. We must assess as best we can what they can or will do, what risks they are willing to take, and what decision criteria are most important to them (price, delivery, quality, or service). The important thing to remember is that your assumptions are just that. They are no better than poorly educated guesses, at best.

Don't fall in love with your assumptions. Check them out. They are neither right nor wrong until proven so.

AUTHORITY TACTICS: COUNTER-MEASURES

Long-run relationships suffer if a company encourages its people to play with authority. Yet many companies have no compunctions about long-run relationships. They operate on the basis that "in the long run there may be no long run." So a person has only one choice: to be on guard. It isn't enough just to ask the question, "Have you got the authority to make a deal?" More is necessary.

1. Know the history of the company and the individual with whom you are dealing. If people have a history of fooling around with authority, you can expect a problem.
2. Have the courage to ask the other person to describe his or her authority as clearly as possible. Do not accept partial or evasive answers.
3. Know your opponent's organization structure.
4. Get the other person's boss to tell you if any authority limits exist.
5. Find out in advance how long it takes to get an approval cleared.
6. Find out if those needed for approval are available.
7. Get a clear idea of all documents required for approval.
8. Do not state your authority unless pressed to. Do not be too clear about it unless you have to.
9. Be prepared to walk out if you are treated to last-minute authority changes. Test them hard.
10. Keep your people informed that the opponent may use such tactics. Don't let them or yourself be surprised.

The trouble with these countermeasures is that they do not guarantee success against those who want to fool around with authority. Nothing does. Nevertheless, an understanding of authority tactics and the countermeasures available against their abuse is bound to help.

AVERAGES ARE ALWAYS NEGOTIABLE

I once read an amazing statistic: "The average American family has one and one-half children." That made me think. Like all averages, it was true and untrue at the same time.

We are often hypnotized by meaningless numbers that look right. No accounting system is perfect. Cost accounts, overhead rates, administrative expenses, profit margins, bad-debt allowances, depreciation schedules, and return-on-investment figures all fit the "one-half" fallacy. They are simply more subtle, not more accurate.

Be skeptical the next time someone shows you a number like 120 percent overhead or a standard interest charge. Ask whether the average (and that's what it is) should really apply to your transaction. Is the depreciation rate the one you should pay, or does it include costs on buildings and equipment at the North Pole? Perhaps the high interest you are being asked to pay includes the amount set aside for deadbeats. Should you pay their tab if your credit record is good? Why pay a percentage for an engineering department you don't need when all you buy is nuts and bolts?

The next time someone says, "I'll sell it to you at cost," watch out. You may find that cost includes a big salary for the merchant's long-retired grandfather.

List prices, standard products, and discount schedules are negotiable. Why? Because they represent averages. They were designed to fit the average customer at some average period of time. You are you. You are not the average. Take it from there. *Averages are always negotiable.*

BEFORE NEGOTIATIONS BEGIN: A MONEY-SAVING IDEA

The buyer should try to begin negotiations after getting the seller to commit to as low a price as possible. The seller, on the other hand, should try to leave as much room as possible by starting as high as competition or experience will permit. This not only makes good sense but is sometimes forgotten in the heat of getting things done.

When a buyer is desperate for a quick delivery, a high-quality product or round-the-clock maintenance service, he or she should not start the negotiation by emphasizing these points. The seller who is aware of these strong needs will be likely to stand firm and bid higher. The prudent buyer will keep sellers anxious about making the sale at the bidding and early stage of bargaining so that they will set their sights lower. The need for the hot delivery or the special service should be one of the issues discussed much later.

This strategy permits the seller to get more involved with closing the deal. Once he or she works to prepare the proposal and starts to make price concessions, it becomes harder to risk losing the job for delivery, quality, or service reasons.

BIG-POT TACTIC: REAL AND STRAW ISSUES

Once upon a time there was a wise man who lived in a Russian village. An unhappy woman came to him, seeking advice. She lived in a small hut, barely large enough for her husband and two children. It came to pass that hard times befell her husband's parents. They had no place to live. Being kind, she let them move into the already-crowded hut. The crowding soon got on her nerves. "What should I do?" she cried to the wise man.

He stroked his beard, thought awhile, and asked, "Have you a cow, dear lady?"

"Yes," she said, "but what has this to do with my problem?"

"I have an answer," he advised. "Take the cow into the hut for a week and then come back." She followed his advice reluctantly. After all, he had a good reputation as a wise man.

A week passed and things got worse. Every time the cow turned, the six occupants had to change seats. It was impossible to sleep. The woman returned to the wise man in tears. "I am more miserable than ever," she said and told him the whole story.

He stroked his beard, thought awhile, and asked, "Have you any chickens, dear lady?"

"Yes," she said, "but what has that to do with my problem?"

"I have an answer," he advised. "Take the chickens into the hut for a week and then come back." More skeptical than ever, she again took his advice, for he was a wise man.

A week later, hysterical, she returned. "You are insane," she said. "Your advice is bad. My hut is now impossible to live in. The cow turns, the chickens fly, the in-laws cough, the children find feathers in their soup, and I fight with my husband. It's all your fault."

He stroked his beard, thought awhile and said, "Dear lady, try one more thing when you go home. Take out the cow. Come back in a week."

"This man is a bit of a fool," she thought, but decided to follow his advice for the last time.

A week later she returned. "How do you feel, dear lady?" he asked.

"This is ridiculous," she said, "but I feel a little better now that the cow is out of the hut."

He stroked his beard, thought awhile and said, "I have a solution to your problem. Take out the chickens."

The lady took out the chickens and lived happily ever after with her husband, her children, and her in-laws.

In essence, that's the way buyers use the big-pot tactic in dealing with sellers. They create issues, some of which are real and some of which are made of straw. They do so with four purposes in mind: (1) to reduce the seller's aspiration level; (2) to provide themselves with trading room; (3) to assure others in their own organization that they are hard bargainers; and (4) to make it easier for the salesperson to take a lower price package back to his or her own people. When the salesperson tells management that the buyer has agreed to remove the cows and chickens, everybody breathes a sigh of relief. It could have been worse.

There is reliable evidence supporting the big-pot tactic. Experiments by me and others confirm that people who start with higher demands come out better. Union negotiators know by practical experience that the more they ask for, the more they get. They started using the big-pot tactic long before any experimenter thought of proving it.

What can a salesperson or labor-relations negotiator do to offset the big-pot tactic?

1. Have patience. Some issues lose importance.
2. Penetrate the real issues by engaging in off-the-record discussions.
3. Ignore or bypass some issues.
4. Suggest sweeping trades of unrelated issues.
5. Protest that the opponent is clouding matters and wasting time.

Above all, don't be satisfied with a bone. Some demands are nothing but straw issues. The buyer wants to trade the bone for something of value. Don't let him or her get away with it. In fact, with some imagination, sellers can build their own straw issues into the proposal. The big-pot tactic gives you room to negotiate and compromise. In the absence of other concessions, it gives your opponent something to take home.

BODY LANGUAGE: IS IT A PUT-ON?

Body language is getting a big play these days. It is being plugged by people who know better as the key to instant perception; the easy way to read people. Nonsense!

Business interest in body language comes and goes like the tides. There are years when four or five books reach the bookstores annually, and then long periods where none are published. These are people who contend that body language is the key to instant perception. That, in my opinion, is nonsense; but there are some things negotiators should be aware of as they deal with others.

When smart liars want to hide the truth, they usually hide their body signs as well. Some years ago, a reclusive billionaire hid from the world. Many writers tried to contact Howard Hughes because he was so prominent in Hollywood, in the defense industry, and in the airlines business as majority owner of Trans World Airlines. Anything written about Howard Hughes was headline material and a potential best-seller.

One person who claimed to have interviewed and written about Hughes was a writer named Clifford Irving. Anyone who watched Clifford Irving tell bold-faced lies about Hughes will recall how cocksure he appeared on television, how directly he looked into people's eyes when answering their questions, how relaxed he was. How could you disbelieve a person who was so open about his answers? You couldn't. What brought Irving down was Mr. Hughes who, angered at being used in this way, sent a personal message from his hiding place denying all Clifford Irving had said. Irving's book about Hughes was laughed out of the stores.

Those of us who saw the Senate Iran-Contra hearings heard men and women contradict one another without batting an eyelash. Somebody was lying, but who? Body language gave us no insight whatsoever.

If ever there was an opportunity to read a person's body language, it was at the Clarence Thomas Supreme Court hearings, at which Anita Hill claimed that Mr. Thomas had sexually harassed her. Those who watched the hearings are still arguing about who was telling the truth. Body language played a very ambiguous role in justifying the contentions of both Mr. Thomas and Ms. Hill.

Body language is not the quick fix it is played up to be. It is ambiguous, easily misinterpreted, and highly subjective. It may, like a Rorschach test, give a deeper insight into the viewer than the person being viewed.

Most of the research in this field is superficial. Julius Fast wrote a book about body language based on observations on subway trains. Others have used videotape under uncontrolled conditions and came up with whatever they wanted to. The best work has been done at the University of California (Los Angeles) by Professor Albert Mehrobian. His book, *Silent Messages,* is worth reading. It describes his carefully controlled experiments and findings.

Professor Mehrobian came to two clear conclusions:

1. *The Rule of "Liking":* This principle says that when you like people, things, ideas, or yourself, you open up, remove barriers, and move toward the people, things, and ideas. When you don't like people, things, ideas, or yourself, you hide, close up, build defenses, and move away.
2. *The Rule of Dominance:* This principle says that those on top of situations, people, things, ideas, or themselves are relaxed, take center stage, project outward, and encompass the interaction. Those not on top of situations, people, things, ideas, or themselves are tense, take peripheral positions, project inwardly, and are engulfed by the interchange.

My own interpretation of the professor's writing has a third conclusion: When people have mixed feelings and have not made up their minds about other people, things, or ideas, they act guarded, controlled, and uncommitted. They suffer from the tension of indecision and want to make up their minds one way or another. To carry them through this difficult period, people search for reassurance. They stroke their chins, rub their faces, play with their arms, legs, or head.

Most of the body signs you observe fit one or more of these three categories. There are dangers in drawing big inferences from tiny clues. You may be seeing what the other person wants you to see.

People put on a good front when they have to.

BOGEY TACTIC: THIS IS ALL I'VE GOT

The bogey works. It is simple, effective, and ethical. In the hands of a skilled buyer, it can benefit both parties. As for the salesperson, the bogey may well be an opportunity to close the sale and improve the profit margin.

Here's how the bogey works: A homeowner wants to landscape and fence the backyard in an unusual way. The job is reasonably complex due to the layout. A bid of $15,000 comes from a local outfit. It is neither the lowest nor highest bid, but it is the most reliable and responsive. The trouble is that the buyer wants to spend $10,000, not $15,000.

"I love your proposal," says the buyer, "but I have only $10,000," then tries to make the dollar limit as believable to the seller as possible. The seller generally responds to the $10,000 bogey by either changing the proposal or showing what alternatives are available. The buyer learns things he or she never knew existed about fencing, lighting, brickwork, planting, and waterfalls, and is then in a better position to buy sensibly.

The bogey should *always* be considered when purchasing a relatively complex product or service. Uncle Sam uses it when he gets a defense contractor to take a close look at his million-dollar proposal because the government budget is only $700,000. A school district uses it when it tells its architect to redesign the high-school building to fit the $22-million limitation imposed by the bond issue. An industrial buyer does it when showing the salesperson that the amount budgeted by the accounting department is less than what the seller bid. What happens in each of these bogey examples is similar to what happened to our landscape buyer earlier. All of them learn about the product and the alternatives available to them.

Why does it work? When a buyer says, "I love your product but have only so much money," the salesperson tends to respond in a positive, friendly fashion. How can you be hostile toward someone who likes you and your product? The salesperson gets involved with the buyer and his or her problem. All that remains between them and a closed sale is a little problem-solving.

The negotiation moves away from a competitive affair to one of cooperation. The salesperson, knowing that budgets do exist in the real world, tends to feel sorry for the buyer. His or her frustration is directed against the "system" that senselessly and unfeelingly created the obstacle. The salesperson starts taking a new look at the buyer's real needs. Before long it is discovered that some items in the original price can be trimmed away, others can be changed, and still others can be adjusted by the buyer to meet the budget. Each party has helped the other reach its overall goals.

"Tiger teams" are highly effective bogey users. Every once in a while, purchasing managements are faced with an especially difficult assignment. They are asked to buy all the material necessary for a complex program at 50 to 80 percent of the originally estimated cost. This usually happens because the company finds itself losing large amounts of money on a job. A "tiger team" consisting of purchasing, engineering, and production people is put together to meet the seemingly impossible bogey.

The amazing thing is how often "tiger teams" *do* reach their targets. Ordinarily, it is hard to get people with different functions to work together closely. Not so with the "tiger teams." Their morale is high. They get seller after seller involved in the problem. Specifications are changed, quality standards restudied, and frills eliminated. What often results from this close buyer-seller coordination is a functionally usable product at a lower price.

Part of the reason that the bogey is so effective is that it involves the salesperson's ego. People like to help others in need. The bogey gives the salesperson a chance to show his or her knowledge of the business and dedication to the buyer's well-being. The bogey may not necessarily lead to a lower price for the buyer, but he or she will be better off by learning a lot more about the product than was known before.

BOGEY-TACTIC COUNTERMEASURES FOR THE SELLER

Can sellers handle the bogey tactic and make it work? Yes, they can. This is what the seller should think and do when a buyer throws a bogey.

1. Test the bogey. Most budgets are flexible.
2. Have alternate designs, delivery, and price packages available *before* you come to the negotiation.
3. If you are not prepared for the bogey, ask for time to study the problem.
4. Find out who the real decision makers are and whether they have already made a decision as to what they want. They may like what you have offered and not want it changed at all.
5. Change the time shape of money. If the buyer doesn't have enough money now, he or she may have it later, may prefer to stretch out the payments, or pay after Christmas.
6. Find out who has the money and who pays the final bill.

7. Let the buyers do some things for themselves to meet their own bogey.

The salesperson who is prepared to handle a bogey can turn it into an opportunity. He or she can provide the buyer with a product that meets needs but still leaves a greater profit for the seller than before. The path to better results for the seller lies in saying, before negotiations begin, "What will I do if the buyer throws a bogey at me?" If the bogey is handled right, he or she will close the sale while the competition is still floundering around.

BOGEYS THAT A SALESPERSON CAN USE

The essence of the buyer's bogey is "I love what you have to sell, but I have only so much money. Please help me." The seller's bogey, in response, should be "I'd love to make this sale to you, but cannot unless we solve a few simple problems first."

These seller bogeys fit the model above:

1. The minimum order is $100.
2. If you want size 42, you'll have to buy some size 48.
3. This machine must be sold with the two-year warranty.
4. If you want this price, we can do it only if the delivery is in six months.
5. We can meet your requirements if you give us 100 percent of the order.
6. This is our standard model. If you can change your specification to fit it, we will be in a better position to meet your price needs than anyone.
7. We can do it, but you will have to change the design like this to fit our production line.
8. We will do it if you give us an advance payment of $10,000.

Bogeys make sense for buyers and sellers alike. For the seller, bogeys can help close a sale, increase an order, offer a better product, or zero in on the buyer's real budget.

BOOBY TRAPS: BLUFFING, LYING, AND POKER PLAYING

To what extent are the ethics of the poker table applicable to negotiating? In poker we know that there are rules of play. Bluffing is certainly within the rules. In poker, as in negotiation, a person is not expected to reveal strength or intentions prematurely. However, there are prohibitions against certain kinds of bluffing. Opening with less than a pair of jacks is taboo, for example. Also taboo are such tactics as keeping an ace up one's sleeve, collusion between players, or setting up ceiling peepholes, as was once done cleverly by a team of cheats at a prominent Beverly Hills social club.

The ethical problems associated with misrepresentation are not easy for those engaged in diplomacy or bargaining. The British civil service once published this interesting guideline for its personnel:

> The rule as regards statements which are intended or are likely to become public is simple. Nothing may be said which is not true; but it is as unnecessary as it is sometimes undesirable, even in the public interest, to say everything relevant which is true; and the facts given may be arranged in any convenient order. It is wonderful what can be done within these limits by a skillful draftsman. It might be said, cynically, but with some measure of truth that the perfect reply to an embarrassing question in the House of Commons is one that is brief, appears to answer the question completely, if challenged can be proved to be accurate in every word, gives no opening for awkward "supplementaries," and discloses really nothing.

I am inclined to view the matter as the British do. Discretion in making claims and statements should not be confused with misrepresentation. Business bluffing is part of negotiating. However, the rules forbid and should penalize outright lying, false claims, bribing an opponent, stealing secrets through electronic devices, or threatening the physical well-being of the opponents or their families. Those at a high level are responsible for delineating that fine line between legitimate and illegitimate practice in matters of fact-finding and disclosure.

The following guidelines make sense to me as a businessman in a highly competitive society:

1. Never condone lawbreaking, outright lying, confidence games, or gross misrepresentation.
2. Make the negotiating team sensitive to the importance of avoiding deliberate misrepresentation or exaggeration.
3. Select ethical people as team members.
4. Avoid playing on the edge of bad faith. Try to keep out of the ethical no-man's-land.
5. Follow the Golden Rule: Do unto others as you would have them do unto you.
6. Favor a policy of factual truth.
7. Insist on enforceable mutual penalties so severe that no company would dare use what the rules forbid without fear of exposure.
8. Avoid overkill in fact-finding. It's all too easy to become overzealous.

A negotiator should be alert to signs of deliberate lying. One man I know calibrates his opponent by asking a few loaded questions to which he already knows the answers. He learns quite a lot from his opponent's reaction to these probes and the accuracy of the responses.

Bluffing, while ethical, involves risk. The bluffer who is called loses credibility. Bluffing also has a way of getting out of hand. It tends to lean too far in the direction of exaggeration. As a general rule, I prefer that my people lean the other way; that is, toward understatement and underselling. In business there is wisdom to the expression "Less is more."

BREAKING AN IMPASSE

Too many negotiations break down for the wrong reasons. There is nothing wrong with deadlock in itself. Sellers have every right to prefer no deal to one at too low a price. Buyers may prefer impasse as a tactic for reaching their objective. What is of concern to us is how to break the deadlock we don't want.

I have found these fifteen moves useful in averting or breaking an impasse:

1. Change the shape of money. A larger deposit, a shorter pay period, or an otherwise different cash flow works wonders even when the total amount of money involved is the same.
2. Change a team member or the team leader.
3. Change the time shape of uncertainty. This can be done by postponing some difficult parts of the agreement for renegotiation at a later time when more information is known.
4. Change the time shape of risk sharing. A willingness to share unknown losses or gains may restore a lagging discussion.
5. Change the time scale of performance.
6. Change the shape of future satisfaction by recommending grievance procedures or guarantees.
7. Change the bargaining emphasis from a competitive mode to a cooperative problem-solving mode. Get engineers involved with engineers, operations people with operations people, bosses with bosses.
8. Change the type of contract.
9. Change the base for percentage. A smaller percentage of a larger base or a larger percentage of a smaller but more predictable base may get things back on track.
10. Call a mediator.
11. Arrange a summit meeting or "hot-line" call.
12. Add options of a real or apparent nature. The offer of

options that are unlikely to be taken may sweeten an otherwise questionable deal.
13. Make changes in specifications or terms.
14. Set up a joint study committee.
15. Tell a funny story.

Impasse breakers work because they reinvolve the opponent in discussions with his or her team and other members of the organization. These icebreakers help create a climate in which new alternatives can be developed. Surprisingly, the introduction of new alternatives sometimes has the effect of making old propositions look better than ever.

People often wonder whether they should make the first move after deadlock or let the other person do it. Common sense says that you ought to let him or her do it. The trouble is you can never be sure it will happen. All you can count on is that the deadlock is likely to put severe pressure on both parties and their organizations. Even if they don't make the first move, they are likely to welcome yours.

Think through *in advance* what can be said or done to provide a face-saving way for you to open the discussion and for the other party to listen. If you set the stage before the impasse sets in, you can better handle the problem.

Breakdowns are not always caused by world-shattering issues or great matters of economics. In my experience, many breakdowns are the result of simple things like personality differences, fear of loss of face, troubles in the organization, a poor working relationship with the boss, or the sheer inability to make a decision. Any consideration of how to break an impasse must take into account the human factor. It is not what you do but how you do it that may be the critical factor.

BRIBERY

Bribery is a way of life. It shouldn't be, but is. When Paul Powell, the secretary of state of Illinois, died, $800,000 was found in his closet. Paul Powell was on the take. He could never have accumulated $800,000 legally on his meager salary as secretary of state of Illinois.

Does bribery fit anywhere in a book on negotiation? Of course. The reality of every negotiation is that there are hidden issues. Artie Samish was a lobbyist who used to say that "with broads, bribes, and baked potatoes" he could buy any vote in the California legislature. What put Artie into jail was adding the fourth "B"—bragging.

I know a vice-president of a trucking company who keeps $30,000 in cash available at all times. He chuckled when I told him I was writing a book on tactics. He said, "Whenever I have a tough bargaining problem with the union, I call my 'consultant' in San Francisco. He picks up a phone, calls somebody, and the problem goes away. I send him ten thousand dollars and a thank-you note. Put that in your book." The VP is a good family man. He attends church on most Sundays. By no means does he view himself as a bad man. To him it's just business—nothing more. He is convinced that all business is conducted in much the same way.

I have a theory that those of us who have never given or accepted bribes really don't understand how seductive they are or how widespread the practice. Those who give bribes tend to believe that everyone has a price. Therein lies the danger. Those on the take know how to do it. Those responsible for policing it don't know where, how, or even whether to look.

Big-company executives should worry more about bribery than they do. They would be wise to remove their rose-colored glasses. Newspapers are full of city officials who sell their souls for a few thousand dollars. If widespread corruption and lawlessness can creep into the White House, it can reach any corporation. A tough-minded approach to conflict of interest is called for along lines like these:

1. An active rotation policy.
2. Continuous internal audit investigations.
3. A policy that exposes any violator to full public view and automatic criminal prosecution.
4. A policy that makes certain that every bribe attempt is reported. Any employee failing to do so should be fired.
5. Gratuities should be defined carefully and limited to free lunches and nothing more.
6. An active promotion of high standards through executive leadership and example.

Don't be naïve and assume that the price in a negotiation is always equal to the dollar value of the purchase order. Corruption and bribery do exist in business. For some people it is a way of life. This is not to suggest that management be paranoiac about it. Just check up once in awhile.

BUY NOW—NEGOTIATE LATER

Buyers prefer to negotiate before they buy. That makes good business sense. However, there are times when "buy now—negotiate later" is the better approach. The important thing, whether you sell or buy, is to be open-minded about both approaches. Failure to do so can be costly.

"Buy now—negotiate later" works like this. A buyer needs something done. He or she authorizes the seller to begin immediately on a prearranged contractual basis. Limited funds, sufficient to maintain a level of effort, are provided the seller. Both parties agree to finalize the contract at a specific date in the future. Similar agreements are called by such names as advanced authorizations, letter contracts, or letters of intent.

As a rule, I prefer to settle before work begins. It is hard to change vendors after a commitment has been made to go ahead. Financial, schedule, and psychological constraints make it difficult to back off from the original decision. The commitment, despite its temporary nature, tends to get the buyer locked in.

Purchasing management looks at "buy now—negotiate later" with a jaundiced eye. Buyers who make such contracts are badgered to finalize them quickly. However, in my opinion, the case *for* "buy now—negotiate later" deserves to be looked at. It can work for purchasing under the following circumstances:

1. When there is no time to negotiate.
2. When the buyer believes that the seller's price is padded with costs unlikely to occur.
3. When the buyer wants to find out if the seller knows what he or she is doing.
4. When the seller is willing to commit to a reasonable "not-to-exceed" price.
5. When the buyer can gain a better insight into the work to be done.
6. When the seller's bargaining position will be worse later because he or she has committed resources and is afraid to lose the contract.
7. When the seller's track record shows that he or she is unlikely to exploit the buyer.
8. When the work cannot be estimated until enough is done to provide visibility.
9. When competition can be developed later.

Sellers generally like to grab a "buy now—negotiate later" authorization. My suggestion is that you hesitate the next time a buyer offers it. Don't grab it until you think it through. You may discover that a better price can be gotten at that moment, and never again.*

---

* *For what can happen to a seller who completes a job before the price is settled, see page 30, "Call the Plumber."*

CALL A CACTUS

Once, at a seminar, we were heatedly discussing a thorny problem in negotiating: how to handle the other party's "bad guy." A lot of good ideas had already been suggested. In the rear of the room sat a quiet, well-dressed young executive from IBM. He slowly raised his hand.

"How do you handle the bad guy?" I asked.

He said, "We call a cactus."

Surprised, I responded, "You mean a caucus, don't you?"

"No" said he, "we call a cactus. We figure out how to get the thorn out of there."

CALL THE PLUMBER

This is a rule of economic life that every seller should remember. It's called "the plumber principle." The value of services is greater before they are rendered than after.

Plumbers know that the time to negotiate a price is when the basement is full of water.

CAR DEALERS AND ACCOUNTANTS

Car dealers and accountants are like fire and water: each watchful of the other; both, clever and quick. Car dealers love to use the "car dealer's delight" on accountants especially.

At some point late in the discussion, the dealer runs an adding-machine tape on the basic car and accessories. In doing so, he or she purposely fails to include a $100 line item on the tape. The accountant is asked to check the tape and easily discovers this "God-sent" bargain. His or her eyes light up and take on a strained but happy anticipatory look. The error is not reported. From that point on, the accountant is hooked. He or she is distracted from negotiating properly for fear that a new tape will be run and the mistake found. The accountant tries to close quickly at or around the bottom-line figure.

Alas, once the deal is made, the dealer takes it to the manager for approval. The error is magically discovered. The "embarrassed" dealer tells the accountant that a $100 error had been made and must be added to the price. Accountants usually give in to somewhere between $50 and $100 after a short hassle. Why? Because they feel somewhat guilty for not reporting the mistake as a good accountant should. Also because they find it difficult to support a logically inconsistent position. To an accountant, the parts must equal the whole.

CATCH-22: DUMB IS SMART AND SMART IS DUMB

In Joseph Heller's acclaimed novel *Catch-22*, the Air Force bombardier Yossarian goes to a psychiatrist and tries to get out of the service because he is crazy. But the psychiatrist says something like, "If you were really crazy, you would want to stay in the Air Force. Since you want to get out, you must not be crazy. Therefore I can't let you out."

The Catch-22 of negotiation is "dumb is smart and smart is dumb." It is not smart to be decisive, brilliant, quick, fully knowledgeable, or totally rational. You'll probably get more concessions and better answers if you are slow to understand, less decisive, and slightly irrational. The trouble is that most of us want to look good. We find it hard to say "I don't know" or "Tell me that again."

CAUCUS: WHEN TO CALL ONE

Diplomatic negotiations are usually 10 percent conference and 90 percent time-out. Most business deals reverse this time relationship. When and how a caucus is called can affect the final settlement. I am in favor of lots of time-outs. They make more sense than long talks and short breaks.

Gordon Rule, perhaps U.S. Navy's toughest bargainer, once said, "Never negotiate an issue unless you are prepared for it." Something unforeseen always seems to come up. When it does, a caucus is called for. Call a meeting among your own people to discuss the new issue. Don't plunge into it half-cocked.

I have found caucuses useful for a wide variety of purposes:

1. To review what was heard or learned
2. To think of questions
3. To develop new arguments and defenses
4. To explore possible alternatives
5. To develop better proof statements
6. To review strategies and tactics
7. To discuss possible concessions
8. To determine how to react to new demands or whether to make additional demands
9. To consult experts
10. To check rules or regulations
11. To analyze changes in price, specification, time, or terms
12. To analyze costs
13. To forestall embarrassing questions
14. To get rid of "bad guys"

A caucus gives you time to think, to make a point more effectively, to check your facts, or to show your resolve. It gives you a chance to put all your people to work on the problem. In her ten years of collective-bargaining research, Ann Douglas, author of the book *Industrial Peacemaking*, found that tension was reduced at the crisis stage by having short sessions and long time-outs.

The head of the team is responsible for seeing that everything needed for a good caucus is available. As in any conference, it is important to have a comfortable meeting place, an agenda, blackboards, displays, calculators, and copying facilities. Privacy is a critical requirement. Many a caucus room has been "bugged" and more will be, Watergate notwithstanding.

If time-outs are so critical to a football coach, they ought to be even more important to a negotiator. The stakes are far higher.

CHANGE OF PACE IN TACTICS

The best pitchers in baseball are not those who specialize in fastballs or knuckleballs. Change-of-pace pitchers win the most games in the long run. In negotiation, too, change of pace counts.

A sense of timing is crucial. There is a time to get involved and a time to be aloof. A time to be open and a time to be inscrutable. A time to talk and a time to stay quiet. A time to probe and a time to accept. A time to be firm and a time to be soft. A time to give and a time to get. The change-of-pace theory ties all this together.

The theory says that a negotiator should not telegraph his or her motivations or the desire to close. It suggests that *it is better to move patiently toward a deal and then away from it, toward and away, again and again. In that way, the other party alternates between the pleasure of seeing the objective within reach and the anxiety of watching it escape.* He or she wavers continuously between holding out and giving in. He or she is never too sure of the next pitch.

CHANGE-THE-NEGOTIATOR TACTIC

"Change-the-negotiator" is a tough tactic to cope with. Once we grow accustomed to dealing with someone, it becomes uncomfortable to start all over again with a substitute. The typical reaction tends to be "Here we go again."

The tactic generally favors a new negotiator. This person has a chance to retreat from previous concessions, introduce new arguments, delay agreements, or change the nature of the discussions from one subject to another. The pressure falls upon the other person to bring the newly introduced negotiator up to par with respect to past arguments and agreements.

People are creatures of exposure. We grow accustomed to enemies as well as friends. We demand predictability from both. A change in the opposition's team is disconcerting. Does the new person like us or not? Does he or she really mean it? Is he or she better or worse? What does the change signify? We prefer stability even from those who oppose us.

A purchasing manager I know uses this tactic deliberately. He instructs his subordinates to bog down discussions with tough demands. When both sides are exhausted and about to deadlock, the manager takes charge of the negotiation. The salesperson is thrown off balance. He or she is afraid to say anything to offend the buyer or the buyer's boss for fear of losing the account. The manager takes the initiative by forcefully demanding lower prices and greater services from the disconcerted salesperson. The manager usually succeeds.

The introduction of new blood does not always signify something sinister. It can be a good way to promote a conciliatory posture. A deadlock can be averted or constructive ideas promoted by introducing a new leader. Sometimes, when tempers are hot, a change in negotiators is the face-saving way to get talks back on the track.

What should you do when the other party's negotiator disappears or the team changes?

1. Do not exhaust yourself repeating old arguments.
2. Be patient if the new person reneges on past agreements. He or she will probably come back to them later.
3. You can find good reasons for breaking off talks until the original person is available.
4. Anticipate how you will handle a change if confronted with it.
5. Feel free to change your position if they change theirs.
6. Some changes signify weakness. Probe for a new offer or concession.
7. Talk to the new person in private.

Changing the negotiator is an old tactic of diplomacy. It is by no means unethical, nor is its use restricted to any national or professional groups. Businesspeople, government negotiators, and car dealers in every corner of our globe have been known to try it on occasion.

CHERRY PICKING: THE OPTIMIZER'S TACTIC

Buyers like cherry picking, but sellers don't. It is an optimizing tactic, and it works in this way: The buyers get bids from the five sellers on a large number of items. They compare bids and find that some are low on certain items but high on others. The buyers then exercises one of three choices:

1. They can break their requirement and place the order for each item with the low bidder for that item. That would give them the lowest overall price but the biggest administrative headache.
2. They can give the order to the seller who can be negotiated down on those items they are high on.

3. Cherry pickers usually take the third choice. They want the best of all worlds: the lowest price on every line item and the lowest total cost.

Most sellers have so little faith in their own pricing system that they succumb to the cherry picker without much resistance. They should recognize that the buyers dislike breaking up the order between vendors and will usually pay a premium for not doing so. The salesperson who can give a reasonable explanation for higher-priced items has a very good chance to prevail. If that strategy doesn't work, a tiny drop in price may be enough to help the buyers justify their position to their own people. In any case the seller should be tightfisted about making reductions on cherry-picked items.

Sellers can counter cherry picking by tying all items together and making the bid contingent on an all-or-nothing basis. But this strategy can backfire because they may end up losing a substantial order.

Cherry picking is hard on the seller but is essentially ethical. The better a salesperson knows the buyer personally, the less is to be feared from cherry picking. When buyers have warm regard for their salespeople, they are likely to give them more accurate information upon which to base a price-lowering decision. Buyers who value their relationship with the salespeople as individuals are less likely to optimize short-run pricing. They tend instead to optimize longer-run business and personal considerations.

CLOSING THE DEAL: ELEVEN WAYS THAT WORK

Jack Smith is a reporter for the Los Angeles *Times* who owns a house way down the Baja Peninsula in Mexico. It's primitive there. The house was built by his friend Gomez, a sort of contractor-handyman who does things at his own pace. It seems that Gomez made the top of a cabinet out of pebbles from a nearby beach. Jack and his wife lived with it for a couple of years and then decided that the pebble top was a mistake. They wanted a top made of white tile. So they asked Gomez to drop over to the house. The negotiation was fascinating. Jack describes it in the *Times:*

> Gomez drove over Sunday morning in an old Jeep wagon. . . . The Jeep was for sale, a fact that did not interest me. As soon as we were both satisfied that I didn't want the Jeep, I took Gomez into the bathroom and told him my plan.
>
> "I want to take this out," I said, "and replace it with white tile. It's too dark to see the pebbles. Then I'd like to have a table made the same size as the pebble top, and put the pebble top on the table. It would make a beautiful cocktail table."
>
> Gomez looked at me with the expression of a man who has heard something he not only does not wish to believe, but is not going to believe.
>
> "You want to get rid of this beautiful top?"
>
> "Not get rid of it, no," I said, feeling strangely guilty. "I want to convert it into a cocktail table, so we can see it better. I'm sure it will be very beautiful."
>
> He shook his head. "What you need, Jack," he said, looking up at the ceiling, "is a skylight. I'm going to put in a skylight, and then you will have the sunlight on your pebbles."
>
> "A skylight?"
>
> "Of course. Leave it to me. It will be very beautiful."
>
> "Are you sure it won't leak? When it rains?"
>
> "Don't worry, Jack. It will not leak."
>
> I knew he would never take out the pebble top. He would regard it as a crime; a sin against the harmony of our house, his masterpiece.
>
> "Well," my wife said when we went back into the living room, "are you going to take it out?"
>
> "No," I said. "We're going to have a skylight."
>
> "A skylight?"
>
> I didn't actually tell Gomez to go ahead with it, though.
>
> On our way to Los Angeles we stopped at his little store

and Gomez put out the salt and a sliced lime and opened the jug of tequila and we had a drink. . . .

"You didn't decide to go ahead with the skylight?" my wife said as we set out over the road.

"Yes, of course," I said. "It's a deal."

"I didn't hear it mentioned."

"We didn't have to," I explained. "Whenever Gomez pours tequila, whatever you've been talking about is a deal. It's automatic."

I just hope he didn't think it meant I was buying the Jeep.

Gomez knew how to close a deal. Once he brought out the bottle, that was it. In Jack's words, "Whenever Gomez pours tequila, whatever you've been talking about is a deal. It's automatic."

How do you bring negotiations to a close? We know it happens when each party expects that the other has conceded all that it will and that further efforts are not likely to be very productive. At closure, the parties insulate their minds to further information and make a final decision.

The reason for the final decision may be based on fact or intuition. That is immaterial. What is important is that the expectations of both parties come together and closure follows. The eleven techniques below are designed to nudge an opponent into agreement:

1. Start with a positive attitude about closing. Make repeated requests for agreement in a matter-of-fact fashion. The theme should be "If not now, when? We know everything we need to know to agree."
2. Don't talk too much in requesting closure. Talking prevents listening to the opponent's response. Excessive talking may be interpreted as a sign of anxiety.
3. Keep asking the opponent what the problem is if no agreement is reached. He or she will probably explain the reason for reluctance if provided an opportunity.
4. Repeatedly assure the other person that he or she is wise in settling. Keep giving good reasons.
5. Don't be afraid to assume that things are already settled. If

you are a buyer, ask the seller for a pen to write the memo of agreement or ask how the check should be made out. If you are a seller, ask the buyer where the delivery is to be made.

6. Walk the opponent into settlement by talking about details like the wording of a clause or delivery instructions. Act as though agreement has been reached on the main issues and price.
7. Take a physical action toward closure. Salespeople can start writing the sales order. Buyers can give the seller a purchase order number and start to shake hands. A physical action on behalf of an idea reinforces a commitment toward closure.
8. Emphasize the possible loss of benefits now available if agreement is not reached soon. Some people are unmoved by gains but are strongly motivated to avoid loss. As a buyer, you can point out that you are stretching your authority in making such a generous offer and that your boss may not go along if there is a delay in closing the deal. You can also make clear that other competitors are anxious to prove that they can perform well if given the opportunity. A seller can help a buyer move toward closure by politely showing that the inventory might not be available if too long a time passes in tying down the deal.
9. Provide a special inducement for closing that cannot be offered later. This can be in the form of a price bonus, progress payments, equipment furnished, or special services.
10. Tell a story legitimizing the deal. Show how somebody got into a difficult situation by passing up an opportunity for settlement. Make a closure a real and desirable experience.
11. Don't give up until you get many nos. A famous mutual-fund salesman once said that he never gives up until he gets at least seven nos.

These techniques have probably been used for centuries by negotiators and salespeople throughout the world. They seek to nudge the other party into an agreement by projecting an attitude that is pleasant, persistent, and positive without being overbearing. At that point, whatever you've been talking about is a deal.

CONFESSION CAN BE GOOD FOR YOU

1. Give yourself room to negotiate. Start high if you are selling and low if you are buying. Have a reason for starting where you do.
2. Get the other party to open up first. Get all his or her demands on the table. Keep yours hidden.
3. Let the other person make the first concession on major issues. You can be first on minor points if you wish.
4. Make them work for everything they get. People don't appreciate something for nothing.
5. Conserve your concessions. Later is better than now. The longer they wait, the more they'll appreciate it.
6. Tit-for-tat concessions are not necessary. If they give sixty, you give forty. If they say, "Let's split the difference," you can say, "I can't afford to."
7. Get something for every concession.
8. Give concessions that give nothing away.
9. Remember: "I'll consider it" is a concession.
10. If you can't get a dinner, get a sandwich. If you can't get a sandwich, get a promise. A promise is a concession with a discount rate.
11. Don't negotiate with funny money. Think of every concession as real money.
12. Don't be afraid to say no. Most people are. If you say no enough times, they will believe you mean it. Be persistent.
13. Don't lose track of your concessions. Keep a tally of yours and theirs.
14. Don't be ashamed to back away from a concession you have already made. It is the final handshake that ends the deal, not the agreements in between.
15. Don't raise the other party's aspirations by giving in too much or too fast. Watch the amount, the rate, and the change of rate of your concessions.

CONCESSIONS: THE IDEAL CONCESSION PATTERN

Is there such a thing as an ideal concession pattern? Evidence is beginning to accumulate that there is. Here is what I found in my experiments:

1. Buyers who started with low offers did better than those who didn't.
2. Buyers who gave a large amount in a single concession raised the expectation of sellers.
3. Sellers who were willing to take less got less.
4. People who gave just a little at a time did better.
5. Losers made the first concessions on major issues.
6. Deadlines forced decisions and agreements.
7. Quick negotiations were very bad for one party or the other.
8. People who made the largest single concession in a negotiation did poorly.

CONCESSIONS: WHAT SELLER CONCEDES AFFECTS BUYER DEMANDS

The economist John Maynard Keynes once said that the trick to stock-market success lay in anticipating how the average person would believe the average person would act. He died a rich man. Others have gone broke using the same theory.

How a buyer responds to a seller's concession can be affected by the concession itself. If it is a large concession, the buyer, instead of being satisfied, may react by making greater demands on the seller. What we do or say affects and is in turn affected by what the other party does or says. It's like a chain reaction.

Where does all this lead us? A seller has to think through the effect that each concession he or she makes will have on what the buyer will then do. The seller has to ask, "If I make this concession, what should I do next, and what will they do after that?" A little question like that can help you see your concession from the other person's viewpoint.

CONCESSIONS: WHEN ONE IS MORE THAN FOUR

Most of us have an innate desire to be fair. Justice dictates that if I make four concessions to you, you will feel obligated to make at least one to me.

The central question in negotiation is not whether I made four and you made one, but whether your one was more valuable than my four. Many a negotiator has done well by making a series of minor concessions and then saying, "Now, what are you going to do for me?" That's the one point that really matters.

CONCESSIONS THAT GIVE NOTHING AWAY

How would you like to make concessions that give nothing away—not goods, money, or services? The beauty of this tactic is that anyone can make these concessions and, by doing so, make better deals.

Assume for a moment that you are a salesperson. Your sales manager has instructed you not to make any concessions in the sales package or its terms. He or she also asked that you leave the buyer as satisfied as possible with the deal even though no concessions can be made. At first glance it looks like an impossible job, but it isn't.

Below are but a few of the concessions you can make that give nothing tangible away.

1. Listen attentively to what the other person has to say.
2. Give him or her the best explanation possible.
3. If you say something, prove it.
4. Be prepared to talk at length even if it means covering the same ground again and again.
5. Treat the buyer nicely.
6. Assure him or her that other buyers are treated no better.
7. Point out as many times as necessary why and how the deal will provide the future satisfaction promised.
8. Show how other competent and respected people have also made a similar choice.
9. Let buyers check some things for themselves.
10. Make promises about future transactions, if that is possible.
11. Have someone at a higher level in your organization commit to the satisfaction of the buyer.
12. Give the buyer knowledge of the product or the marketplace.

In *The Merchant of Venice*, Shakespeare wrote, "He is well paid that is well satisfied." Each of the above concessions contributes to the buyer's satisfaction. Can any seller afford not to make them?

CONFESSION CAN BE GOOD FOR YOU

Confession is not only good for the soul, but it can be good for the negotiator. The confessor puts it all on the line. He or she not only tells all he or she knows, but reveals motivation and assumptions as well. It's a high-risk tactic that sometimes pays off.

Confession is a good way to gain sympathy. People tend to be charitable toward the person who tells everything. Confession produces other benefits in that it flatters the listener's ego and gives a sense of power. Few of us have not at one time or another expressed compassion for those who confess. Conversely, we tend to be angry and vengeful at those who do not.

Some years ago, I attended a rate hearing. The trucking company not only laid out all the facts, but confessed to the board that a 90-cent rate was sufficient to make a profit. For a few seconds, nobody said anything. Suddenly the review-board chairman blurted out, "We can do better than that. How would a dollar suit you?" Benevolence got the better of him.

Confession can be an effective tactic for gaining concessions. *Getting or giving the full story is always part of the price.*

CREDIBILITY HAS A PRICE

Price is not money. It is a combination of benefits. Hidden in the price that a buyer pays is the seller's credibility. From the buyer's point of view, the right to inspect and verify what he or she has been told is as much a part of the deal as the goods and services for sale.

To negotiate with others effectively, we must give some information about ourselves. That is the only way to make a better deal for both parties. The question is not whether we will, but how much and what. Credibility involves what is said, how it is said, when it is said, and who says it. All of us know how hard it is to deal with people whom we do not believe or trust.

Our society is moving quickly into a new phase. Some time ago, sellers could insist that their information was private. "Let the buyer beware" was the cry of the nineteenth and the first half of the twentieth century.

Buyers are getting smarter, thanks to people like Ralph Nader. They are demanding proof. Credibility and the right to get the full story are quickly becoming ever-increasing parts of the price. The new business creed is "Let the buyer be aware!"

DEADLINES: WHY AND HOW THEY WORK

Deadlines force action. It is no accident that income-tax returns are filed on April 15, that Christmas presents are bought on December 24, and that planes are caught at the last minute. For years lobbyists have taken advantage of the fact that legislators pass all kinds of dumb bills just before adjournment.

Time limits are part of daily living. Work starts at 9:00 and stops at 5:00, trains leave on schedule, dental appointments must be kept, and bills are due on the tenth of the month. Time is a factor in every human transaction. We respond to deadlines almost without awareness.

Deadlines pressure people into making an either-or choice. If they choose to accept the deadline, they get the deal over with. If they don't, the consequences are unpredictable. It's a question of the bird in hand or the uncertain one in the bush.

You can never be sure that a negotiating time limit is real. You can rarely predict with accuracy the cost of not meeting a deadline. Experience tells us that some deadlines mean dead, others don't. Some are costly, others inconsequential. People who accept a deadline do enjoy one pleasure: They have the satisfaction of dealing with a less-uncertain future. They can rationalize that things might have been worse had the deadline not been met.

Be skeptical of deadlines. Time limits, like trains, come and go. The IRS will negotiate an extension beyond April 15. Hotels will let you stay beyond 1:00 P.M. without charge. Bids due on the tenth may be accepted by the buyer on the eleventh. A report promised on Wednesday probably won't get you fired if it is delivered on Thursday. The offer that was to expire on June 1 is usually available on June 2. Reporters don't meet all their deadlines, but I've yet to run into a blank column in a newspaper. Deadlines are as real as the beholder thinks they are.

Of course there is a risk in not believing a deadline. When a buyer says, "I'm going to place the order by Wednesday," he or she just might leave you high and dry. When the salesperson says, "If you give me the order today, I can guarantee delivery," perhaps it is best to give the order today. The inventory may be sold to someone else if you wait. The more you know about the other party's organization, production schedule, inventory picture, and money pressures, the better you can determine if the deadline is real.

Time is power. Most of us go into a negotiation with a self-inflicted weakness. We are always aware of the time pressure on ourselves. That knowledge makes us less effective than we could be. What we should concentrate on are the deadlines that constrain the other person. If there are deadlines on us, there are probably deadlines on him or her. These three questions will help guide you out of the deadline trap:

1. What self-imposed or organization-imposed deadlines am I under that make it harder for me to negotiate?
2. Are the deadlines imposed on me by myself or my organization real? Can I negotiate an extension with my own people?
3. What deadlines are putting pressure on the other person and their organization?

Time limits have a way of hypnotizing us. We tend to accept them even when we shouldn't. That's why it is good to put a deadline on any offer you make for a house. It helps the seller make the decision you want them to make. Deadlines work even when they shouldn't.

DEADLINES THAT GET A BUYER TO BUY

Salespeople know from experience that certain deadlines cause a buyer to buy. Below are a few that get buyers moving even when they aren't quite ready to:

1. The price goes up July 1.
2. This offer is good for fifteen days.
3. The option expires June 30.
4. Inventory subject to prior sale.
5. If you don't send us more money, we will have to stop work.
6. If you don't give me the order (or the specification) by June 1, I can't deliver by June 30.
7. It will take eight weeks to get it through our production plant.
8. Better place the order immediately to assure availability of long-lead-time items.
9. The cargo ship leaves at 2:00 P.M. Do you want space on it?
10. If we don't get your deposit tomorrow, we can't hold it.

DEADLINES THAT GET A SELLER TO SELL

Sellers are responsive to time pressures—perhaps more than buyers, though most buyers would swear otherwise. Some deadlines imposed by buyers are actually good for salespeople because they may make it easier for the salespeople to negotiate with their own management, pricing, or engineering people. These buyer-imposed deadlines shown below can electrify sellers into action:

1. The money to buy it won't be available after June 30.
2. I need a price by tomorrow.
3. I'm going to place the order by Wednesday.
4. If we can't agree, I'm going to start talking to your competitor tomorrow.
5. Bids will not be accepted after June 1.
6. Just give me a ball-park estimate of what it will cost. I need it tomorrow.
7. I'm not going to be responsible for buying this after Friday.
8. My boss has to approve, and he's leaving tomorrow for a week in Europe.
9. Here's my production schedule. If you can't meet it, that's it. I'll have to place the order elsewhere.
10. The fiscal year ends December 3.
11. The buyer is going on vacation Monday for three weeks.
12. The procurement-approval committee meets tomorrow. Do you want the order at that price or not?

DEADLOCK

Deadlock is one of the most powerful tactics in negotiation. There is almost nothing that so tests the strength and resolve of an opponent. Yet most people avoid deadlock like a disease. They are afraid of it.

People who deadlocked in my experiments were frustrated. They kept trying for agreement well after the experiments were over. They were angry—angry at each other, angry at me, angry at their teammates, and angry at the time limits imposed on them. They were unhappy. Deadlock was no fun under experimental conditions. In the real world, it's even worse.

A psychiatrist I know likens deadlock to alienation. He tells me that one of people's greatest fears is separation from others. People go to great lengths to avoid breaking valued relationships. Experiments likewise confirm that men and women distort reality rather than disagree with peer groups. Alienation and deadlock have a traumatic effect on people.

All of us have deadlocked at some time. We know how uncomfortable it is. Having gone into a negotiation desiring agreement, the impasse leaves us with a sense of failure. We tend to lose confidence and question our own judgment. "Was there something we could have said or done differently? Were there any other concessions that could have been made? How will our boss look at the deadlock? Should we have accepted the last offer? Will the deadlock reflect on our reputation?" These questions haunt both parties.

No wonder businesspeople are afraid of deadlock, especially when they work for a large organization. The truth is that a bad settlement is easier to explain to management than a deadlock. What makes it worse is that others can break the impasse merely by making a small concession. The fact that the deadlock served to soften up the opponent is quickly forgotten. If you put yourself in the position of either the buyer or seller, it's easy to see that deadlock is not to their personal advantage. It is not worth the risk or the extra work that goes with it. From a personal standpoint, it often looks like a dumb move.

Deadlock is just one of many tactics available to a negotiator. It deserves to be considered like any other alternative. It is not always appropriate. Of course not. Neither is any other tactic always appropriate. Negotiators who do not have the backing of management will hesitate to deadlock even when it makes sense. However, it is my opinion that the manager willing to open his or her mind to deliberate deadlock is bound to improve his or her settlements.

What should management do to help its people use deadlock more often? It should make sure that deadlock is weighed routinely as a viable alternative in planning. It should provide the time for coordination and patience without which deadlock becomes ineffective. Perhaps, most of all, it must reassure its people that deadlock is not equated with failure. People in the organization should not fear that deadlock will cause others to question their business judgment.

The power of deadlock lies in understanding what it does to both parties. It is a severe test of their resolve and strength. The buyer and seller are softened up after deadlock. Both are more willing to compromise, especially if a face-saving way out is found. Those willing to try deadlock are in a position to get better results. However, as all of us know, deadlock does involve risks. Some deadlocks can't be unlocked. They stop at the word "dead."

DECISION MAKERS

The real decision makers are rarely the people who sit facing each other across the table. Both buyer and seller have to deal with other people in their organizations. These people have different motives and priorities from the negotiators themselves. They are also measured by their bosses in different ways.

You cannot negotiate effectively unless you think about the decision-making process of the other party. By doing so, buyers may find that they have more in common with the salespeople than the salesperson has with his or her own pricing person in Chicago. Once the buyers think this through, they will recognize that their role is to help the salesperson negotiate more effectively with the real decision maker.

DECOY: BR'ER RABBIT AND THE BRIAR PATCH

Once upon a time, according to Joel Chandler Harris's *Uncle Remus* stories, Br'er Rabbit was caught by Br'er Fox, who had every intention of eating him. Br'er Rabbit said to Br'er Fox, "Please don't throw me in the briar patch." The fox, thinking that this was the worst thing that could happen to the rabbit, threw him in. Once the rabbit was in the briar patch, it was the fox who was afraid to go in and get him.

Sometimes an opponent can be dissuaded from taking an action we really are worried about if we direct their attention to an area that is less threatening or better protected. I remember a small manufacturer who was in serious financial difficulty with his many suppliers. Under heavy pressure to pay, the manufacturer advised each supplier that he would be driven into bankruptcy if sued for payment. He told them that this was the worst fear he had because it would ruin his financial and social standing in the community. Each supplier took the cue by writing a nasty letter threatening to force the manufacturer into bankruptcy unless paid in full. The manufacturer then accumulated the letters, showed them to each supplier, one by one, and negotiated 50 percent off each debt. His briar patch was bankruptcy; his goal was negotiating debt relief.

DEFAULT IS AN UNFAIR TACTIC

There are some holes in every contract, even the best of them. Certain parts of the deal are ambiguous, unclear, and unsettled. This occurs because the negotiators are content to leave a number of procedural and operational matters to those people who will actually do the work. These gaps can be very expensive if you are dealing with someone who wants to take advantage of them.

The default tactic takes advantage of omissions and ambiguities by interpreting every gap in one's own favor. This is done in three steps:

1. The agreement is studied with the intention of discovering holes in its structure.
2. The gaps are plugged by writing a memorandum to the other party stating that a certain action will be taken by a specific date in the future.
3. If no reply is received in a reasonable length of time, the action is taken unilaterally.

Here's a good example: A paper mill gives terms of net thirty days. The paper buyers write a letter saying that it is company policy to pay cash in ten days and take a 2 percent discount. If no answer is received in a reasonable period of time, they take the 2 percent discount. In many cases, nothing further is heard of the matter. I have seen the same tactic used in matters involving specification changes, credit, inspection procedures, repairs, and sales add-ons. The pattern remains much the same whatever the matter at issue.

The countermeasures are obvious. Prevent default by incorporating understandings and procedures into agreements. If you receive a memo, answer it promptly. Even if you fail to answer, don't be ashamed to point out that the unilateral action taken was not in accordance with your interpretation of the basic agreement. The default tactic is unfair. You have every right to protest loudly and at a high level. Don't let the defaulter get away with it. Call the bluff.

DELIBERATE ERRORS

Some people make deliberate errors. They add or multiply wrong, change meanings, leave out words, or make incorrect statements. Deliberate error makers do so for a purpose: they want to misdirect or deceive.

I once saw an aerospace contractor make a deliberate $10,260 mistake in a proposal. The government found it by accident two years later. In this case, the proposal involved hundreds of spare parts. The pricing man multiplied 380 × $3 wrong. Instead of $1,140, he wrote $11,400 in the "total" column. Since the full package totaled $842,000, nobody noticed the difference. The customer just assumed that the arithmetic was all right and settled on a lump-sum basis.

The worst case of a deliberate error I was ever subjected to was a two-bit movie producer who had the audacity to change one clause after an agreement had been reached. The change was quite fundamental. Instead of giving the actor a percentage of gross receipts, the producer changed it to net receipts. In the movie business, the accountants see that net receipts are zero or less, even for successful projects. The contract was mailed to the actor and to me simultaneously. I can only assume that the producer hoped the anxious actor would sign and mail it back. When I confronted the producer with the mistake, he simply insisted that he could not live with the prior agreement and decided to send the version he preferred. What nerve!

The possibility of error is great at all times, but during crises it is especially so. Figures are added wrong, multiplied by wrong factors, left out, or changed even when intentions are honorable. The opponent with larceny in mind is counting on passing a mistake through. If negotiators discover it later, they must have the courage to explain to management why they did not check things under pressure. This requires the kind of courage some people do not have.

For an unethical opponent, the penalty is low and rewards high. After all, anybody can make a mistake by changing 5 percent of gross to 5 percent of net or adding a long column of figures incorrectly. If the mistake is discovered, excuses can be made and discussions reopened. I have seen shady operators make no mistakes in price agreements, but quietly change page 10 of a fifteen-page specification to favor their objectives.

When these things happen, negotiators should get angry and insist that they have been duped. Protest at the highest level. There is no point in becoming a tacit accomplice by covering up the error.

Here are four variations of the deliberate error to be aware of:

1. *The "Phony-Offer" Lure:* A mistake is made that offers something for sale at a very good bargain. When the buyer shows interest, he or she learns that the advertisement or figures were wrong. Buyers sometimes make high offers for a seller's product in order to eliminate competition. Later the buyer explains that the original offer was a mistake. (See "Phony Offers," page 150.)
2. *The Billing Error:* A deal is made at one price but acknowledged and paid at another. Businesspeople like you and me get confused. Some pay twice, some pay for what they never get, some get things they never pay for, and others pay more or take less than they agreed to.
3. *The "Car Dealer's Delight":* An error is made that diverts the attention of the buyer. (See "Car Dealers and Accountants," page 30.)
4. *The "Specification Mistake":* A specification is written that is much easier or harder to meet than the one agreed to. The trouble is that the change is subtle. It is hidden in the fine print.

Never assume that everything is all right! Be skeptical and check. Force yourself to read the fine print and add the figures.

DEMANDS AND OFFERS

People who give themselves room to negotiate do better than those who don't. My experiments with over three hundred executives confirm what good negotiators already know.

1. Buyers do well when they make low offers.
2. Sellers do well when they make high demands.
3. Sellers who make unexpectedly high demands tend to do very well if they are persistent and do not deadlock.

High demands proved one more thing in my experiments, something that many merchants and buyers in Third World countries know by instinct. The high demand of the seller often caused the buyer to open with a higher offer than originally intended. For example, a buyer and his partner might agree prior to negotiation to offer $10 for a moderately attractive wristwatch. Upon hearing the seller demand $100, the buyers usually felt silly offering only $10. What followed was an opening offer of $20 or $25 in response to the seller's high demand. In experiments, it happened time and again.

Labor negotiators add another dimension to the high-demand approach. They go into the talks with a "big pot" of issues. Not only does the large number of demands satisfy different segments of the membership, but it also allows straws to be given away. The unions have found that the "big pot" creates trading room. Sweeping exchanges of issues can be made.

The case for high demands and slow, hard-fought concessions is a strong one. They help reduce the opponent's aspiration level. Together they give the negotiator a chance to test the strength of an opponent and his or her willingness to stand firm.

My advice: If you buy, start low; If you sell, start high. In either case, have a good reason for starting where you do to avoid an appearance of flippancy. By giving yourself room to negotiate, you may discover that you are better off than you thought.

EMOTIONS: HOW TO COPE WITH EMOTIONAL OUTBURSTS

Emotions play a powerful role in negotiation because people find it difficult to tolerate unexpected outbursts. We go to great pains to hide anger, fright, apathy, or depression. When the other party lets loose, we find it hard to cope.

People who, by their own behavior, cause another person to become emotionally agitated begin to wonder whether they themselves have pushed too far. They become afraid that things will get out of control. Emotional actions breed emotional reactions. An emotional opponent can gain the initiative. The surprise outburst may be staged to test our resolve, shake our self-confidence, or force us to reassess our targets or position.

Emotions tell a story. Anger is sometimes used to support a position, tears to beg for mercy, fright to tie one's people closer together, apathy to show indifference. Emotions are like a zoom lens. They put into sharper focus words and ideas that might otherwise go unseen or unheard.

The best way to cope with an emotional outburst is to play it cool. If you become perturbed, the negotiation will degenerate into an argument. The person who can maintain composure under stress is looked up to. The Italians call such people "men of respect."

When the climate gets emotional, try to bring issues into focus by centering discussion around facts rather than feelings. Rephrase the other person's comments to show that you understand his or her viewpoint. Call a recess. The more you stick to a rational approach, the harder it will be for them to get excited.

I am not in favor of deliberate emotional displays. Remember that some people stage emotions to communicate feelings they do not feel. Others are adept at covering up intense feelings. Be skeptical and play it cool. Get the story before reducing your demands or aspirations. There are a lot of good actors around.

EMOTIONS: THE PENALTY FOR LOSING YOUR COOL

When people are emotional, they don't think clearly. Experiments confirm that people distort reality, don't listen, and pick up only those inputs most in tune with their emotional wants. When they are afraid, they see others as fearful; when they are sad, others appear sad; when they are angry, others appear angry. The emotional person loses touch with reality.

Two thousand years ago, Aristotle had this to say about distortion and emotion:

> Under the influence of strong feeling we are easily deceived. The coward under the influence of fear and the lover under that of love have such illusions that the coward, owing to a trifling resemblance, thinks he sees an enemy and the lover his beloved. And the more impressionable the person is, the less is the resemblance required. Similarly, everybody is easily deceived when in anger or influenced by any strong desire, and the more subject one is to feelings the more one is deceived.

Emotions are a two-edged sword. They can show that you really care or they can twist you up to the point where even a good deal looks oppressive. I have seen people deadlock for emotional reasons—reasons that made no sense when tempers cooled. But it was too late. The deal, like Humpty Dumpty, could not be put together again. We pay a price for losing our cool.

END RUNS: WHEN IT BECOMES NECESSARY TO BYPASS YOUR OPPONENT

There are times when it is necessary to bypass the person you are negotiating with. Buyers find it a lot easier to get around salespeople than salespeople around buyers. The salesperson is concerned that a buyer will so resent the end run that future business will be lost. He or she knows that a buyer whose competence is challenged or who loses face in the organization will be hostile. The salesperson must ask, "Is it worth the risk?" and, if so, "How can I do it as politely as possible?"

Essentially, the bypass seeks to open new communication channels for a variety of legitimate reasons. They may include breaking an impasse, getting to the real decision maker, insuring that one's viewpoint is being conveyed properly, reversing a prior decision, testing a take-it-or-leave-it offer, or dealing with someone easier to get along with. In this real world of ours, there are end runs designed for the purpose of buying favors from people in high places. These will not be discussed here, but are nevertheless always a danger.

Is there any way for a salesperson to bypass a buyer without getting the buyer angry? None that is perfect. The following suggestions do tend to reduce hostility because they give the buyer a face-saving way out:

1. The boss-to-boss contact.
2. The sales call made while the buyer is on vacation or sick leave.
3. The technical or manufacturing end run.
4. The "bigger-than-both-of-us" operations problem.
5. Change the negotiation site to the golf course, to church, or to a professional association meeting where the right person is likely to be.

6. The "old-school-chum," third-party approach.

The end run can backfire. A buyer may be so angry at being circumvented that a deadlock is precipitated. The person who has been bypassed and placed in an awkward position has three countermeasures available: (1) bypass the opponent; (2) warn his or her people of its dangers so that it doesn't happen again; and (3) take sharp action to discourage further tactics of this sort. The bypass or end run works only against groups that are so poorly coordinated that they let it happen.

ESCALATING-AUTHORITY TACTICS

Years ago I read in *Life* magazine that the Skouras brothers used the escalating-authority tactic to their advantage in movie negotiations. When an actor's agent bargained against the Skouras organization, he started with the youngest brother. After the two had been at it for a long while and reached a tentative agreement, the next older brother was asked to approve. He would not approve, and would then proceed to bargain on his authority. Finally, the process was repeated with Spyros himself. Few agents had the stamina and dedication to withstand such an onslaught.

The purpose of the escalating authority is to pass the approval level higher so that your opponent is forced to literally renegotiate or at the very least repeat the arguments at each level. It is physically and psychologically wearing. The tactic tests the self-confidence of the negotiator. It chips away at his or her aspiration level and demands.

The tactic also drives a wedge between the negotiator and the organization. In a typical situation, the buyer agrees with the seller on a price, the most important issue in the negotiation. No memo of agreement is written because there are several other minor matters to discuss. The salesperson tells his or her boss that the deal is almost wrapped up at a good price. The next day, the buyer's manager reopens the negotiation by lowering the offered price, thereby placing the salesperson in a difficult position with his or her boss.

Escalating authority calls for firm countermeasures. Those shown below help call the escalator's bluff:

1. Put higher-level people into the negotiation if the other party does.
2. Be prepared to walk out.
3. Go directly to the top of the company. Protest.
4. Be careful not to arouse the hopes of your organization too soon.
5. Keep your organization aware that an escalation of authority may be used to chip away at its people's aspirations.
6. Do not repeat your arguments at each level. Sit back and let your opponent do it.

Escalating authority is by no means restricted to the movie industry. Many car dealers are fond of it, too. It takes an exceptional person to stand up to the tactic. The person must be committed to the position and have the courage to outwait the exploiter who tries it.

ESCALATION

Escalation is one of the most effective tactics in negotiation. Business history is full of successful escalations. Whether it is ethical or not depends on how, when, and why it is used. This is one tactic that every buyer and salesperson must understand if he or she wants to avoid being exploited.

In its unethical form, escalation works like this: The seller and buyer *agree* on a price. The next day, the seller raises his price. The buyer gets angry but starts negotiating again. They compromise on a final price higher than the original agreement. The tactic can be and often is used by buyers as well as sellers.

As an example, assume that you want to sell a car worth

$7,200. A buyer answers the ad. After a lengthy negotiation, you reluctantly agree to accept $6,500. The buyer leaves a $100 deposit. The next day he or she returns with a certified check for $6,000, rather than $6,400. He or she cries a lot and explains that this is all that can be raised. Will you accept the deal or not? I believe that most people will.

People do not make decisions easily. Once a decision is made, they begin to convince themselves that it is a good one. Having gone through the effort of negotiating, making up their minds, and proving to themselves that the decision is sound, they are reluctant to reopen the matter. If, in the process of deciding, they have further committed themselves by telling others in the organization that the deal is reasonable, it becomes even harder to resist escalation. The difference between what they thought they were going to get and what they get becomes relatively less important.

Escalation can help a seller prove that the price originally proposed is a fair one. Several years ago, as a buyer for a large company, I received a $500,000 proposal from a seller. The cost analyst and I were convinced that the services could be bought for $440,000. About a month later, negotiations began. The trouble was that the seller opened the conference by demonstrating that his bid was in error. He needed $600,000 to do the job. This announcement knocked a big hole in our aspirations. To this day, I do not know whether the $600,000 demand was the result of an error or not. All I know is how pleased I was to buy the services for "only" $500,000 when it was all over. Escalation is one approach that some sellers use to convince a buyer that they have bid a very tight price. It helps them prove their point.

Escalation can also be used in a perfectly ethical way to discourage additional demands of an opponent. Many years ago, I was buying a small house. The owner and I had dickered for several days and were getting close to agreement. As part of the settlement, he agreed to provide a termite clearance worth about $100. This was not really a concession because California law requires that a seller provide such a clearance automatically unless the parties specifically decide not to.

We met at 9:00 in the morning of the last day. I had decided to nibble for the stove and refrigerator. Both were old. I expected that he would throw them into the deal because they weren't worth moving to Tennessee where he was going. Before I could ask for them, he surprised me. He said, "I've been thinking about that termite clearance, and I can't throw it in." Here he was reneging on a $100 concession when the full deal involved about $15,000. It took me aback.

I put aside my planned demands for the old stove and refrigerator. The next thirty minutes were spent in getting him to reconcede the $100 termite clearance. How good I felt when I persuaded him to throw the termite clearance back in. By the way, I got the stove and refrigerator. Not free, as I had planned, but at additional cost. He had successfully stifled my demands.

Neither party in a negotiation knows how far they can go. As a rule, both know that the longer they bargain, the better one or the other is likely to do. I was convinced that I could get the stove and refrigerator thrown in free if I persisted. By reneging on the termite clearance, the seller sent me the signal that I had gone as far as I could go. In so doing, he discouraged my future demands. He had every right to change his mind on any prior concession before final agreement on the whole deal was reached.

Whenever you as a buyer or seller want to convey your resolve and tell the other party that they have gone as far as they can go, escalation is an *ethical* alternative. The message comes across clearly whether the negotiation involves borders between countries, a billion-dollar contract, or a termite clearance.

Escalation works better than it deserves to. There are people who would not hesitate to use it in a business situation even after a contract is signed. The first line of defense against escalation is a better understanding of how and why it works. A number of countermeasures are discussed next.

ESCALATION COUNTERMEASURES

What can be done to prevent escalation? These actions are available to you:

1. Call the other person's bluff. He or she may be as unwilling to start over again as you are.
2. Get a large security deposit. If you are selling a house or car, be sure to get as much earnest money as you can.
3. Get as many high-level people as possible to sign the contract agreement. There are unethical people who escalate even after a contract is signed. The more names on the contract, the more difficult it is for these people to escalate.
4. Counterescalate. Change your offer or demand.
5. Caucus. Give yourself time to think.
6. Don't be shy. Ask the other party before the contract is signed what assurances will be given to guarantee against escalation.
7. Give strong consideration to walking away from the deal.

These countermeasures are not foolproof. It's safe to assume that the escalator knows what he or she is doing. He or she has decided deliberately that the odds of winning are good. Test the escalation vigorously. You may find that he or she has more to lose than you do. The escalator is no fool. He or she is just a tough gambler who does not deserve an easy victory.

EXPERTS: THE USE AND ABUSE OF

What's an expert? Over the years I've heard experts defined in many ways. Some were none too complimentary. That's good because it reveals a healthy skepticism that expertise like other things in life is not to be taken at face value.

Experts aren't all they are cracked up to be. Some experts are real; others are phony. Some are scientific in outlook; others make up facts and statistics as they go along. Some are secure in their knowledge; others are fearful of contradiction.

Experts play an important role in negotiation. People who are thought to be authorities in a field exert greater influence than those who are not thought so. People tend to be intimidated by experts. They become afraid to express opinions. When an authority speaks, others are reluctant to challenge these assertions. Experts enjoy the initiative in promoting ideas.

Certain experts have greater credibility than others. Those with the highest credibility are people who do original and controlled experiments. Below that are those who do independent analysis. Those who put information into categories and fool around with semantics are at a lower rung of the expert ladder. Research findings also indicate that experts who are not threatening to others and express themselves with confidence exert greater influence.

Knowledge is not enough. Psychologists have discovered that many other factors help determine whether a person will be believed. It appears that older people, white people, those with good appearances, those who are published, those with high academic degrees, and those who are national figures find it easier to sell their viewpoints. Even a small thing like the way the expert is introduced has significance. Psychologists have found that experts who are introduced in a positive, credential-loaded way carry greater weight with listeners than people with equal qualifications not so introduced.

The next time you are up against an expert, stay cool. Don't be put on the defensive. Like all of us, experts have their limits. The following are five suggestions as to how to deal with an expert:

1. Test the person. Expert or not, he or she may know less about a specific issue than you do.
2. Don't confuse wealth, position, or fame with expertise.
3. Expertise is not transferable. An expert in one area is not likely to be equally versed in another.

4. Broaden the subject. Maybe this expert knows more and more about less and less.
5. Be skeptical. Check his or her expertise.

When all else fails, you can always claim ignorance. Ignorance and irrationality are powerful negotiating tools. There are few things as frustrating as dealing with a person who can't or won't understand. Don't be afraid to ask the same question ten times in ten different ways. Probe for the answer you want. Experts don't always have common sense. Like us, they talk too much at times.

Probably the best defense against an expert is getting your own. Remember Karrass's Law of Experts: *For every expert, there is an equal and opposite expert.*

FACE-SAVING: THE BIG HIDDEN ISSUE

Asians are supposed to be more concerned about face-saving than we Westerners. That is nonsense. Americans are as concerned about face-saving as people anywhere. Perhaps our concern is well hidden, but it's there nevertheless. Averell Harriman was once described as a superior negotiator. The foreign diplomat who so described him said that Harriman was an expert in finding face-saving solutions to international problems. Face-saving is one of the big hidden issues in every negotiation.

People negotiate on two levels: personal and business. A bad deal for a person's company may not be bad for him or her. If there's a good explanation, it may permit a person to justify the deal to others and thereby maintain their confidence. Conversely, if an individual suffers loss of face in dealing with another, even the best bargain will leave a bitter aftertaste.

All people have a need to validate their self-worth. Other people are mirrors by which our self-worth is reflected. When others recognize our worth, we find it easier to see it in ourselves. When they don't, there is trouble.

When a person's self-image is threatened, he or she becomes

hostile. Some people attack, some run away, and some become apathetic—but all get angry. Experiments show that people, given a chance, retaliate against the person who attacks their ego. *Those who have lost face are willing to suffer losses to themselves if in so doing they can cause the abuser to suffer.* Research clearly supports that the person whose "face" is threatened withdraws. The more critical the attack, the less information the face-saver communicates. Loss of face becomes significantly more serious when people are abused before friends or those who are important to them.

A negotiation can hardly be conducted without questioning the other person's presentation. One must probe into the facts and assumptions. These probes should not be on a personal level. They should be directed to the business at hand and not the competence of the adversary. I have found that some of the phrases below help reduce tension when a position is questioned:

1. "On the basis of your assumptions, I can see your conclusion, but have you considered . . . "
2. "There is some information you may not have had available."
3. "Let's look at it this way."
4. "The difference between our points of view is not large, but . . . "
5. "I think that your production person may have led you in the wrong direction."
6. "Perhaps there are other reasons I'm not aware of."
7. "It's certainly open to several interpretations, but I believe that . . . "

Can we minimize the hostility created when a person is put into an awkward position? One way is to blame errors and discrepancies on such third parties as accountants, lawyers, or other people no longer with the company. Another is to blame differences on policies, procedures, or data-processing systems. These "bad guys" serve to direct responsibility away from the person and toward nonthreatening channels.

Hostility can also be relieved by positive means. This is done by finding as many common areas of agreement as possible. These common areas are then incorporated into a position that emphasizes what both parties are for, rather than what they are against.

I know some people who still believe that a strong personal attack pays off. I don't. It is dangerous to abuse another person no matter how angry you are or how justified your position. *Always leave the other party a face-saving way out.*

FAIR AND REASONABLE: THE SEDUCTIVE TRAP

Few of us want to exploit the other person. We would rather be fair and reasonable. But fair and reasonable happens to be a very troublesome idea to work with. It looks seductively simple. Below the surface, it raises some difficult problems for those who buy and sell. Both prefer to be fair and reasonable but are bound to have trouble doing so. A few examples will make this clear.

If you were giving prizes and there were two first-place winners, you might give each a honey fudge ice-cream cone. That would be fair, wouldn't it? But if one liked honey fudge and the other didn't, would that change your concept of fair somewhat?

Or what if some billionaire and I were first-place winners and each was given $1,000? Money is not like honey fudge. Everybody likes it. However, the real question might be how much satisfaction the billionaire got from another thousand in contrast to how much I got. I have good reason to doubt that each of us would gain equal satisfaction. If so, does this affect the idea of fair and reasonable? I believe it does.

In the last analysis, the central commodity that is exchanged in a negotiation is satisfaction; not goods or money or services. Satisfaction is the end product. What gives satisfaction to one person does not give equal satisfaction to another. The concept of fairness is subjective. It is never amenable to measurement!

"Fair and reasonable" are Humpty Dumpty words. They mean whatever you want them to mean. I would rather be realistic and use Shakespeare's words: *"He is well paid that is well satisfied."*

FAIT ACCOMPLI: THE DEED IS DONE

"Fait accompli" is a tactic associated with diplomacy. It works as well in business. The principle is simple. Someone takes a surprise action designed to place himself or herself in a favorable negotiating position. The "accomplished fact" cannot help affecting the final outcome. Iraq marches into Kuwait, then the Kuwaitis and their allies try to negotiate. Had the negotiation taken place at the Iraq-Kuwait border, results might have been different.

I once worked for a plastics manufacturer who learned from his Washington lawyer that price controls were soon to go into effect. The manufacturer immediately advised all customers by telegram that prices were increased 50 percent. Shortly afterward, controls were instituted. The owner then commenced negotiations with each customer. Most were delighted to settle for any amount less than 50 percent. The fait accompli was successful.

Action has a way of altering the balance of power. The strength of fait accompli rests in the fact that once a deed is done, it is difficult to undo. In effect, the aggressor says, "I've done it. Now let's talk."

A brief look at some typical seller-buyer fait-accompli actions shows how common the tactic is in the real world:

TYPE OF ACTION	USUALLY DONE BY *Buyer*	*Seller*	*Both*
1. Repair machine prior to price agreement.		X	
2. Make the change, then negotiate.		X	
3. Give seller a "paid-in-full" check which is less than the seller's bill.	X		
4. Ship somewhat defective parts so late that buyer must use them in production.		X	
5. Let seller begin work on basis of an anticipated order, then back off.	X		
6. Start a lawsuit, then talk.			X
7. Stop work, then negotiate new price.		X	
8. Violate the patent, then settle out of court.			X
9. Agree on one set of terms but send purchase order or acknowledgment with other terms.			X
10. Have machine installed or delivered, then reject it and ask for credit.	X		
11. Violate a law, then negotiate.			X
12. Sell grade A but ship grade B.		X	
13. Buy grade B but set so high a quality inspection that only grade B+ gets through.	X		
14. Issue an investigative or audit report, publicize it, then negotiate its points.			X
15. Bypass normal channels.			X
16. "I made the deal. You tell them it's off."			X
17. "I got caught. We'll have to cover up."			X
18. Break the rule, then negotiate.			X
19. "The material is all cut up. I can't return it and I can't pay."			X

TYPE OF ACTION	USUALLY DONE BY *Buyer*	*Seller*	*Both*
20. "I spent the money on something else. I need more to keep on working."			X
21. "I won't move out. Make me."			X
22. "I started the paperwork. We can't reverse it."			X
23. "Sorry about that bum check, but I can't pay."	X		
24. "I did it. What are you going to do about it?"			X
25. "I'm bankrupt. Will you settle for ten cents on the dollar?"	X		

The expression "Possession is nine points of the law" is a familiar one. Fait accompli is based on the same general concept. There are several countermeasures available against this essentially unethical tactic:

1. Anticipate the tactic. Protect against it by putting heavy penalties into the contract.
2. Protest at a high level.
3. Start a lawsuit.
4. Take your own aggressive action. Then trade off.
5. Get public opinion on your side.
6. Get a big deposit.
7. Never pay in advance of work done without good security.

It is not easy to deal with the person who executes a fait accompli. The best approach is to make the costs so high that the aggressor is afraid to try it or is forced to retreat if he or she does.

FAMILY ASSOCIATIONS PAY OFF

When we looked at the most powerful people on earth years ago, we saw not individuals, but families. Those most influential were not presidents or prime ministers. They were the Rockefellers, the duPonts, the Rothschilds, the Tafts, and a few other key families in Europe and Asia. Presidents came and went, but these families remain strong for centuries.

Family associations pay off. When two brothers join to buy refrigerators from Sears, they get a better deal than if they bought individually. When two buyers in the same company combine requirements, their purchasing power is increased. The low prices achieved on corporate agreements confirm this. Yet buyers are usually so busy that they fail to implement this commonsense idea. What's worse, purchasing management not only lets it happen but contributes to defeating family associations by lack of communication between end users in different areas of the company.

Most buyers in big organizations don't know what the person at the next desk is doing. It is axiomatic that the buyer has no idea of what is being bought in other parts of his or her division, in other divisions of the company, or in other companies within the corporation. There is scarcely any communication link between buyers. What little there is, is complicated by petty jealousies. It's every one for himself—the company be damned.

This is not the fault of the buyer. Management is to blame. Despite the proliferation of computers, it is still very hard to find out who in a company is buying what from whom. Computer data are generated for reasons other than purchasing negotiations. The information necessary for that purpose is missing. To compound the buyer's problem, it turns out that the typical computer run can be hard to read. It can show little if any delivery or quality history and fails to differentiate well between types of products purchased. I am not familiar with any computer setup that tabulates purchases about to be made. There are many, however, that permit a buyer to trace what has been purchased, but they can be hard to follow. Buyers sometimes find the typical tab run so complicated that they do what comes naturally. They place the order as though they were the only people in the company doing business with the seller. It doesn't make much sense, but that's the way it is in a lot of purchasing organizations.

The way out of the dilemma is to organize corporate information so that the buyer can get an easy answer to five questions:

1. Who is dealing with the supplier or is about to?
2. Are there any problems with the supplier on existing orders?
3. Can buyer requirements be combined?
4. Is there any information about the seller's people or organization that will help the negotiator?
5. Does a corporate purchase agreement make sense based on estimated quantities? (Remember that 90 percent of the requirements on any item comes from 10 percent of the people using it.)

No purchasing manager should let his or her people go into a negotiation without raising these basic questions.

As for those on the selling side, what surprises me is how often sales managers fail to take advantage of their own "family associations." Having sold to one department or division of a company, they fail to find out which other divisions have similar requirements. The easiest sale of all is through a reference from a satisfied customer in the same company or the same industry. "Family associations" make sense for buyers and sellers alike. Why not use them more?

FATIGUE

The research is clear that people deprived of sleep, food, or drink function poorly. People who are tired are influenced easily and make dumb mistakes. Those who have to negotiate through the night know that almost any deal can look pretty good at 3:00 in the morning.

Many a negotiation has been set up to go through long daytime sessions followed by all-night talks or nights devoted to replanning and reestimating. Those who set it up were aware that this treatment, if applied for a period of time, would make the negotiators irrational, depressed, and error prone. It would also get their spouses darned angry.

Bargaining is a tough physical process. It requires clear wits and large reserves of energy. People are not equal in their ability to stand stress. The strain of long plane trips, tight schedules, and new surroundings takes an awful toll on good judgment.

The team leader is responsible for conducting business at regular hours. He or she should see that the team eats at normal times and gets enough rest. If the trip is a long one, spouses should be encouraged to come along at company expense. The stakes are too high to be chintzy with per-diem allowances and first-class accommodations.

FINE FOOD AND SMALL FAVORS CAN INFLUENCE BIG DECISIONS

Buyers are more susceptible to sales influence while they are eating and after they are well fed. What every good salesperson knows has been confirmed experimentally. The salesperson who takes the buyers out to lunch is doing the right thing.

Small favors can influence big decisions. A desert land-sales firm has learned that profits can be made by giving away three $10 bills in Las Vegas. All a person has to do for the $30 is to listen to a one-hour presentation.

I asked the developer why he gave money away. He said that four principles were going for him: (1) everybody likes something for nothing; (2) people like to gamble with free money; (3) they don't want to feel cheap; (4) they open their minds to the presentation to rationalize taking the money. As he put it, "The amazing thing is that they pretend to themselves and to the land salesperson that they are attending the talk because of a genuine interest in the land." For a mere $30, a skeptical audience becomes responsive.

Good food, a nice evening, and small favors are not bribes. There is nothing corrupt about offering these common amenities. What they do for the salesperson is make the buyer more receptive to the sales message. A company that is stingy about allowances for lunch and drink expenses is making it harder to sell. Conversely, salespeople who pocket the allowance when they should be spending it are fools.

FORM AN ASSOCIATION WITH YOURSELF

Associations are good for business. There is one association anyone can join, and that is an association with himself or herself. People pass up an opportunity to make better settlements in their rush to get orders placed. They forget to form an association with themselves.

Ordinarily, a single buyer with modest needs has little bargaining power against a seller. This lack of bargaining power need not exist. A buyer can increase his or her leverage by searching for ways by which to make the overall deal more attractive to the seller. This can be done simply by asking a few questions before negotiating a purchase.

1. Can I cause the seller to lower his price by promising future business or by ordering more now?
2. Can I increase the seller's business by permitting him or her to use me as a reference?
3. Can I help the seller get more business by actively soliciting accounts for him or her (without a conflict of interest)?
4. Can I bunch purchases together to increase the seller's interest in making the sale?
5. Can I increase some open purchase order to the seller for the same item?
6. Can I increase the dollar size of an existing order by adding a new item?
7. Can I take options on future requirements and thereby beat the price or get better service?

I know a man who saved $1,000 on a swimming pool by forming an association with himself. He found a builder who wanted to break into a newly developed housing tract. The contractor was willing to build a superb pool at a substantial discount to the first homeowner who would allow it to be shown to neighbors. When the pool was completed, my friend asked the builder to clean it regularly as part of the deal. The builder protested, but then decided that it was to his best interest to keep the pool sparkling clean. They compromised by sharing maintenance costs for three years. The total deal was good for both parties, but especially for my friend.

Form an association with yourself! It works just as well whether you buy or sell.

FULL AUTHORITY: THE BUILT-IN TRAP

Four hundred years ago, Sir Francis Bacon advised heads of state to negotiate through intermediaries rather than face to face. His advice is well taken. The history of summit meetings is paved with blunders. There are good reasons for this.

Full authority accentuates other imbalances in power between parties. While each can speak for and bind his or her organization, they may not be equal in other more important ways. One may be in poor physical shape, as President Franklin D. Roosevelt was at Yalta, while the other is in the prime of life. One may be carefully prepared while the other is too busy to get ready. One may be harassed by problems while the other is well staffed and free of smaller cares. One may be emotionally secure, the other anxious and unstable. One may be financially sound, the other living like a prince on credit. One may feel the need to play "big shot," the other less concerned with image making. One may have risen to high status by hard work and great risk while the other lived a life of leisure. These differences can affect any negotiation even when authority is limited. When the negotiators have full authority, it can result in disaster.

Top people go into a negotiation with special problems in contrast to people lower on the authority pyramid. The chiefs are generally less knowledgeable and less likely to have prepared in depth. They do a poorer job of coordinating and negotiating with their own people. They tend to feel that they can and should speak for the needs and priorities of those below. However, in any complex organization, "Father does not know best." He just thinks he does. We have more than our share of fools, blunderers, and ideological misfits in high business and political offices. The top person tends to suffer from one other disease: the need to play the role of an all-wise politician or businessperson.

Those with full authority must take special precautions. They must not be pushed into quick decisions. They must build into their planning time to rest, to think, to check facts, and to touch base with others. They must feel free to ask dumb questions and to say "I don't know" as often and as casually as other people do. The stakes are higher when high people meet. Bruised egos and bad mistakes are more costly. Beware of summit meetings. You are generally better off dealing through intermediaries with limited authority.

FUNNY MONEY CAN WORK FOR YOU

Don't negotiate with funny money. That is a rule you should never forget. Once you see the difference between funny money and real money, it becomes easier to avoid giving the store away.

What in the world is "funny money"? We are surrounded by it. Chips in Las Vegas are funny money. So are credit cards, monthly payments, and interest rates. Funny money is the income tax deducted from your salary and the insurance payment tacked onto your house mortgage. All these have one thing in common: While they really concern money, they do not seem quite real. Each seduces us into spending more by taking our eyes off the real target: "What does it cost in hard cash?"

Gamblers in Nevada know human nature. People will lay a $10 bet with a plastic chip faster than they will put a $10 bill on the line. Land developers know that it is easier to sell lakefront lots at $360 a month than at the scary full price of $100,000. What difference does 9 percent or 10 percent interest make unless you look at it over the thirty-year mortgage span. A. P. Giannini founded the Bank of America and made it prosper because he understood that people were more concerned with their money payments than the total cost. Funny money is "easy-come, easy-go" money. Ask Visa if it isn't so.

Whenever you negotiate, discipline yourself to think of real money. Below are two columns. The one on the left is funny money. The one on the right is the real issue you should be thinking about.

FUNNY MONEY	REAL MONEY
1. The buyer says, "You are asking 20 cents a pound. We'll give you 19 cents a pound. What's a lousy penny?"	1. The seller should be thinking, "With 2 million pounds involved, that man is asking us to cut our profit margin from $60,000 to $40,000."
2. The transportation seller says, "We charge you only $5 to fill out an export document. You know that it would cost you three times that if you did it yourself."	2. The transportation buyer should be thinking, "With 3,000 foreign shipments a year, that person is asking us to give $15,000. Why, that pays for a full-time clerk for a year."
3. The construction buyer says, "We can't give you the 10 percent fee you ask; 9½ percent is all. What difference does it make?"	3. The contractor should be thinking "A ½ percent fee on a $3-million job represents $60,000 added profit. Wow! That can buy that new piece of equipment we need."
4. The building material salesperson says, "We'll sell you those beautiful used bricks at $650 a thousand."	4. The customer should be thinking, "But I need 10,000 bricks. That comes to $6,500. I'll bet I can make a deal for $5,500 if I take the lot."

FUNNY MONEY	REAL MONEY
5. The banker says, "We can't reduce the interest rate from 9½ to 9 percent on your new manufacturing plant mortgage."	5. The controller should be thinking, "Over a thirty-year period that ½ percent is worth $150,000. Wow! $150,000 is worth negotiating for."
6. The union negotiator says, "We need an extra two minutes on the break to allow people to go to the bathroom."	6. Management should be thinking, "Two minutes a day for 2,000 men for one year is worth $80,000. Wow!"
7. The big executive says, "Let's make a million-dollar concession on this $50-million deal."	7. The president should be thinking, "Our whole company earned only $5 million all last year. Maybe we ought to try a $250,000 concession instead."

People with business sense train themselves to think of real money whenever they transact business. Only then do they decide whether they want the discussion to revolve around such unrealities as percentage rates, cost per pound, price per unit, employee-hours, overhead rates, or labor rates per hour. They prefer to let the other party think in terms of funny money while they do not.

The funny-money principle states: "People who deal in funny money spend more and give more away."

GET-EVERYBODY-INVOLVED LEVERAGE

Many years ago, the Students for a Democratic Society (SDS) used the "get-everybody-involved" tactic to create turmoil on American campuses. They succeeded far beyond their expectations.

The SDS packaged issues together to exploit the unrest of antiwar groups, black activists, students who were displeased with curricula, and professors disturbed by budget cutbacks. Police violence followed the first demonstrations. This did what SDS could never do. It got the vast majority of nonpolitical kids angry at authority. What followed were massive demonstrations and a shutdown of the institutions. A handful of activists leveraged their power and thereby succeeded in disrupting the lives of millions of people.

The idea behind "get everybody involved" is inducing groups with different interests to commit themselves to a position in a negotiation. The number of issues is so broadened that as many people as possible become involved in the outcome.

The tactic is used commonly in collective bargaining. Quite a while back, the United Farm Workers and the grape growers entered negotiations. Before long, its leader, Cesar Chavez, included among the issues such divergent matters as housing, education, immigration policies, the store-clerks' union, other labor organizations, and Democratic party politics. Soon the public and so many other people had an equity in the outcome that a settlement was bound to follow.

There is nothing unethical about this tactic as such. It happens in business every day. A buyer friend was recently shipped some shoddy but usable goods. When his request for a price reduction was refused, he registered complaints with the license department, the Better Business Bureau, and the local trade association. In addition, complaining letters were sent to the seller's marketing, production, finance, and engineering executives. He got the reduction.

"Get everybody involved" works because power coalitions develop around issues. The phrase "Politics breeds strange bedfellows" is quite understandable in that light. If a negotiator raises enough issues, he or she is bound to find supporters somewhere for a number of them. As the conflict grows, there are always people on the other side who get a greater and greater equity in settling the dispute before it gets completely out of hand. If the problem grows large enough, neutral third parties and the public are inevitably dragged into it.

The best countermoves against "get everybody involved" are patience and public relations. The common sense of neutral third parties should be given time to prevail. If those who are uncommitted believe that grievances will be heard fairly and acted upon, they will act as a force toward moderation. The uncommitted resent being manipulated for the purposes of others. Restraint, open-mindedness, and good public relations will help cool the power of the loose-knit "get-everybody-involved" coalition.

GOOD-COP/BAD-COP TACTICS

We have all seen "good-cop/bad-cop" tactics in the movies.

Here's how "good-cop/bad-cop" works. A suspect is caught and interrogated. The first detective puts him or her under a glaring light, asks questions relentlessly, roughing up the suspect. Then the tough detective leaves. In comes a nice detective who shuts the light off, gives the suspect a cigarette, and lets him or her relax. Soon afterward, the suspect spills all. "Good-cop/bad-cop" works better than it should.

How does "good-cop/bad-cop" work in negotiation? One person takes a tough stand, makes large demands, and acts in an aggressive manner. Next to him or her is friendly old Smiley, who says little during the discussion. After a while, the "bad cop" shuts up and the "good cop" takes over. When he or she makes demands, they seem reasonable by comparison. Why not? It seems a pleasure dealing with such a nice person after being worked over by that meanie. You can't help feeling that things could have been worse.

"Bad cops" come in all shapes and forms. They can be people or nonpeople, real or make-believe. Pricing people, lawyers, accountants, and even bosses make good "bad cops." They are very believable. Committees, regulatory bodies, and bankers often act in the role of hard-liners. Nonhuman "bad cops" include company policies, standard terms and conditions, credit rules, and procedures of all kinds. After all, if you, as the opposing negotiator, don't like my company policy, whom can you talk to? I don't even know who writes "our" policies. They can't help becoming part of your problem if they are part of mine.

When you are up against "bad cops," there are a number of good countermoves you can take:

1. Let them talk. Often their own people will get fed up.
2. Protest to higher authorities.
3. Walk out.
4. Blame them in public.
5. Use your own "bad cop."
6. Predict very early in the talks that the "bad cops" will soon take that role. This helps neutralize them.
7. Call a caucus.

The best defense of all is a recognition that the "good cop" and "bad cop" are on the same side. They both want to get as much as they can get. "Good-cop/bad-cop" is their way of doing it.

HARD TO GET

A fact of life: *People put greater value on things that are hard to get.*

Buyers don't appreciate easy victories as much as they should. So, if you really want to make them happy, make them work hard for everything they get. Don't be in a big hurry to make concessions, to offer extra services, to promise quicker deliveries, to give away free training, to tighten a specification, to provide easy terms, or to take a lower price.

Don't be easy to get!

HECKLERS

I don't like hecklers. They shake me up. There is a pro tackle who drives the opposing quarterbacks crazy by making biting remarks. In baseball it's not uncommon for the catcher to rattle a batter with a torrent of inane chatter. Buyers sometimes heckle salespeople for the same reason. The heckler wants to reduce the other person's capacity to deal with the job at hand.

Heckling is hard to take. While most people go out of their way to treat others courteously, the heckler does the opposite. He or she seeks to exploit weaknesses in an opponent's personality. Many union negotiators like to use this tactic on management.

A person can be heckled verbally, physically, or psychologically. Verbal abuse may consist of unnecessary noise, kidding, or nonsense talk. Physical heckling often includes uncomfortable eating and seating arrangements. Psychological abuse takes many forms, such as subtle attacks on a person's status or intelligence, deliberate inattention to what he or she says, or threats against job security. The heckler hopes that the victim will subconsciously want to relieve pressure by settling quickly.

In the long run, hecklers hurt themselves. In baseball they find themselves ducking close pitches. In football they are at the bottom of the pileup. In business, eventually they get squeezed out of their own organizations. People who play foul are foul. Nobody trusts them.

Yet, I'm afraid to say, heckling works in the short run. Hecklers shake people up more than they want to admit. That is what the hecklers count on. Therefore you have little choice but to raise their cost for this cheap trick. The countermeasures available to you are much the same as against the "bad guy" shown on page 82. In life as in negotiation, people are abused to the extent that they permit themselves to be. Force the heckler to find another "victim," and he or she will.

HOLY WAR: WHY WE NEED OUR "ENEMIES"

One way to muster the total resources of an organization, a political party, or a nation is to convince its people that their cause leaves no room for compromise. The "holy-war" tactic is effective because it marshals the psychological and material strength of an organization against the "villain" across the table. Internal squabbles are diminished. Everybody is expected to contribute toward victory by submerging their own self-interest.

Our "enemies" serve a purpose. They allow us to focus the self-righteous attention of our people on the petty measures of the other party. In doing so, the organization around the buyer rallies against the seller, and vice versa. People within the buyer's organization who hardly speak to one another normally join together against the outside threat. All this may be well and good, but there are dangers.

The trouble with holy wars is that people get tired of them. It is hard to maintain a fever pitch about any cause in the face of day-to-day problems. Furthermore, some people submerge self-interest less than others. Grumbling is bound to start the moment a holy war gets bogged down in setbacks, frustration, or corruption.

Another difficulty in starting an all-consuming conflict is that it inspires the opponent to do the same. The normal divisions found in any organization give way to a unified front against the unreasonable "enemy." In fact, the group on the defensive has less reason to manufacture reasons for the holy war because it is they who have been attacked. They also gain by having "enemies."

One source of real power in a negotiation comes from your ability to rally support. If those at home are united behind the negotiators' objectives, bargaining becomes easier. The "holy-war" tactic helps rally people to the cause, but it can get out of control quickly. The Iran-Contra scandal and the strange mentality it encouraged proved that the judgment and value system of zealots leaves much to be desired.

HOSTAGE TACTIC

Every month we read about a kidnapping somewhere in the world. Someone is captured and held until a ransom is paid. The price is exorbitant, but the alternative is far worse. One has but to remember the prisoner-of-war issue in the Vietnam War. The North Vietnamese built the issue man by man. They knew that these hostages would become important bargaining collateral. The Communists understood this tactic well. We did not.

The "hostage" tactic is common in business, but the victim is different. The hostage in business transactions is never a person, but something else of value. Typical hostages include money, goods, property, or a person's good reputation. The business kidnapper says, in effect, "If you don't meet my demand, you won't get back what I'm holding."

I ran into a hostage situation yesterday on my way from work. The auto mechanic took my transmission apart to fix a seal. The job was estimated at $550. When I dropped into the shop after work, I learned that a rebuilt transmission was necessary. The transmission lay on the floor, half taken apart. Little pieces were all over. He gave me a choice. I could pay for the seal and pay for putting it together again, or pay $1,500 for a rebuilt and guaranteed one. I chose the latter, as I'm sure most people would have. The repairman knew that he was in a better negotiating position after the transmission was apart in his shop than before. He had the body.

A friend of mine got into a lawsuit and had her bank account attached the day before her property taxes were due. She was forced to settle. If she had not done so, a number of checks for tax payments would have bounced, and the penalty cost would have been exorbitant.

I know a tenant who kidnapped a house. The tenant wanted to break the lease. He proceeded to change all the locks and then refused to pay rent. At night he played bongo drums, to the despair of his neighbors. When threatened with eviction, he quietly told the landlord that the interior of the house would not look very good if he were forced out. The landlord capitulated.

A supplier bid wrong on a job and lost money. He knew that the buyer needed the parts desperately, so he held them as hostage for a higher price. The buyer paid and got the parts on time.

We know how hard it is to deal with a kidnapper or skyjacker. There are no easy answers. The business kidnapper is not as difficult because life is not at stake. The countermeasures that follow apply to business hostages. Human hostages are quite another problem because the risks are far greater.

1. Get your own hostage. Then trade.
2. If you must pay ransom, pay it—but get ready to renegotiate through the courts.
3. Scream, picket, and protest at a high level.
4. Get an arbitrator.
5. Put severe penalties into the contract. The severity of the Lindbergh law reduced kidnapping.

Unfortunately, the payment of ransom encourages kidnapping. Unscrupulous businesspeople who try it and succeed look for other victims. That is why we who are exploited should contact the police, the public, legislators, and trade associations. They will help make the price too high for the exploiter.

HOW TO PUT YOURSELF IN THE OTHER PERSON'S SHOES

The next time you are in a business or social negotiation, ask yourself three simple questions. They will put your thinking on the right track. The questions below are oriented from the seller's viewpoint, but they apply to anyone anywhere.

1. What decision do I "realistically" want the buyer to make?
2. Why has he or she not already made that decision?
3. What action can I take that would make it easier for the buyer to make the decision I would like him or her to make?

These questions will help you think more constructively about your own actions and how they relate to the decision-making process of the other person.

ICEBERG THEORY: WHEN A LITTLE MEANS A LOT

There are not very many people we get to know well in life. Most business transactions are between people who do not have close personal ties. Yet, by the nature of things, we are forced to make important decisions involving others on the basis of relatively little information.

Ted Kotsovolos has a theory that he calls the "iceberg theory." Ted was the director of purchasing for a company that buys almost a billion dollars worth of goods and services a year. He believes that most of us try to appear as attractive as we can. We want people to associate with us in order to make a better social or business deal with life.

People stage performances. What shows is scenery, dress, mannerisms, and the words we speak. These are like the tip of an iceberg. The bulk is below. If, with all our efforts to look good, the tip shows flaws, one can only assume that the bottom is worse. If early signs indicate broken promises, questionable integrity, mealymouthed commitments, exaggerated facts, faulty knowledge, or deficient planning, don't be optimistic about the future. The situation is worse than it looks.

IDEAL NEGOTIATOR: THE MOST IMPORTANT TRAITS

I am convinced that negotiation is one of the most difficult jobs a person can do. It requires a combination of traits not ordinarily found in the business world or professions. The process of negotiating demands not only good business judgment, but also a keen understanding of human nature. The bargaining table is the center of a tense drama. I know of nowhere in business where the alchemy of power, persuasion, economics, motivation, and organizational pressure come together in so concentrated a fashion and so narrow a time frame. Nowhere is the return on investment potential so high.

These are thirteen traits I look for in a good negotiator:

1. An ability to negotiate effectively with members of his or her own organization and win their confidence
2. A willingness and commitment to plan carefully, know the product, the rules, and the alternatives; the courage to probe and check information
3. Good business judgment; an ability to discern the real bottom-line issues
4. An ability to tolerate conflict and ambiguity

5. The courage to commit oneself to higher targets and take the risks that go with it
6. The wisdom to be patient and thereby to wait for the story to unfold
7. A willingness to get involved with the opponent and the people in his or her organization—that is, to deal in personal and business depth with them
8. A commitment to integrity and mutual satisfaction
9. An ability to listen open-mindedly
10. The insight to view the negotiation from a personal standpoint—that is, to see the hidden personal issues that affect outcome
11. Self-confidence based on knowledge, planning, and good interorganizational negotiation
12. A willingness to use team experts
13. A stable person; one who has learned to negotiate with himself or herself and to laugh a little; one who doesn't have too strong a need to be liked because he or she likes himself or herself.

Can anyone fit a bill as tough as this? Probably not. However, when the stakes are high, it pays to find the right person. Common sense and research tell us that skilled negotiators come home with better settlements.

IGNORANCE CAN WORK FOR YOU

If you have ever tried to negotiate with someone who can't or won't understand, you know how hard it is. They wear you down until finally you decide, "The hell with it."

Sir Francis Bacon, sensing the frustration that is felt when someone deals with foolish or ignorant men, suggested almost 400 years ago, in his essay "Of Negotiating," that an absurd man be used to negotiate business which, as he put it, "doth not bear itself out well." He knew how hard it was to do business with people who were indecisive, disorganized, foolish, or fanatical about their viewpoint.

As a tactic, ignorance offers many benefits to the person courageous enough to try it. It can give a person time to think, time to check with experts, or time to test the resolve of the other party. The salesperson who is ignorant of costs cannot be interrogated about them. The buyer who says, "I don't know a thing about your problems. All I know is that I can pay this much and nothing more," is a tough person to deal with.

Ignorance may not be bliss, but it can help you in negotiating. Try it occasionally. Your opponent may find, like so many of us have, that it's hard to negotiate with a horse's ass.

INDIRECT INFORMATION CHANNELS

There are two levels of communication in every negotiation. One is direct, consisting of information passed across the table. The other is indirect, consisting of information passed through a variety of off-the-record channels.

Indirect channels exist because they must. On the one hand, a negotiator may have to appear tough in order to satisfy the expectations of those at home. On the other hand, he or she must appear reasonable to the opponent if he or she wishes to leave the opponent satisfied with an agreement. Both buyer and salesperson share these conflicting motives. This helps build an unspoken kinship between them.

Not everything that must be said can be said at the table. Indirect-communication techniques permit information to flow from one person to another with a minimum of friction. If a position is advanced informally and subsequently rejected, both parties are aware of it but need not fear any loss of face. When a formal offer is made and later results in a formal rejection, recriminations and hard feelings are more likely to follow.

Informal-communication channels permit goals of a personal

and organizational nature to be changed quietly. Some are abandoned, others deflected, and still others modified by the flow of semiofficial and unofficial information. The indirect channels listed below are necessary to supplement open communication. They provide a deeper perspective to the oratory of the bargaining table:

1. Polite end runs by people at higher or lower levels
2. Off-the-record or secret discussions
3. Price drops, trial balloons, and rumor leaks
4. Lost memos, notes, and documents which are deliberately left around for the opposition to find and study
5. Third-party intermediaries
6. Committee study-group reports and analyses
7. Press, publication, or broadcast media.

INTEGRITY

A negotiation is more than a discussion of issues or a signed agreement. It is an *unwritten* judgment on the quality and character of the participants. In reaching that judgment, integrity is the key element. Integrity makes the deal work. There is no substitute for it.

The absence of integrity cannot be offset by intelligence, competence, or tight legal phraseology. Without this quality, no deal, however carefully written, is worth much. Built into the transaction must be a high sense of values, the generosity to resolve subsequent difficulties equitably, and a commitment to meet the intent of the agreement. Integrity is always a big part of the price. Wherever it is lacking, you'll find yourself shortchanged.

KINDNESS CAN WIN YOU OVER

Many foreign businesspeople are gracious hosts. When you visit their country, they literally "win you over with kindness." After thirteen grueling hours in the air, you are ready to go to bed. There, to greet you at the airport, is a bright-eyed young person in a well-pressed suit. He or she is quick to tell you that a marvelous evening has been arranged. Your claim to being tired is to no avail. "Oh, no," says he, "all the reservations are made. We will have an exciting evening. It will be good fun." You don't want to hurt his or her feelings, so you go along.

That night you eat too well, drink too much, stay up too late, and have a hell of a good time. The next morning, the negotiation begins. There, across the table, is a brand-new young person in a well-pressed suit. Fresh, clean, and bright-eyed. Ready to go at it issue by issue.

Rich food and strong drink can dull wits as quickly as physical exhaustion. When good living is mixed with lack of sleep, the combination is lethal. A tough negotiator can turn into a passive cooperator almost as fast as it takes to say "Chateaubriand and champagne."

They that take up the cocktail shall perish by the cocktail.

"KRUNCH" TACTICS: YOU'VE GOT TO DO BETTER THAN THAT

There are seven magic words that drive a salesperson crazy: "You've got to do better than that." The "buyer's krunch" doesn't deserve to work as well as it does. In fact, a salesperson who understands it can make it work for him or her.

Imagine for a moment that we are sellers of a highly competitive standard chemical like salt. We bid $1 per pound on 100,000 pounds. Seller B bids $1.02 and Seller C $1.04 a pound. All others bid a good deal higher. Now the buyer tries the krunch. All he says to the three lowest bidders is "You've got to do better than that."

Do they do better? You bet they do. In fact, if the buyer says, "You've got to do *significantly* better than that," they have a good chance of doing even better.

Why does the krunch work so well? The answer lies in the pricing system of most companies. There is generally slack in bid prices. Even when the seller proposes a tight price, it rarely represents the least he or she will take. Pricing is not a science. Honest cost accountants differ on what something costs. Honest pricing people differ in their interpretation of what the market will bear. It isn't surprising that even the low bidder is mentally prepared to take less.

When salespeople hear the krunch, they tend to feel that the buyer likes them. They are grateful for a second crack at the job. All they need to do is drop the price and all will be well. Not necessarily. The buyer has krunched the competition as well. They are also willing to drop their price. The buyer has improved their position just by using seven magic words.

I believe that this tactic is ethical. There are many who do not.

Most people seem to agree that it is inherently dangerous for the buyer. It may do more harm than good. Purchasing managers should have a clear policy as to whether and when the krunch is to be used. As a manager, I instructed my people to use the tactic only with prior approval and under four conditions:

1. When all qualified buyers were given a second chance to improve their bids
2. When a severe budgetary limit existed
3. When there was doubt as to whether the bids reflected a true market sample
4. When there was a need to determine whether seller services were or were not included in the price and whether they were worth paying for.

The uninhibited use of the krunch by every buyer ultimately results in false economy. Sellers soon learn that they had better add 10 percent to the bids in order to subtract it later. In a small community or one in which there are few sellers, the krunch can lead to collusion, price-fixing, and lower overall quality.

What should a salesperson do when caught in the krunch? First, find out what the problem is. Ask the buyer whether others are offering the same product and service mix at a lower price. If you have gotten to know the buyer on a personal level, the answer may be surprisingly candid. It is not easy for a buyer to be inscrutable with somebody he or she likes.

The salesperson should recognize that every competitor offers a different package. Price is not money alone. It is a combination of benefits, including services, quality, delivery, competence, reliability, peace of mind, and lots more. No two "price" packages are alike. Let the buyers know what you can do for them. If they say "So what?" or "Everybody does that," remember: They know that there is a difference between promises and performance. Many make promises; not all perform.

Defend your price as persistently as possible. Show the buyer why it makes sense. Don't be shy. Point out in subtle ways how some people degrade quality or fail to provide services. Tell about the problems other buyers have run into. You don't have to mention names to prove your argument.

If, after all this, a concession seems necessary, don't rush into it.

Think first. Perhaps you can sell paintbrushes with the paint. Perhaps you can make the concession subject to instant acceptance for one reason or another. Handled right, it is possible to make an opportunity out of the krunch. A salesperson should not go into a negotiation without asking himself or herself, "What will I do if the buyer says, 'You've got to do better than that'?"

LAST AND FINAL OFFER

All of us have heard terms like "This is my last and final offer" or "This is my doorknob price." The trouble is that you never know whether it is or isn't the final offer. If you believe it, you agree. If not, you either keep talking or lose the deal.

It is possible to phrase a "last and final offer" so that it sounds final but permits you to retreat gracefully if necessary. The answer to the paradox lies in finding a method that will obscure the phrase in some way. This can best be illustrated by a series of examples related to buying a house.

Assume that you are the buyer and have told the seller, "This is my final offer for the house and furniture. If you don't accept it in three days, return my check." There are other ways of saying much the same thing available to a buyer. Each of the phrases below changes the meaning:

(A) "CONTENT" ALTERNATIVES (This is what we are talking about.)

1. This is my final offer for the house, fixtures, and patio furniture.
2. This is my final offer for the house (other items assumed from prior discussions).
3. This is my final offer considering all factors. (All factors may include escrow fees, financing, tax carryovers, interest penalties, and property.)
4. This is my final offer for the house. I will also offer you so much for the fixtures and patio furniture.

(B) "CONSEQUENCES" ALTERNATIVES (This is what will happen if we don't agree.)

1. If you don't accept my offer in three days, please return my check.
2. If you don't accept my offer in three days, call me.
3. If you don't accept my offer in three days, I'll call you.
4. If you don't accept my offer in three days, I'll consider that you are not interested.
5. If you don't call me in three days, consider the deal dead.

(C) "FIRMNESS" ALTERNATIVES (This is how sure the opponent can be about possible consequences.)

1. If you don't agree in three days, tear up the check and forget the deal. I'm going to Europe.
2. If you don't accept the offer in three days, I will buy the other house.
3. If you don't accept the offer in three days, we'll still be friends.
4. If you don't accept the offer in three days, good luck. Return the check and forget it.
5. If you accept the offer, present the check personally at my bank. The attached stop-payment letter goes into effect on the fourth day.

(D) "TIME" ALTERNATIVES (When will it happen?)

1. If you don't agree in three days, I'll be back in a month.
2. Take a few days to think about it.
3. Think about it and return the check to me in three days if you are not interested.
4. I've postdated the check three days so you can think about it.
5. The agent on the other house says I can conclude the other deal in less than a week or so.
6. Let me know whether or not you accept the offer.

Each revision to the original statement was designed to convey an aura of commitment and at the same time leave room for possible retreat. *There is no way to predict exactly how opponents will listen to or perceive what is said. For practical purposes, if they believe a commitment has been made, it has been made. If they don't believe it, then no matter how real the negotiator's intentions, they will challenge it. People read more into a statement than the speaker usually intends. They fill the blank spaces.* It is this tendency that permits a negotiator to retreat gracefully if he or she has framed the commitment well.

In the last analysis, the "last and final offer" can assist or impair bargaining power. If your claim is not believed, then your bargaining leverage is weakened. The wording and timing are important because they will determine whether the tactic will be productive or counterproductive. From the standpoint of a negotiator faced with a "last and final offer," an understanding of its subtleties is imperative. The stakes are too high not to listen carefully. The other party may not be bluffing.

LAST AND FINAL OFFER: COUNTERMEASURES

When someone gives you a "last and final offer," don't accept it at face value. Test it. These suggestions will help:

1. Listen to the exact words. He or she may be hedging.
2. Interpret the phrase without overreacting. Act as though you heard it in the way that best reflects what you want to hear.
3. Give the other party a face-saving way out from the "last-and-final" commitment.
4. Get angry if it suits your purpose.
5. Let him or her know what can be lost by deadlock.
6. Consider whether you should test it by walking out.
7. Change the subject.
8. Introduce new alternatives and possible solutions.
9. If you think the other party is going to come up with a "last and final offer," perhaps you should beat him or her to it.

"Last and final offer" has a good deal in common with "chicken." Daredevils sometimes test the courage of other drivers by heading straight at them at high speed. Somebody has to give to avoid a collision. It works the same way in negotiation. When you are given a last clear chance to take the final offer or risk the consequences, you are in a "chicken" situation. Fortunately, in negotiation, there's a middle road. You can usually keep talking. *But not always.*

LIMITED AUTHORITY

Limited authority is a source of power. People are generally better off if they don't have full authority. One bachelor I know likes to tell those he deals with that he must talk to his wife. No one has yet denied him that privilege. It gives him the time he needs to think things through.

Negotiators with limits can prove to be tough. They can say no gracefully. It is never they who say no, but someone or something else. That something else turns out to be a procedure, a policy, a budget, an engineering standard, or a government regulation that cannot be budged. The salesperson who lacks authority to give credit, or to change a price, or to settle a claim, or to grant a discount, or to absorb freight doesn't make concessions in those areas. He or she can't. The buyer who cannot exceed his or her budget, or cannot approve an order greater than the dollar limit, or cannot accept an off-standard product is hard to negotiate with.

Some funny things happen in negotiation. I am always surprised at how often one person's limits become the other person's problem. If I have limits to my authority, it is you, my opponent, who have to figure out a way around them. You are forced into a strange choice: to accept the deal at my limits, or to make a lot of work for yourself and maybe get no deal at all.

If you challenge my lack of authority by bumping the problem upward, other apprehensions set in. Now you must take on my boss or my boss's boss or our legal counsel, all of whom represent new status relationships and a greater degree of preparation on your part. Also, if you decide to go to higher levels, there is a chance that the other party will get angry. This especially bothers salespeople who are in no mood to jeopardize long-term accounts by frosting the buyer. Some would rather accept a lower price than risk a higher-level confrontation.

There is greater strength in not having authority than having it. Most buyers and sellers complain about the limits imposed on them. I feel that they should welcome such limits because they make their jobs easier. A person going into a negotiation would do well to ask, "What limits do I want imposed upon my authority?" Well-chosen limits can make a big difference in the final outcome.

LIMITED AUTHORITY: LIMITS I'VE BEEN GLAD I HAD

Authority limits can work for you. Below are limits I've been glad I had because they helped the other person make up his or her mind:

(A) DOLLAR LIMITS

1. Capital versus expense limit
2. Low purchase limit
3. Petty-cash limit
4. Signature authorization
5. Director approval
6. Budget limit
7. Standard-cost limit
8. Government-approval limit
9. Maximum or minimum price limit.

(B) TERMS LIMITS

1. Credit amount limit
2. Credit time limit

3. Advance-payments limit
4. Progress payment
5. Quantity discount schedules
6. FOB points
7. Warranty limit
8. Trade- and cash-discount limit
9. Interest-charge limit.

(C) PROCEDURE AND POLICY LIMITS

1. For types of contracts
2. For estimating, pricing, and audit
3. For labor projections
4. For overhead rates
5. For contingencies
6. Procedure for approving changes
7. Rules against revealing cost
8. For in-house transfer charges
9. For revealing information
10. For handling payments and billing
11. For handling terminations
12. Proof of work and payment methods
13. Charging for engineering assistance on training.

(D) LEGAL AND INSURANCE LIMITS

1. Company and standard terms and conditions
2. Rights in data
3. Insurance-coverage requirements
4. Government regulations
5. Limits of liability
6. Liability to third parties
7. Bonding requirements
8. Robinson-Patman compliance
9. Most-favored company or voting clause.

(E) ENGINEERING LIMITS

1. Limit on changing specifications
2. Changing package size
3. Input and output limits
4. Shelf-life limits
5. Revealing secrets.

(F) COMMITTEE LIMITS THAT HELP

1. Purchasing committee
2. Standards committee
3. Finance committee
4. Engineering-evaluation committee
5. Material-review board
6. Make-or-buy board
7. Salary-review board
8. Grievance committee
9. Source-selection committee
10. Negotiation committee.

(G) OTHER LIMITS THAT HELP

1. Price-rise limits
2. Limits to settle claims
3. Crediting limits for defective parts, overshipments, late delivery
4. Time limits of all kinds
5. Manufacturing-schedule limits.

Limits have served me well. Some gave me time to think, to hold tight, or to get the full story. Others gave me a chance to ask better questions or give better answers. Perhaps most importantly, they gave me a face-saving way to test my opponents' resolve and gave them a face-saving way to give in. The case for authority limits is a strong one.

LIMITED INSPECTION

"Limited inspection" is the most prudent approach for sellers who want to build credibility. The buyers are given only the amount of information consistent with their minimum needs. Guidelines are negotiated in advance that restrict what they may look at and whom they may contact. Contact people are briefed by the sellers to say as little as possible and to provide only what is asked for. The buyers are granted the privilege of looking and asking, but are made to work for what they get.

Limited inspection requires courage. Sellers must be prepared to say no to some requests and thereby risk reprisal. If the contact people have good judgment, all can go well. If not, customers may grow more distrustful than ever and go elsewhere for their needs. The key to making limited inspection work is good sense on the part of contact people.

In part, limited inspection works because people have a cultural aversion to prying into other people's affairs. They carry this aversion to the bargaining table. There is a tacit recognition in our free-enterprise society that sellers have the right (within reason) to conduct business as they see fit and to keep secrets from their competitors.

Limited inspection also works because it is so hard for people to ask good questions. Most interrogators are not willing to put in the effort. Others lack the time to do so. It takes more than the right to look to guarantee good answers.

Buyers who are offered limited-inspection rights should be unafraid to ask for more. The more they ask for, the more they will get. If rebuffed, there is nothing wrong with protests to higher buyer authority to stimulate further disclosure. When necessary, other people should also make demands for information. Squeaky wheels get action. *Many* squeaky wheels get *more* action.

Buyers who have the guts to be skeptical and to demand evidence get more information. They are likely to succeed because it is hard for a salesperson to look a buyer in the eye and say no. Test it and you'll see.

LISTENING: THE LEAST EXPENSIVE CONCESSION YOU CAN MAKE

How would you like to give the other person a concession without giving away anything of tangible value? It's easy. Just listen to him or her. Listening is the least expensive concession you can make. It can well be the most important.

Are you listening? Probably not. Research indicates that immediately after people have listened to someone talk, they remember only about half of what they have heard—*no matter how carefully they thought they were listening.*

Negotiation requires hard listening. It is too bad that most of us do not know how. Listening is the easiest way to recognize needs and discover facts. If you take the time to listen, you can't help learning. The trouble is that you have to get out of some bad habits. It means that you must look the speaker in the eye, be alert, sit straight, get close, and *be greedy to grasp new information.* He or she will reward your efforts by making it easier to pick out his or her points.

Why don't we listen? Of the eleven reasons below, only the first is the responsibility of the speaker. The rest are self-inflicted impediments to good listening.

1. Most people speak before they think. Their speech is disorganized and hard to listen to.
2. We have a lot on our minds that cannot be switched off at a moment's notice.
3. We tend to talk and interrupt too much.
4. We are anxious to rebut the other person's arguments.
5. We dismiss much of what we hear as irrelevant or uninteresting.
6. We tend to avoid listening to hard material because it is too technical or detailed.

7. We allow ourselves to get distracted and don't concentrate. The distractions are more fun than the topic under discussion.
8. We jump to conclusions before all the evidence is in.
9. We try so hard to remember everything that the main points get lost.
10. We dismiss some statements because they come from people whom we don't consider important.
11. We tend to discard information we don't like.

A close look at the bad habits reveals that they center around one theme. Poor listeners permit themselves to drop out of the conversation in the hope of catching up later. Unfortunately, they don't.

Constructive listening begins with a realization that a speaker is presenting himself or herself for your approval. He or she wants you to see and believe the presentation. Like an actor on a stage, he or she will perform better if you open your senses to what he or she says.

When people speak, they have a main theme, a few major supporting ideas, and proof that their ideas are sound. The trouble is that people don't follow that simple pattern. They mix things up. Anecdotes, ideas, irrelevancies, proof, and empty clichés are thrown together for the listener to unscramble.

How can we cope with this jumble? We can ask the other person to summarize main points and reasons. At times we can summarize the statements and ask whether or not our summary is correct. There is nothing wrong with saying, "I don't quite get the point," or "Let me get it straight," or "Do you mean to say . . . ," or "I'm not quite sure how that ties in." The other person wants you to understand. He or she will welcome the chance to make the point clear. You are doing a favor.

Listen actively. Listen as though you will have to summarize the main points to your boss. You will find that supporting details will fall in place if you catch the main points. Get into the habit of repeating what has been said so that the speaker knows you understand.

Another good idea is to assign one person on your team as an official "listener" who can take notes and observe what is said, how it is said, the order in which things are said, and what is not said. You will be surprised at how much a perceptive listener can see and hear that others at the table fail to pick up. One company I know of went too far. They had a group of psychologists on the staff and decided to put them into negotiations as listeners. It should have worked, but didn't. The psychologists turned out to be harder to understand than the opponents.

Below are a few more listening tips that work every time:

1. Give full attention. You just can't listen and do anything else at the same time.
2. Don't interrupt.
3. Discourage cute side remarks and distractions.
4. Don't cut off listening when something hard comes up.
5. Practice listening to ideas you don't like. Try to repeat what you've heard.
6. Let the other person have the last word.

Listening is the one concession you can give that is guaranteed to get you more than you gave.

LONG-TERM VERSUS SHORT-TERM RELATIONSHIPS: THE BIG TRADE-OFF

What works for a one-shot deal may be inappropriate in a long-term relationship. One vice-president of a prominent conglomerate, as exploitative a man as you would ever expect to meet, put it this way: "In the long run, there is no long run." This man and those who work for him in sales and purchasing tend to see every negotiation from an overly competitive viewpoint. Now that the company is in a battle for industrial survival, their people are learning at great cost that in business there is indeed a long run which can and must affect tactical choices and attitudes.

One of the big trade-offs in negotiation is that of balancing short-term victories against long-term goals. An opponent can be badgered, coerced, or threatened into doing what you wish. People who give in under these conditions remain hostile. Lord help the coercers if they ever need assistance or goodwill later.

People who know where they are going and why, make better negotiators. They don't win Pyrrhic victories that sow the seeds of later defeat. A good long-term strategy is more important than short-term gains. Part of the price in every negotiation is the flow of future satisfactions and dissatisfactions. It's a trade-off that only a person of good judgment knows how to make.

LOST MEMOS, NOTES, AND STOLEN DOCUMENTS

Sometimes the best way to reveal a position without taking responsibility for it is by losing your unsigned notes in the corridor or putting them in a wastepaper basket where an opponent can find them easily. Diplomatic messages are often exchanged by the convenient loss of an attaché case. Military plans of an apparently secret nature are found from time to time on the body of an officer on the battlefield.

Information obtained from indirect sources has more credibility than that provided openly. Lost memos, notes, and stolen documents are studied line by line by an opponent. The same information passed freely across the table might not be looked at. Producers hope that censors will attack a movie on the basis of sex. That practically guarantees a good box office for an undeserving picture.

I knew a man in the machine-shop business who made a lot of money leaving information where others could find it. He did a big business in getting machining jobs from giant aerospace corporations and promptly subcontracting them to small shops at lower prices. Whenever a prospective bidder came to him, that bidder would accidentally find a handwritten list of presumably competitive bids. All the prospective supplier had to do was bid lower to get the job. The trouble was that the list was a false plant meant to be read while the buyer left the room momentarily on some pretense. The buyer knew that few sellers could resist the temptation to outsmart their competitors. They invariably bid lower than the make-believe low bid on the list.

Another version of the same tactic was used by an opponent one time who deliberately let me learn something by writing so large that I could read it upside down. I felt rather proud of myself until I began to get suspicious. I know many buyers who are not averse to letting a salesperson read upside down occasionally if it suits their purpose.

Don't trust data you get too easily. People who negotiate are not fools. Some information is designed to mislead. Some is planted deliberately to test what a seller will take or a buyer pay. The next time your opponent forgets his or her attaché case with all those papers in it, be wary. Few things in life are free. Especially good information.

LOWBALLING: THE ATTRACTIVE OFFER THAT TURNS OUT NOT SO ATTRACTIVE

Lowballers lure people into a deal by offering a low price. They do so with no intention of coming through. Their plan is to make big profits by adding high-priced extras or causing expensive changes to be made. Knowing how to defend yourself against the lowball can save you lots of money whether you buy or sell for a living.

Car dealers have developed the lowball into an art form. They aren't alone, however. Boat dealers are coming up fast. In either case, the base car or boat is offered at a very low price and the trade-in deliberately quoted high. The buyer checks around diligently and learns that the price offered is a very good one. By this time, the buyer is tired and confused. When he or she returns to the dealer who made the attractive offer, it turns out to be somewhat worse than thought earlier.

Before the deal is closed, the buyers find themselves saddled with extras, finance charges, and maintenance contracts they never knew existed. All at high prices. As for the trade-in, it becomes apparent that a mistake has been made. The old boat suddenly needs lots of work and isn't worth nearly as much as the dealer thought. Sure, by that time lowball victims should be running in the opposite direction. But they don't. All they want is to get the whole thing over with.

"Changes are profits in escrow." That's the way one vice-president of a construction firm put it. He likes to "buy in" on a contract at a low price. Later he takes advantage of product changes, replacement parts, and continuing maintenance to put himself into a good profit position. He added with a knowing smile, "You'd be surprised to know that a clever project manager or engineer can earn his salary many times over by encouraging customer changes. That's where the real money is made." When you think about it, the "buy-in" is not so different from what the car salesperson does.

The lowball works best on buyers who don't know what they want. Instead of doing research on the various options available to satisfy their short- and long-term needs, they find themselves enticed by extras later. Sometimes it is not the buyer but his or her organization that is to blame. The typical project or engineering manager tends to downgrade needs due to budget problems. Only later do they admit to needing changes and extras to do the job the way it should be done. What it boils down to is that most of the add-ons could have been negotiated by the buyers more effectively as part of the original deal had they done their homework.

Thus far we have talked about how sellers lowball buyers, but the reverse is also true. Buyers can—and often do—lowball sellers. They do so with promises of big orders that never materialize, with easy job specifications that turn out to be hard, with reasonable delivery requirements that accelerate, with promises to pay that are not lived up to, with guarantees of quick decision-making that turn out to be slow and thereby result in expensive delays. Buyer-initiated lowballs are based on the same basic principle: Get the seller hooked, then tighten up the deal.

Is there any way to keep out of trouble with somebody who has lowballing in mind? I believe so. These suggestions help:

1. Know what you want.
2. Don't get hung up on price.
3. Get the seller to declare himself or herself on the full price with all add-ons included.
4. Take an option on those you don't need immediately.
5. Get full price breakdowns whenever you can.
6. Have a tight change-control procedure to insure that specification changes are carefully understood and priced.
7. Resist the tendency to be greedy. There is no such thing as a free lunch.

Probably the best advice is to be prepared to walk away from the lowballer. You may have to start all over again, but it's better than letting him or her gain from this unethical tactic.

MAKE THEM AN OFFER THEY CAN'T REFUSE

"I'm going to make him an offer he can't refuse." So said the Godfather in Mario Puzo's novel.

Some negotiations are settled by a block of cement in the East River. Organized crime can settle a debt, buy a business cheaply, resolve a labor dispute, fix a price, or make things happen.

When businesspeople get involved with organized crime, they inevitably find themselves at the short end of "an offer they can't refuse."

MAKE THEM AN OFFER THEY MUST REFUSE

There are times you should "make them an offer they must refuse." But why should anyone give other people such an offer? There are lots of reasons. Such proposals set the stage for making later offers look good by comparison. They can serve to get other people off your back or give you a chance to think things through. They can tie negotiations up, force talks to break down, or postpone decisions. I have seen unacceptable offers made simply as an ego kick—just to show the opponent how independent the negotiator was.

One of the best reasons for making an offer he or she can't accept is to help zero in on what will be accepted. The magic of such an offer is that it opens up a flow of conversation. When people believe that no deal is likely, they talk candidly with one another. It is then that real motivation and goals are revealed. There is no reason why a person cannot then follow up with bargaining in good faith.

Make "them" an offer "they" must refuse.

MAKING STRONG ASSERTIONS: UNLESS YOU'RE SURE, YOU'D BETTER SAY "I RECKON"

I attended college in Colorado at a time when there were still a few cowboys around. One used to say to me, "You'd better say 'I reckon' unless you're damn sure." Benjamin Franklin said it another way in his autobiography. His thoughts about making strong assertions are especially relevant in this era of the "hard" sell.

> I make it a rule to forbear all direct contradictions to the sentiments of others, and all positive assertion of my own. I even forbade myself the use of every word or expression in the language that imported a fix'd opinion, such as "certainly," "undoubtedly," etc., and I adopted instead of them, "I conceive," "I apprehend," or "I imagine" a thing to be so or so; or "it so appears to me at present." When another asserted something that I thought an error, I deny'd myself the pleasure of contradicting him abruptly, and of showing immediately some absurdity in his proposition: and in answering I began by observing that in certain cases or circumstances his opinion would be right but in the present case there appear'd or seem'd to me some difference, etc. I soon found the advantage of this change in my manner; the conversations I engag'd in went on more pleasantly. The modest way in which I propos'd my opinions procur'd them a readier reception and less contradiction; I had less mortification when I was found to be in the wrong, and I more easily prevail'd with others to give up their mistakes and join with me when I happened to be in the right.
>
> And this mode, which I at first put on with some violence to

natural inclination, became at length so easy, and so habitual to me, that perhaps for these fifty years past no one has ever heard a dogmatical expression escape me. And to this habit (after my character of integrity) I think it principally owing that I had early so much weight with my fellow citizens when I proposed new institutions, or alterations in the old, and so much influence in public councils when I became a member; for I was but a bad speaker, never eloquent, subject to much hesitation in my choice of words, hardly correct in language, and yet I generally carried my points.

MASLOW'S NEEDS THEORY

In 1954, Abraham Maslow wrote a good book called *Motivation and Personality.* He said that people organize their needs by ranking them from most to least important. Since it is never possible to satisfy all needs, those most pressing get in line first. One can imagine those wants as a five-story pyramid. The structure shown below is based on Maslow's Needs Theory.

Those needs at the base are the strongest. A thirsty person will search for water and let desire for love wait. A company on the verge of bankruptcy will contribute little to the community hospital. A person grown accustomed to a full stomach puts a higher value on salary-continuation insurance. A successful businessperson with millions says, "Now I'll live my own lifestyle and help humanity at the same time." When needs at a lower level are reasonably satisfied, energy is then directed upward toward higher needs. It makes sense from an individual and corporate-business standpoint.

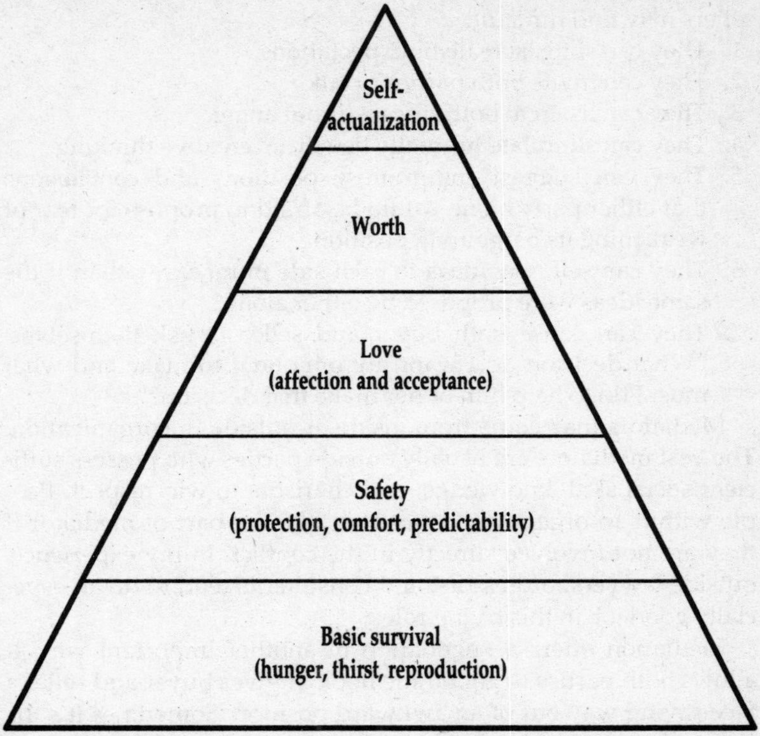

MEDIATOR: A KEY ROLE

A mediator is not often used in buy-sell negotiations. One should be. Mediators have had a key role in reconciling seemingly impossible international conflicts for centuries. The concept of mediation is certainly as applicable to business as it is to diplomacy.

Here are a few things that mediators can do that buyers or sellers may find difficult:

1. They can suggest realistic expectations.
2. They can invite both parties to talk.
3. They can listen to both sides without anger.
4. They can stimulate mutually beneficial creative thinking.
5. They can suggest compromise positions and conclusions that either party alone would be afraid to propose for fear of weakening its bargaining position.
6. They can sell new ideas to each side more easily than if the same ideas were proposed by either alone.
7. They can cause both buyer and seller to ask themselves: "What decision do I want my opponent to make and what must I do to help him or her make that decision?"

Mediators may come from inside or outside the organization. The best mediators are usually outside parties who possess sufficient social skill, knowledge, and charisma to win respect. People within an organization can also take the part of mediator if they are not involved directly in the conflict. In my experience, outside lawyers, professors, and consultants tend to do an especially good job in this trying role.

Mediation offers a negotiation in another important way. It allows both parties to get off the hook. It gives buyer and seller a face-saving way out of an awkward position. Sometimes it's the only way to break an onrushing deadlock.

MEDIATORS WHO ARE BIASED

Mediators are supposed to help separate heat from light, emotions from facts, and wishes from reality. They act as filters to improve communications between participants. The mediator passes information between parties and in so doing is bound to highlight some points and play others down. Presumably all this is done in an unbiased way—but not always. There are plenty of biased mediators.

The problem is that everyone is somewhat biased. We cannot escape seeing things in a personal way. Facts, means, goals, and values are interpreted by us in terms of our personality and experience. There is no escape from the built-in bias. Experiments with translators prove that they distort meaning in translation even when they don't want to.

Bias can creep into the mediation process in other ways. A person may be biased because he or she shares friends or values with one or the other party. These may be mutual business interests or political considerations that bind the negotiator to a position. Bias is rarely obvious in mediation. You've got to be alert to spot it.

When choosing a mediator, keep these points in mind:

1. Know the mediator. All are somewhat biased.
2. Beware of built-in procedural biases.
3. Recognize that some mediators are actually paid off or have other powerful conflicts of interest.
4. If you have any reason to doubt a mediator, choose another one.

I know a very rich man who likes to negotiate through biased mediators. He lets a small group of trusted long-time employees act as go-betweens. These men are given no authority to make a deal. They are used to carry messages, reflect attitudes, and propose solutions. They are obviously part of the rich man's team, but they act as mediators nonetheless.

Why bother to talk to them? The opponent *does* bother because he or she has no choice. Since the rich man makes himself unavailable, the opponent has to do business through the biased mediator or not at all. In this way, the billionaire makes the biased-mediator tactic work for him.

MEMOS OF AGREEMENT: WHAT TO WATCH OUT FOR

It is impossible to recall the events of a negotiation. Too much goes on to be remembered in detail. A negotiator should take notes as he or she goes along. Discussions and agreements on issues must be recorded as they happen. The most important record of all is the memorandum of agreement, which is a written account of the major terms of settlement. It is signed by both parties and becomes the basis of a formal contract. The conference should not end until all *essential* issues have been resolved and a memo written and signed.

You are better off writing the memo than letting the other party do it. The person who pens the deal has an advantage. You can express your concept of the agreement. You can interpret meanings and shape the words to reflect your understanding of the discussions. The question is not one of exploiting the other party or catching him or her in some stupid legal trap. Not at all. It is simply one of getting the areas of agreement laid out in your own way rather than leaving it to your opponent.

Before presenting the memo, a negotiator should have it reviewed by teammates. Errors of omission as well as commission are bound to arise. The opponent should be given an opportunity to review the agreement as carefully as he or she wishes and to amend what is believed to be in error. He or she should be made comfortable about the legal ramifications of the memo by putting in a clause that makes the agreement subject to legal approval.

The memo should emphasize intent rather than detailed phraseology, simplicity rather than legal jargon. The negotiators should record and cross-reference all agreements made so that those who draft the final contract will be able to do so without confusion. Whenever possible, specific references should be made to detailed statements of work, terms, conditions, and specifications that have been discussed. Issues like price, delivery, warranties, and quality standards that are of major significance should also be covered. Experience shows that a few minutes taken in writing down the agreement can save trouble later.

It takes good judgment to write a memo of agreement. Courage is necessary. I have seen good settlements bog down into an impasse because one party was too insecure to take the other on good faith where a minor point was concerned. They made legal mountains out of small issues that had little likelihood of ever arising. Legal extremists tend to have trouble agreeing on the contents of a memo. They see a lawsuit in every word. Negotiators should not be afraid to leave details to the people who draft the contract. In a well-constructed memo, the intent of the parties and the major terms of agreement are specified, but details are not.

A negotiator has to be careful whenever the other party writes the memo of agreement. He or she must not be lazy or naïve. Force yourself to take these precautions:

1. The memo should be read carefully by more than one person. Errors of omission and commission do arise. They may prejudice your position without meaning to.
2. Face real problems immediately. It takes judgment and courage to open an issue thought to be closed. Don't make problems, but don't run away from them either.
3. Have faith in your opponent if you have reason to. If you are unsure, then button down details to a greater extent.
4. If you don't like the wording, rewrite it yourself.
5. No matter how late the hour, do not sign the memo until it reflects the agreement as you perceive it.
6. Feel free to change your mind up to the last minute.

One major company has a policy that its negotiators write the memorandum of agreement before going into negotiation. Not only does it permit them to write it more easily later, but it serves as a guide to objectives as well. They know where they want to go before they start going.

The jointly signed memo is an important document. It tends

to keep the parties from changing their minds if they have second thoughts about the deal. They do not want to be considered indecisive, nor do they want to open up the whole can of worms once the lid is on. Writing down points of agreement *commits and involves* both parties.

A word of caution about the final contract: After the contract is written, it should be compared immediately to the memo of agreement. Occasionally essential terms are left out or changed in the drafting process. I have seen agreements proceed to the final contract stage only to have the parties discover that no agreement was ever reached on an essential point. These matters must be faced promptly even when it means that the entire negotiation is reopened. Some people lack the courage to do so. Others are just too lazy to read the contract in detail and to reopen unpleasant matters if differences arise.

MISSING-PERSON MANEUVER

In this maneuver, the person with final authority disappears to Europe just as the parties reach agreement. Nothing can be done until he or she returns, and nobody is quite sure when that will be. I was caught by this tactic a few years ago and have never forgotten. It happened this way.

An actor friend asked me to represent him in negotiating for a part in a TV documentary. The studio was a small one, and only $10,000 was involved. Discussions dragged on and off for three weeks. I negotiated patiently. First with the business manager, then the vice-president, and finally the president. At last we reached agreement. There was a slight problem, he explained as we shook hands. The company had been acquired recently by a California conglomerate that insisted on approving actor contracts. A routine formality. When we called corporate headquarters in Beverly Hills, we learned that the man in charge had just departed for Europe. He could not be reached for three weeks.

We waited. Nothing happened. The deal was never made. I discovered later that someone else was hired at half the price while we waited like fools for the missing man to come back. It did no good to be angry. I've not been caught since, but suspect that part of it is luck.

There are four reasons that people use the missing-person maneuver: (1) to stall final agreement in order to lower the aspiration level of the opponent; (2) to break off talks permanently; (3) to make a better deal elsewhere using the present deal as a floor; and (4) to learn more about the matter while they retain the option to close when they want to.

The effect on the victim is traumatic. The deal he or she thought they had is beyond reach. During the delay, they tend to convince themselves that it made good sense. If the missing person shows up and demands further concessions, the negotiator and his or her people are ripe for the plucking. They will generally prefer to close the deal at a lower price than risk blowing it entirely.

The following countermeasures are appropriate against this unethical tactic:

1. Test to find out if the missing person is in the next room or whether agreement can be reached without him or her.
2. Consider walking out.
3. Put a time limit on your offer.
4. Go higher in the missing person's organization.
5. Recognize that there is no deal until there is one. Make this clear to those in your organization.

The best defense against the "missing-person" maneuver is to guard against it in the first place. Try to understand the authority structure before you negotiate. Ask the other party questions. Make him or her draw organization charts. Have him or her put authority statements in writing. The greater his or her degree of commitment, the less you have to worry about.

When somebody tries this tactic, you can make it work for you. Feel free to negotiate openly with others while the missing person is gone. Missing persons have a way of showing up when their best interest is involved.

MOTIVATION IN NEGOTIATION: WHAT THE OTHER SIDE REALLY WANTS

1. They want to feel good about themselves.
2. They want to avoid being boxed into a corner.
3. They want to avoid future troubles and risks.
4. They want to be recognized by their boss and others as a person of good judgment.
5. They want knowledge.
6. They want to keep the job and get promoted.
7. They want to work easier, not harder.
8. They want to meet their personal goals and needs without violating their integrity.
9. They want to feel that what they are doing matters.
10. They want to avoid the insecurity that comes from surprises and changes.
11. They want to count on you now and in the future.
12. They want to be listened to.
13. They want to be treated nicely. They want excitement, adventure, travel, sex, and good food.
14. They want a good explanation.
15. They want to be liked.
16. They want to get the negotiation over with and get on to other things.
17. They want to know the truth.
18. They want to be thought of as honest, fair, kind, and responsible.
19. They want money, goods, and services.

MOVES AND WILDCAT-WALKOUT TACTICS

"As long as people talk, they don't fight" is an old adage. It's not true. Talking and fighting go together. Bargaining in conjunction with outside moves is an integral part of the negotiating process.

The power of moves and wildcat walkouts is readily seen in labor negotiations. Talks coordinated with events that take place away from the table can be persuasive. A wildcat strike in Los Angeles may be all that is necessary to convince management in Detroit that auto workers feel strongly about an issue. A newspaper announcement that a chemical is in short supply can convince a buyer that he or she had better close a deal immediately. Sending the fleet out on maneuvers can persuade a foreign power that we mean what we say.

A move outside the conference room adds emphasis to the words. It escalates risk. There are moves that make sellers apprehensive. There are others designed by sellers to keep buyers on their toes. First we will look at the moves that worry sellers and then those that make a buyer anxious:

Buyer moves that worry sellers:

1. Talking to competitors
2. Letting salespeople wait in the reception room while competitors are waiting
3. Sending out new requests for quotations
4. Showing that the buyer's boss is angry at the delay
5. Going over the head of the salesperson
6. Rejecting a shipment while talks on the new order are going on
7. Demonstrating that a new design is in the works that may eliminate the requirement

8. Showing the seller that the buyer may make it rather than buy
9. Surprises of all kinds.

Seller moves that worry buyers:

1. A press release that prices may soon rise
2. A tightening of credit terms
3. Rationing of material
4. Longer delivery promises
5. Stopping work if funds are not forthcoming
6. Seller employees preparing for a strike
7. A growth in out-of-stock items
8. News that a seller is negotiating with someone else for a very large order
9. Rumors that a product line is unprofitable and will be dropped
10. A memo to salespeople that marginal accounts are to be dropped.

We know that strike votes, lawsuits, secondary boycotts, wildcat walkouts, hunger strikes, and massive demonstrations do influence progress at the table. Moves affect the expectations of the parties and alter the balance of power.

NEED TO BE LIKED: WHAT A GOOD NEGOTIATOR SHOULDN'T FEEL

Everybody has a need to be liked and approved of. Experiments indicate that people with enough power to influence others want those whom they influence to like them. In effect, they are saying, "Do as I say, but be sure to love me at the same time." There is one source of strength that those with little power have: They can withhold their love and approval.

Can someone be a good negotiator if he or she has a strong

need to be liked? I think not. Negotiation involves a conflict of interest between parties. One must be willing to risk doing some things that may lead to being disliked. It is not easy to take a stand on an issue, or ask a question, or say no. The person who is afraid to confront conflict is likely to give the store away.

This is not to say that a good negotiator need be belligerent. Too much belligerence is as bad as a strong need to be liked. Negotiation involves a mix of competition and cooperation. The belligerent person finds cooperation difficult. People who need to be loved tend to run from conflict. They're just people who can't say no.

NEGOTIATION GRID: WHAT KIND OF PEOPLE SHOULD YOU HIRE?

A manager is responsible for hiring the kinds of people he or she feels will best get the job done. I've known purchasing managers who were sweet, likable, cooperative people who hired negotiators in their own image. They leaned heavily toward a cooperative approach and shied away from the competitive aspects of bargaining. Other negotiators lean in the other direction. There is no precise answer because it depends on the marketplace and what you are negotiating for. The key point is to hire people to fit the negotiating needs of your organization.

The negotiation grid helps a manager focus on the problem. Do you want your people to be 1–1 people or 3–3 or 4–3 or 5–5 or what? Somewhere in the grid is the competitive-cooperative mix that makes most sense for your business.

THE NEGOTIATION GRID*

Competitive Negotiator
(Self-Centered)

Slightly Competitive	1-1	1-2	1-3	1-4	1-5
Somewhat Competitive	2-1	2-2	2-3	2-4	2-5
Moderately Competitive	3-1	3-2	3-3	3-4	3-5
Quite Competitive	4-1	4-2	4-3	4-4	4-5
Highly Competitive	5-1	5-2	5-3	5-4	5-5
	Slightly Competitive	Somewhat Competitive	Moderately Competitive	Quite Competitive	Highly Competitive

Cooperative Negotiator
(We-centered)

* *This kind of layout owes its origin to the Blake and Mouton managerial-grid concept.*

NIBBLING: IF YOU CAN'T GET A DINNER, GET A SANDWICH

I know an army colonel who never buys a suit without nibbling for a tie. He's been doing it for twenty years all over the world. It rarely fails. He usually gets a free tie. In the parlance of negotiation, my friend has become a skilled nibbler.

Nibbling pays. Somebody once said, "If you can't get a dinner, get a sandwich." Nibblers go for the sandwich. It may not do much for their egos, but it sure helps their pocketbooks.

Buyers nibble on sellers and sellers on buyers. Both should understand how and why it works. In the word of business, it is generally better to be a nibbler than a nibblee.

Why does the nibble work? It works because most people are impatient. They want to close one deal and get on with another. People want to be liked. They want to show how fair they are and they want to build future relationships. Businesspeople are willing to make concessions to achieve these goals.

Perhaps most important, the nibble succeeds because it is small compared to the whole deal. In the case of the army colonel, the merchant has mentally completed the transaction. The sales ticket is written, and tailor chalk marks are all over the suit. All that prevents closing the deal is a slight impediment—a free tie. "Will the colonel walk out if he doesn't get the tie?" the merchant wonders. Rather than take the risk, he throws in a $30 tie and rationalizes that it cost him only $8 anyway.

Do professional buyers and salespeople nibble? Of course they do. In fact, the really costly nibbles occur after a deal is made.

Sellers nibble by making overshipments, by supplying slightly inferior merchandise, by not performing promised services, by delivering late, by adding special charges, or by tying the sale of a shirt to the sale of a suit.

Buyers nibble by paying bills late, by taking discounts not earned, by requesting special delivery or warehouse services, by asking for slightly better quality than contracted for, by demanding extra reports, certifications, or invoices, by getting free engineering changes, and by requesting free extra consulting and training help.

Can sellers handle the nibble effectively? I believe that they can stop it whenever they wish. These countermoves work:

1. Do not give the salesperson authority to provide little extras.
2. Have a published price list and policy on extras. Make it as visible to the buyer as possible.
3. Resist the tendency to give in. If you are patient, the nibbler will give up.

4. Insist that a suit is a suit. The shirt is not part of the deal.
5. Ask the nibblers if they are kidding. It will probably shame them into forgetting about it.
6. Price the nibble into the sales price.

In combating nibbling, recognize that most nibblers in our society feel "chintzy." They retreat from the nibble when confronted by tactful and persistent resistance. Yes, nibbling works; but with a little firmness, the nibbler—be it buyer or seller—can be stopped. The countermeasures above are applicable when either party starts taking small bites.

Nibbles that occur after a contract is signed are the most dangerous. They eat up profits like a termite. Worse yet for the seller, the buyer is often oblivious to receiving them. At the very least, when the seller's engineer gives the buyer's engineer free services, the seller ought to be gaining the buyer's goodwill. At best the seller should be charging for the services.

NIBBLING ON A COST BREAKDOWN

Architects give clients a cost breakdown of their fee structure. I don't think they should. They leave themselves open to small nibbles that add up. Look at the effect of a 1 percent nibble in each of the areas of labor, overhead, administration, and profit:

Before the Nibble		After 1% Nibble	
Labor, 1,000 hrs @ $100 hr	$100,000	990 hrs @ $99 hr	$98,010
Overhead @ 100%	100,000	Overhead @ 99%	97,030
Consulting	10,000	Consulting	9,900
Subtotal	210,000	Subtotal	$204,940
Administration @15%	31,500	Administration @ 14.85%	30,434
Subtotal	241,500	Subtotal	235,374
Profit @ 10%	24,150	Profit @ 9.9%	23,302
Total	$265,650	Total	$258,676

The little nibbles of 1 percent add up to more than 2½ percent of the whole banana. Not bad for a few hours' work.

"NICE PEOPLE" AND "RELIABLE NICE PEOPLE"

My brother-in-law George is a wise man. He worked as an electrician until he retired. General Motors is having a lot of trouble these days in keeping its people productive. Nobody seems to care much about meeting work or quality standards. Money and the fear of getting fired don't seem to be as inspirational as they were once thought to be. The Japanese and just about everybody have caught up and may be getting ahead of us. So I asked George what had made him work harder and who was the best boss he ever worked for.

The best man George ever worked for was one he remembered from twenty years before. From a lifetime of bosses, good times and bad, one man stood out. He was, as George put it, "a reliable nice guy."

"We broke our backs for that man," said George. "He got to know us. He knew what we could do well and what we couldn't. He knew about our families and our little problems. He was like a good neighbor. But most of all he never let us down. When the going was tough and we couldn't deliver because we were sick or tired or drunk, he understood and treated us like human beings. He never turned on us when things didn't go right for him. Good or bad, he gave us our paychecks with a kind smile. So we broke our backs for him."

"Is there a difference between nice people and reliable nice people?" I asked.

"There sure is," George said. "Nice people treat you nicely as long as things are going their way. Reliable nice people treat you nicely even when things are bad. They stick with you no matter what, so you stick with them no matter what."

A short time ago, I spoke to a friend who was unhappy with his boss, whom I also know. When I asked about the problem he said, "I just don't know about Blaine. I don't know how he feels about me or my work after five years of reporting to him." What a sad thing that is. As we talked, it turned out that Blaine was a nice guy but you couldn't quite trust him. He wasn't a reliable nice guy. That lack was already slowing down his upward progress in the company. People were not working hard for him.

Long-term relationships based on integrity are essential to negotiation and to the day-to-day administration of agreements that follow. But there is one step beyond integrity. We want the other party to show sincere goodwill and compassion if things do not go as well as they should. We want them to be "reliable nice people." For that most of us will bend over backward and give more than we get.

90-10 RULE: HOW TO MAKE IT WORK FOR YOU

Peter Drucker once pointed out that the key to good management lies in understanding the "90-10" rule. Ninety percent of the sales of a company are generated by 10 percent of its products. Ninety percent of the work of a purchasing department is directed to 10 percent of what it buys. The 90-10 rule has broad application in negotiation.

By a strange quirk, 90 percent of the time spent in session concerns matters that have little importance. Of all the issues we discuss, those that represent 90 percent of the value take up 10 percent of the time. Ten percent of the concessions involve 90 percent of the price movement.

In negotiation as in management, perspective is important.

Before you go into a negotiation, arrange your priorities. Ask yourself whether it might be best to give equal time to all issues. Perhaps it is to your advantage to leave just a little time for big matters and lots of time for little ones. Perhaps it is you who should make the nine small concessions for the one big one.

NO DEAL WANTED: THE BIG STALL

Buyers and sellers do not always negotiate to reach agreement. Some negotiations are conducted to forestall decisions or delay undesired actions on the part of the other party.

I have known buyers to initiate discussions with sellers solely to tie up their inventory while they fished for better prices elsewhere. Sellers who are already doing work on a time-and-material or cost-plus basis have been known to purposely delay reaching a fixed-price agreement in the belief that a later settlement would be better. Diplomatic negotiations are often conducted for no other reason than to cover up an intended attack or to divert attention from an arms buildup.

"No-deal-wanted" negotiations are part of the bargaining process. While often unethical, they are not always so. These are some of the purposes I've seen them used for:

1. As leverage elsewhere
2. To set the stage for real talks later
3. To set the stage for someone else
4. To tie up production or inventory
5. To fish for information
6. To delay undesired decisions or actions
7. To talk while searching for outside alternatives
8. To stall for time in order to get the public or third parties involved
9. To show a willingness to compromise (even where there is none)

10. To force conflict into arbitration after testing for the bottom line
11. To divert attention.

The next time you go into a bargaining session, it will be well to ask yourself, "Is this one of those no-deal-wanted negotiations?" Your basic approach may be a lot different if you suspect that the other person doesn't really want a deal.

NONNEGOTIABLE DEMANDS: ARE THEY NEGOTIABLE?

Are nonnegotiable demands negotiable? Do they serve a purpose at the bargaining table? The answer to both questions is yes.

Nonnegotiable demands are demands so extreme that compromise appears virtually impossible. At stake are deep-rooted values that may be of an ethical, religious, professional, or economic nature. The introduction of such demands creates hostility because it threatens important beliefs.

The strange thing about nonnegotiable demands is that they can help negotiators rally their own people at the same time that they diffuse the opposition. By making extreme demands, a negotiator can demonstrate his conviction. When nonnegotiable demands are mixed with more moderate ones, the negotiator has a chance to give large numbers in the organizational spectrum an equity in the outcome.

Nonnegotiable demands lower the expectations of an opponent. They make him or her more willing to compromise somewhere rather than risk so serious a confrontation of values. There are usually some people in the opponent's organization who believe that the extreme demands have partial merit. When certain African-American groups demanded reparation for 300 years of slavery, most people thought it apropos.

Is there room for such demands in buy-sell negotiations? Of course. It happens every day. Sellers tell buyers: "We cannot reveal our costs." "We will not give you our trade secrets." "We cannot reduce the price because government regulation prohibits us from doing so." "We will not permit your people to interfere with our management decisions." These demands may or may not be nonnegotiable but they sure sound like it to the inexperienced buyer.

Nonnegotiable demands are appropriate under some circumstances. You should not make them unless you have considered the cost of deadlock, the degree of mutual dependence, backlash, face-saving, and your own ability to muster internal support for the extreme demand.

Nonnegotiable demands are part of bargaining. They are inherently neither good nor bad. When you hear them for the first time, your reaction is to get angry and lash back. The following countermeasures will help keep tempers under control even when deeply held values are threatened:

1. Conduct off-the-record talks.
2. Don't provoke further hostility.
3. Explain why the demands are nonnegotiable.
4. Strengthen the resolve of your people by getting them involved.
5. Let the public understand how reasonable you are.
6. Be prepared to discuss those issues that are negotiable.
7. Don't be afraid to use your strength with discretion.
8. Don't panic.

Nonnegotiable demands are dangerous for the party making them. They can so inflame the other person that deadlock becomes inevitable on all issues. Yet, in my experience, most such demands turn out to be somewhat negotiable if good reasons are given and sufficient time is provided for acceptance of the "nonnegotiable" idea.

NONPERFORMANCE: THE INSURANCE-CLAIM GIMMICK

Most insurance companies are honest. Some are not. Those who aren't have been known to use nonperformance as a means of negotiating lower settlements with people who have been injured in an automobile accident. The insurance company signs an agreement to pay a lump sum of $50,000 and $1,000 a month for five years.

The trouble begins when the checks fail to arrive as promised. Whenever the poor person tries to find out what the problem is, he or she is told that something is in process or that somebody has to approve it. In the meantime, bills accumulate, and the person's position becomes more desperate. A person knows he or she can sue, but is afraid to because the lawyers may get it all. After months or perhaps years, the insurance company makes up a story as to why it can no longer pay the settled-upon sum. A new offer of $70,000 cash is made, and the victim grabs it.

Nonperformance is sometimes used by sellers to force a better price. A buyer contracts for a job he or she needs done by a certain date. The seller stalls around, letting time run out. Then the seller tells the desperate buyer that it cannot do the job without extra funds to pay subcontractors for what is now a "crash" job. The seller usually gets what he or she wants.

Nonperformance is an unethical tactic designed to place someone into a deep and difficult financial or schedule position and then "help" him or her get out of trouble by coercing him or her to accept a lesser deal. The nonperformer's plan is to wear them and scare them down. It's a dirty trick.*

* *For countermeasures against this dirty trick, see "Escalation Countermeasures" on page 63 and "Shyster Tactics" on page 198.*

NUMBERS THAT MIX ME UP

I've taken all kinds of math courses, but I get screwed up by some things that look simple.

1. I get paid by the month and have trouble figuring out what my weekly salary is.
2. Compound interest confounds me. I know what it is but can't work with it.
3. If I borrow money from January 2 to January 28, I'm not sure how many days I should pay interest on. Is it twenty-six or twenty-seven?
4. I can do percentages but have trouble with 8¼ percent for six months on the unpaid balance. I also get mixed up when someone says it's only ⅜ of a percent.
5. I forgot how to do long division.
6. I add wrong if the columns of numbers aren't lined up just right. I subtract well because there is only one number on top and one on bottom.
7. I can multiply 496 × 1387 but am likely to get it wrong under pressure.
8. I get mixed up reconciling my checkbook.
9. 6½ yards at $13.25 a yard kills me.
10. It's almost impossible to figure out if the big box of cornflakes (24 ounces for $2.49) is less expensive per ounce than the smaller one (11 ounces for $1.47). I've given up.
11. When the building-material man brings 3,000 bricks that are wrong and picks up 2,500 of them and then drops off 5,000 of the good ones, I get confused. What should he be paid for?
12. I never know what time it is in Chicago. Indianapolis is impossible.
13. I have trouble figuring out the return on an investment if the time period isn't exactly one year long. It never is.

14. When I'm in Italy and they say, "That will be ten million lire," I stick out my money and hope for the best.

When I was a kid I took those exams that were supposed to measure your skill with numbers. I remember one question I never did answer: "What part of a foot is ⅘ of an inch?" For all the world, I didn't know what they wanted to know. I looked at the paper. I looked at my foot. And I gave up. Maybe that's where my problem began.

It's true that one of those little pocket calculators will help, but I don't know how much. The problem goes pretty deep. Deeper than computers, I suspect. Perhaps right into our educational system.

These illustrations have a good deal of significance for those who negotiate. By and large, people are poor at handling figures. They make dumb mistakes. So do you. Go slow. Double-check. Have somebody else do it also. Especially when you are under pressure. Some people make a living on other people's mistakes.

What part of a foot *is* ⅘ of an inch?

OBJECTIONS: HOW TO HANDLE THEM

There are two sides to every story. If a Republican were to discover a way to abolish poverty, some Democrats would find objections to it. Every buy-sell transaction involves satisfaction and dissatisfaction. Both parties are bound to have some objections that must be overcome. The difference between a successful negotiation and one that is not may rest on how well you handle objections.

The fundamentals of handling objections are the same for buyer and seller. However, we will consider them from the seller's viewpoint. The seller has the tougher problem because he or she must handle objections without offending the buyer. The buyer has somewhat more leeway in this regard.

Quite some time ago a jeweler handled my objections with

finesse. He was a pro. My wife doesn't see well. The only kind of watch she can use is one with large hands that contrast sharply with the face. Such a watch is hard to find, but we found one that she could read. It was rather ugly and had not sold for that reason. It seemed that the $300 asking price was too high for this ugly watch.

When I told the jeweler that the price was too high, he said that the item was, at that time, fair-traded and therefore not subject to his judgment. Next he told me that it was accurate to seconds a month. I responded by pointing out that such accuracy was unimportant. As evidence I showed him my wife's Timex. "She's worn that thirty-dollar Timex for seven years," I said, "and it's been good enough."

"Ah," he answered, "after seven years she deserves a good watch."

Later in the bargaining, I pointed out that it was a funny-looking watch. His response: "I have never seen a nicer watch designed for people with visual problems." We settled for $225.

Objections can be handled effectively once you get the hang of it. Practice following these nine commonsense steps and you'll start getting better tomorrow:

Step 1. Before meeting the buyer, write down the benefits and disadvantages of your product and the competitor's product.

Step 2. Write down every buyer objection to your product or service you can think of.

Step 3. Have others in your organization raise objections in a brainstorming session. Practice answering the objections as though they were raised by the customer.

Step 4. When an objection is raised by the buyer, be sure you understand it clearly before answering.

Step 5. After you understand the objection, determine whether it is easy or hard to handle. Easy objections are those that can be refuted with readily available proof or evidence.

Step 6. Rephrase the objection in question form demanding a yes answer from the buyer. For example, "Do I understand that you are worried about the high operating costs in running the car?" This question would elicit a "yes" answer from a potential Cadillac buyer who expressed an objection to the high gas and repair costs.

Step 7. Do not reinforce the buyer's objection by agreeing with it. The salesperson above would be unwise to say, "Yes, Cadillac operating costs are high but . . ."

Step 8. If the objection is easy to counter, give your proof and ask for a *positive* reaction to the evidence. For example, the salesperson might say, "While you might expect that operating costs on some luxury cars are high, this one isn't. Do you know that *Motor* mag ran tests and found that Cadillacs get twenty-five miles to the gallon. Isn't that something?"

Step 9. If the objection is hard to handle rephrase it as a "yesable" question. Then answer the objection to the customer.

If, for example, the Cadillac buyer objected to its high price, the salesperson might say, "I take it then that you like the car but are concerned with the price. Is that right? Well you can't find another car like this on the road. It has power, is absolutely safe, maintains its resale value, and is truly economical in an overall sense. Everybody can own a car, but not everybody can own a car as fine as this. There's a reason why people of means own Cadillacs. They know what good value is."

The key to answering objections lies in giving the buyer the satisfaction of knowing that his or her viewpoint is understood. By rephrasing the objection in question form, you simultaneously convey your understanding and elicit a "yes" mode of thinking. When a hard objection is raised, it is more difficult to move the buyer into a "yes" mode. There is a natural tendency on the part of the salesperson to voice agreement. This should be repressed because it is generally unwise to reinforce negative responses. Only positive responses are worth reinforcing. If a strong hard-to-handle objection is raised, the salesperson should respond by stressing those product benefits most important to the buyer. Tough price objections are always best handled that way.

The principles above are applicable not only in business, but also in the social world. Objections always come up in life. It pays to know how to handle them wherever they arise.

OFF-THE-RECORD DISCUSSIONS

History is full of examples of negotiations that have run on for years. For example, during the Vietnam War the North Vietnamese and American peace-talk delegations met but once a week for years in Paris. The sessions were vitriolic. Not far away, our top man attended tea after tea with their top man. The teas were cordial even when the delegations were shouting at one another at the table. Formal discussions often serve a propaganda role. Off-the-record talks permit things to be said that give both a glimpse of the real issues and problems. Such discussions best set the stage for later compromises.

In her ten-year study, Ann Douglas discovered that in the last phase of labor bargaining formal meetings were shorter, caucuses longer, and private talks more frequent. Business negotiations are no different. It's good to have a drinking buddy throughout negotiations, but at the last stage it's essential.

Social or off-the-record discussions are a form of legitimate communication between buyer and seller. In an informal setting, they can let their hair down and discuss person-to-person problems. They can express gripes against constraints imposed by unreasonable people back home. They can share those things that unite humans no matter what their cause: children, spouses and high taxes. These discussions act as a safety valve. They permit problems to be solved, assumptions to be tested, and assessments of integrity to be made under nonstructured conditions.

Off-the-record discussions serve another function that is not always recognized. They permit the informal and unofficial leaders of a negotiation to express themselves on a sub-rosa basis. For example, it is common for procedures to designate the buyer as official leader of the purchasing team, but often it is the engineer who really leads the team because he or she has superior product knowledge and may in some cases know more about negotiating as well. Off-the-record discussions on a person-to-person basis permit these realities to surface without disturbing formal status relationships.

Informal talks are mandatory when official positions have hardened and deadlock is imminent. While it may be difficult to say anything conciliatory at the table, a few well-chosen words after dinner can indicate unofficial willingness to compromise. A series of social meetings may be necessary to elaborate on details so that public and private positions on both sides can be coordinated without loss of face.

The effective negotiator knows how important off-the-record or secret negotiations are. However, like almost everything, there are two sides to such negotiations. Their danger should be understood and precautions taken:

1. Be wary of confessional sessions. They may be one-sided.
2. Drinking-buddy setups are common. I know a man who uses this technique because he can control his liquor better than most.
3. Some negotiators have an intense need to be loved. They become generous in a "loving" social climate.
4. Informal discussions may be used to present false pictures. It is easier to plant phony information in an informal setting because people lower their guard.
5. People with "little-shot" complexes exhibit greater status deference in a social setting than under formal conditions.

Private talks are a necessary part of negotiation, not the exception. They bridge the gap between what is wanted and what is possible. Not everything that must be said can be said at the table. A good negotiator knows that.

ON TANGLING WITH AN ELEPHANT

There is no more uncomfortable bedfellow than an elephant with a sense of grievance.

Experiments indicate that people with power tend to be benevolent if they are not insecure. Such expressions as "throwing ourselves on the mercy of the court," "confessing our errors," and "apologizing for wrongdoing" have roots in the idea that people with power tend to be fair if their authority is accepted rather than threatened. As one research psychologist put it, "When up against a superior power, it is best to ask for equity."

Don't get the big elephant mad at you.

ONE-UPMANSHIP

I hate buyers who start a negotiation by telling me:

1. How fat I'm getting
2. How bad my quality was last time
3. How late my deliveries were
4. How I failed to live up to the last agreement
5. How they "told me so" last year
6. How what I propose to do won't work
7. How well my competition is doing
8. About the unimportance of what I'm doing.

These "one-upmanship" remarks are designed to throw me off balance. They do.

OPEN-DOOR POLICY: HOW MUCH SHOULD A BUYER KNOW?

How much information should a seller give a buyer? Some companies have an "open-door" policy. They take the attitude that the customers have a right to know what they are buying and why it costs what it does. Usually such a generous view of the customer's rights is not the result of benevolence, but is based on government regulation or the pressure of competition.

The open-door policy is designed to completely satisfy the buyer's need to know. Members of the buyer's organization can investigate where they please, talk to anyone, and ask any questions that come to mind. The seller's people are instructed to cooperate with any request provided that it is relevant to their function and to the buyer's need to know.

Why should any seller want to be so open with a buyer? Sometimes the answer is simply that the legal rules of doing business make such candor necessary. Sometimes such a policy is best because it permits the buyer to see just how good a deal he or she is getting. The open-door policy tends to promote trust and thereby to set the stage for an open discussion of mutual problems and risks.

The buyer who has free access to a seller's records has an advantage. He or she can probe, challenge, and question in a way that would be impossible without such data. On balance, I am convinced that the less a seller tells a buyer the better off he or she is. Don't give cost breakdowns, detailed labor rates, production records, or profit figures unless the law says you have to.

The buyer who is lucky enough to have full access to information still has several problems. Buried in the data are a mass of facts, interpretations, and assumptions. These must be sifted, verified, and put into context. The records never tell the full story. Neither do the people you ask. They have their own reasons to tell only half the story on some matters and to hush up others.

The "90-10" rule applies especially to the buyer who has full access. Ten percent of the available information represents 90 percent of the useful negotiating data. If the buyer gets bogged down in the 90 percent of information that has little value, he or she is in trouble no matter how open the open-door policy is.

OUTSIDE ASSOCIATES INCREASE YOUR BARGAINING POWER

It's nice to have friends. One of the best ways for a negotiator to increase bargaining power is to find good partners. Outside associates shift the balance of power. They make it easier to take risks, do work, get information, or absorb costs. Good partners can add legitimacy to a position by providing a climate of integrity, friendliness, competence, and financial strength.

Interestingly, perception plays a big part in making outside partnerships work. When the opponent hears that a negotiator has an associate, he or she tends to fill in details of the relationship himself or herself. He or she is apt to perceive a closeness that is not necessarily there. Some partnerships are as loose as mere name-dropping. Others provide for minor mutual assistance. What goes on in the opponent's head may have more to do with the power of an association than the partnership itself.

What kinds of third-party associations give a seller greater bargaining leverage at the table? It is well to note the wide range of partnerships available to a seller in dealing with a buyer:

1. *Technical partners:* An airframe company teams with a missile manufacturer to provide a complete defense system.
2. *Financial partners:* A bank underwrites funds for a seller to buy necessary production equipment.

3. *Political partners:* A senator exerts persuasive power to get a shipbuilding contract placed in his or her state.
4. *Broad-line-of-service partners:* A steel producer joins with a metal fabricator and local distributor to offer a broad line of services to the buyer.
5. *Turnkey partners:* A contractor offers a hotel builder a full turnkey operation, including all electrical, mechanical, heating, refrigeration, and control installation. He or she walks into the negotiation with the major subcontractors.
6. *Trade-association partners:* Sellers exchange information about credit, product standards, ethical principles, government regulations, and lobbying needs.
7. *Geographic partners:* Sellers join together with other businesspeople in a chamber of commerce operation to promote local business.
8. *International partners:* American sellers form a joint venture with Japanese businesspeople to market a product in Japan. Without the partnership, it would not be possible.
9. *Reference partners:* The seller arranges that satisfied customers contact a potential buyer to assure him or her of future satisfaction.

From the buyer's standpoint, third-party associations may include any of the following leverage builders:

1. Cooperative buying organizations
2. Buying through brokers
3. Hidden purchasing through agents
4. Combined contractor and subcontractor buying
5. Using government audit agencies
6. Purchasing trade associations
7. Guarantees of payment through cosigners, banks, or financial backers.

Most outside associations are ethical. Those that are not are usually prohibited by conflict of interest, law, or good taste. Restraint and good judgment are the keys to their use.

A few words should be directed to people who find themselves in front of an alliance or partnership. Be skeptical. Remember that conflicts exist even in the closest of families. Outside partners are unlikely to have the same priorities, motivations, and decision-making criteria. Don't be intimidated by the association before you. It is probably less cohesive than it appears to be.

PACKAGING PERSUASIVE IDEAS: WAYS TO COMMUNICATE YOUR POSITION

If you want the other person to believe what you say, send the message in the best way possible. This is just common sense. Businesspeople would easily agree that a poorly packaged product is hard to sell. The same is true of ideas. The means by which your position is communicated can make or break your position.

Marshall McLuhan's seminal book, *Understanding Media,* showed how messages undergo subtle changes of meaning when they are transmitted through different channels. McLuhan covered a wide range of media, including the telephone, spoken words, print, numbers, appearance, time, visual processes, and even comic strips. How a message is sent in negotiation affects how it will be received. Yet most people pay too little attention to packaging their position in the best way.

Sir Francis Bacon was concerned with the proper choice of media back in 1608. His advice still makes good sense today:

> It's generally better to deal by speech than by letter; and by mediation of a third person than by a man's self. Letters are good, when a man would draw an answer by letter back again; or when it may serve for a man's justification afterwards to produce his own letter; or where it may be dangerous to be interrupted; or heard by pieces. To deal in person is good, when a man's face breedeth regard as commonly with inferiors or in tender cases, where a man's eye upon the countenance of him with whom he speaketh may give him a direction how far to go; and generally, where a man will reserve to himself liberty either to disavow or expound.

In negotiation we can select from a wide array of persuasive tools. Let's look at a few of the choices:

1. *Written and printed media:* Procedures, cost records, Xerox copies, copious amounts of data, technical specifications, statistical tables, surveys, books, regulations, newspaper articles, computer runs, telegrams, references from good customers
2. *Visual media:* Artistic renderings, movies, cartoons, TV displays, comics, graphs, photos, mechanical drawings, videotape, lighting effects, flip charts, slides, viewgraphs, overlays
3. *Models:* Visual models, mathematical models, computer programs, graphic displays, mock-ups
4. *Verbal media:* Person (face-to-face), phone conference calls, tape recordings, records, cassettes, special audio effects, hotline hookup, music, deliberate noise or quiet
5. *Situational and time media:* Stage setting, location, seating arrangement, conference room, clocks, and punctuality effects
6. *Demonstrations:* Simulations, mock sessions, case studies, dog-and-pony shows, on-the-spot interviews, experiments, military-type games, "spontaneous" happenings or demonstrations.

Each of the media choices above has the power to *hypnotize* the viewer. A printed page from a book carries more weight than a handwritten note; a review in the *New York Times* is more important than one in a local paper; an opinion by a recognized expert is more persuasive than one by an ordinary person. Yet, in point of fact, the book may be superficial, the *Times* review silly, and the expert dead wrong. The medium makes a difference even when it shouldn't.

PATIENCE: THE SUPERTACTIC

Americans look at negotiation as a Ping-Pong game. One side serves, then the other. A few quick slashes and it's done. Then on to something else. Not so the Japanese. A quick deal can get a Japanese executive fired. It is a sign of bad judgment.

History shows that the North Vietnamese leased a villa in Paris for two years when talks began. Averell Harriman, our man, probably had a room at the Ritz Hotel on a day-to-day basis. We didn't believe it would take very long. Even three years of negotiation in Korea had not conditioned our people to expect long years of talk in Paris. In Iran, to our surprise, we negotiated for hostages for more than a year. We Americans are an impatient lot.

Patience is the most powerful tactic in negotiation, more powerful even than deadlock or threat. Patience, persistence, and determination can make up for inadequate resources. It works in international negotiation. It worked for Iran and for the North Vietnamese. These relatively small nations held back the United States for many years.

Patience works. This is what it can accomplish for you:

1. It divides your opponent's organization.
2. It can lower the other party's expectations.
3. It leads to concession after concession.
4. It forces a new look at priorities.
5. It separates wishes from reality.
6. It brings new problems and issues to the surface.
7. It gets other people involved.
8. It can cause a change in leadership.
9. It can be expensive for one or both sides.
10. It allows third parties to mediate.
11. It is tiring and takes you away from other work.
12. It provides new information.

Patience fulfills the basic mission of negotiation. It allows a person to get the viewpoint before settling on the price. It takes time to understand issues, weigh risks, test the opponent's strength, find weaknesses, know what he or she wants, and change expectations. It takes time to discover what he or she will do under stress. Patience gives an opponent and his or her organization time to get used to the idea that what they wish for must be reconciled with the realities of what they can get. A quick negotiation has none of these virtues.

Patience has another payoff. It gives buyer and seller a chance to find how best to benefit each other. Before a negotiation begins, it is not possible for either to know the best way to resolve problems, issues, and risks. New alternatives are discovered as information is brought to light. Both sides can benefit at the same time as a result of patient bargaining.

A wise old man once said, "If you can't get the viewpoint, you can't understand the price." The fun in negotiation is getting the viewpoint. There's always a story. Good businesspeople prepare their organization for a slow negotiation. They know that patience is the only way to get the viewpoint, the only way to understand the price.

"PEACE-BY-PIECE" TACTIC

When two parties do not trust each other enough to agree on all issues, they have an alternative. They can settle on a "peace-by-piece" basis. The two reach agreement on low-risk matters, leaving difficult issues to simmer. If, over a period of time, things work out satisfactorily, they tackle a tougher issue. "Peace-by-piece" gives each party a chance to test the intentions of the other without getting hurt too much.

The "peace-by-piece" principle is as applicable to buy-sell negotiations as to diplomacy. A prominent journalist described it in relation to the early talks between the Arabs and Israel. The principle is as true today in negotiating the autonomy of the West Bank as it was then:

> Instead of trying to settle everything all at once in a package deal, the Israelis, the Egyptians, and the big powers are now concentrating on a single possibility—clearing the Suez Canal—which may be a first step toward settlement. . . .
>
> The Israeli leaders need to come to grips with negotiating realities. They need to see that a reopening of the Canal can mean an implicit ceasefire of an enduring kind. They need to see that they can abandon one bit of territory, say the line along the Canal, without abandoning everything. . . .
>
> In short, the Israelis need to stumble into settlement, bit by bit. And a Suez negotiation provides just that kind of framework.
>
> Similarly for the Egyptians, Sadat has made a big step forward in accepting the idea of a peace agreement with Israel. He needs some tangible gains, something to show for his efforts, before he can take the further forward steps.

Trust takes time to build. Buyers and sellers who are unfamiliar may hesitate to commit themselves on all issues. In that case, they can fracture issues into distinct parts. Agreement can then be restricted to these smaller matters. For example, a franchiser may wish to find someone to handle California. A prospect comes along who seems to fit the requirements. An agreement is made with him or her to cover Los Angeles rather than the entire state. If things work out in Los Angeles, the franchise is expanded to all of California. Similarly, buy-sell agreements can be fractured by geographic-area, product-line, or service-center arrangements.

"Peace-by-piece" agreements are often used by buyers dealing with new vendors. Instead of giving them a large order, the buyer gives them a series of smaller ones. If all goes well, the buyer expands the order. Sellers do the same thing when they provide credit to a new account. If he or she pays bills over a period of time, the credit limit is raised. Each success serves to broaden the base of future agreement.

PERSONAL ATTACK: IS IT JUSTIFIED?

Is a personal attack on the other person ever justified in negotiation? There are many people who think so. I don't. I agree with Ben Franklin: "There's no such thing as a small enemy." People who are attacked on a personal level try to get even. It is a counterproductive tactic.

Those who like to use the personal-attack approach do so to destroy the opponent's ego and put him or her on the defensive. They use the tactic under the following circumstances:

1. When the person under attack has a weak ego and will take a passive role rather than face further attack
2. When a split in the other person's organization exists and can be widened
3. When something can be gained by discrediting an expert
4. When opponents are close to a decision but are afraid to make it; sometimes they can be bullied into it
5. When a relationship is short-lived and personal hostility is unimportant
6. When an opponent is likely to express his or her real feelings or to give information while angry.

If you are ever subjected to a personal attack in negotiation, walk out. Protest as loudly and as high up as you can. *The amount of personal abuse a person is subjected to is proportionate to what he or she is willing to endure.* You don't have to take abuse. People respect those who refuse to.

PERSUASION: THIRTEEN TIPS WORTH REMEMBERING

The suggestions that follow are based on some research findings in psychology. Like all research, experiments in persuasion are not exact models of the real world. Good business judgment is the only way to fill in the large gaps left by research.

1. It is better to start talks with easy-to-settle issues than highly controversial ones.
2. Agreement on controversial issues is improved if they are tied to issues on which agreement can easily be reached.
3. A message that asks for a greater amount of opinion change is likely to produce more change. Here, as in other aspects of life, aspiration level is related to achievement.
4. When two messages must be sent, one of which is desirable and the other undesirable, the most desirable to the audience should be sent first.
5. Learning and acceptance are improved if emphasis is placed on similarities of position rather than differences.
6. Agreement is facilitated when the desirability of agreement is emphasized.
7. A message that first arouses a need and then provides information to satisfy it is remembered best. However, when a need-arousal message is severely threatening, the listener tends to reject it.
8. It is more effective to present both sides of an issue than one side.
9. When pros and cons of an issue are being discussed, it is better to present the communicator's favored viewpoint last.
10. Listeners remember the beginning and end of a presentation more than the middle.

11. Listeners remember the end better than the beginning, particularly when they are unfamiliar with the arguments.
12. Conclusions should be stated explicitly rather than left for the audience to decide.
13. Repetition of a message leads to learning and acceptance.

PHONY OFFERS AND WHAT TO DO ABOUT THEM

The "phony offer" is an unethical buying tactic that sellers run into. A buyer opens with a sufficiently high offer to eliminate competition. Once this happens, the offer is taken back and bargaining begins in earnest.

For example, a couple wants to sell their boat for about $40,000, places an ad in the paper, and gets several interested buyers. One offers $38,000 and puts down a $200 deposit. The offer is accepted. The sellers no longer consider other buyers. They wait for the certified check to close the deal. Several days pass and nothing happens. Then a telephone call. The buyer sadly relates that he or she cannot go through with the deal because his or her partner (or spouse) won't allow it. He or she says that they have checked comparable boats and this one is only worth $34,000 because . . . The sellers get angry, of course. By this time they have thrown away the names of other interested buyers. But the sellers begin to wonder what the right price should be. They are reluctant to start over again with new ads, telephone calls, and all the work that goes with selling a boat. A settlement at less than $38,000 usually follows.

The phony offer is common in real estate. It can prove to be a disaster for the seller. A clever buyer with larceny in mind can so tie up the seller in litigation that the property cannot be sold to anyone else. The phony-offer buyer is then in a position to coerce the seller into taking less.

The tactic has a lot in common with escalation, but there is one big difference. The phony offer is made specifically to eliminate competition: to leave the field open for the buyer alone. It works because sellers don't expect it. They breathe a sigh of relief and thank their stars that the boat or what have you has been "sold" at such a good price.

The first line of defense is to recognize that some people make phony offers deliberately. These additional ideas also help minimize its impact:

1. Get a substantial nonrefundable deposit.
2. Draft the offer yourself. Tie it down with deadlines and safety clauses.
3. Check the buyer's litigation track record. If he or she is the suing type, you're in for trouble.
4. Be skeptical of getting too good a deal.
5. Don't throw away the names of competing buyers until the deal is closed.
6. Have the written offer signed by more than one person wherever possible.

These countermeasures are effective in stopping the phony offer. The buyers using the tactic are not interested in paying premium prices. They will run away when their bluff is called.

PIECEMEAL AGREEMENTS VERSUS LUMP-SUM AGREEMENTS

The French believe that negotiation should begin with agreements in principle. Americans lean toward starting with agreement on a fact-by-fact, issue-by-issue basis which leads ultimately to settlement. There are advantages and disadvantages to both approaches. How you start can determine where you end.

Piecemeal bargaining builds gradual trust and permits the parties to get a better feel for the whole story. They learn about each other's needs and priorities. The step-by-step inquiry uncovers the risk areas each wishes to avoid. It works best when detailed cost information is available and overall differences are not too large.

The argument for agreement in principle is that once logical principles are established, conflicts involving specific facts and issues can be fitted into the framework. Issues can be traded in a broad-brush way for other issues. The focus of bargaining becomes related to overall performance rather than detail.

I favor an approach that blends the piecemeal and lump-sum concepts. I like to start by stating the principles that govern my thinking and explore those most important to the other party. I do not seek agreement on principle, but only an insight into the other's viewpoint. From that point I prefer to negotiate on a piecemeal basis for these tactical reasons:

1. People have a need for closure that is satisfied in part by piecemeal agreements.
2. Piecemeal agreements can reveal much about a person's personality and the intensity of his or her wants.
3. Perceptive listening may reveal weak areas in the other party's power structure.
4. Item-by-item discussion permits a person to retreat gracefully from high sham positions and, at the same time, to fulfill the behavioral expectations of those he or she represents.

An agreement is not reached until it is reached. If one agrees in principle, one need not agree on the parts. If one agrees on the parts, one need not agree on the whole. Some people sell themselves short by feeling that their integrity is at stake on each issue. Once committed on a point, they are embarrassed to retreat. Nonsense! In negotiation the sum of the parts need not equal the whole. The deal is done when we shake hands. Not before.

POWER OF LEGITIMACY: SIGNING THE LEASE—A HORROR STORY

Most people don't bother to read a standard lease before signing. They feel somewhat helpless in front of all that fine print. What they don't know is how stacked against them the typical standard lease is. Some of the terms date back to the Middle Ages, and nobody has bothered to change them since. Standard terms and conditions exert a power of their own that I call "the power of legitimacy."

When you sign the lease, you have probably agreed:

1. To let the landlord visit you anytime without notice
2. To pay the rent even if the landlord doesn't keep his or her promises
3. That the landlord can reject any prospective sublease tenant you find for whatever reason he or she wishes
4. That if you have a claim for injury, you waive your right to collect from the landlord to the extent the law allows
5. To pay the landlord his or her legal costs if he or she sues you, but if you bring suit, he or she pays none of yours.

Why in the world would anybody sign something as dumb as this? People do it every day. These standard terms are so ingrained in our landlord-tenant relations that one feels powerless to change them. They shift the balance of power to the landlord without even the dignity of a negotiation.

That's the way the power of legitimacy works. It hypnotizes you into compliance. The next time you are asked to fill out the standard finance-charge form, accept the terms on the fine print of the contract, follow the regulation or procedure, pay the ticketed price, or pay extra for the warranty, watch out. These things are more negotiable than they appear to be.

POWER OF SIMPLE SOLUTIONS

There is a subtle power in simple solutions. People yearn for simplicity. Part of the hidden price in every deal is the ease by which a settlement can be understood and explained.

Simple solutions focus attention on relationships and numbers that seem natural. Splitting the difference or sharing a pie equally among four children can be understood easily. In fact, if you don't split the pie equally among the four children, how do you split it equitably?

Settlements may be made on the basis of how things were done in the past. Published standards, averages, and changes in the cost-of-living index affect settlements even when their relevance is questionable. Comparisons between things only remotely comparable sometimes help parties find a compatible agreement. In the absence of other criteria, we tend to relate the price of a 30-foot boat to that of a 40-foot boat. When we learn that a 30-foot boat costs $60,000 and a 40-foot boat costs $160,000, we find it hard to believe. Prices of $80,000 and $100,000 would appear to make more sense.

I like round numbers. Thomas Schelling did research at Harvard on what he called "focal" power. His findings confirmed that nice, round numbers like $1, $10, $100, $1,000, $100,000, and $1,000,000 tend to command attention. Prices like 96 cents each, $9.65 per piece, and $96.43 per unit are harder for us to deal with. Like most people, I never learned to multiply easily by anything but 10.

The next time a seller asks for $102,400, why not offer to settle for $100,000? You are likely to earn over $2,400 for only a moment's work. Round numbers are nice numbers.

Simple solutions send up signals. They say, "If not here, where?" That is their power.

POWER TO THE BUYER: NEGOTIATING WITH A SELLER WHO HAS NO COMPETITION

Buyers fold like a tent in front of a seller who has no competition. When there is only one seller, the balance of power certainly tips in his or her direction. Still, there are real limits to a seller's ability to exploit this superior bargaining position.

Competition between firms is only one source of power. The seller with no competitors may be exposed to other sources of buyer power. A buyer can sometimes create competition by doing it himself or herself or by doing without. He or she can point out to the seller that his or her long-range interest in keeping the customer is more important than any short-term price advantage he or she might gain. The seller may be in competition with himself or herself by being torn between getting rid of the heavy inventory of late-season goods or holding out for a higher profit. Sometimes the seller with no competition needs money to keep the factory going, to keep talented people on the payroll until business gets better, or to pay taxes before the Internal Revenue Service closes the door.

There are other sources of power available to a buyer if he or she understands them. They are:

1. *The Power of Commitment.* Commitment, loyalty, and friendship are bastions of power. People who are committed to their goals or to the satisfaction of others have a hidden strength. People who are loyal to their company, its management, and its product negotiate more effectively in their behalf.

2. *The Power of Legitimacy.* No source of power so hypnotizes people like the power of legitimacy. We have learned to accept the authority of things like procedures, laws, standard forms,

and price tags to such an extent that we fail to question their applicability in changing situations.

I was recently in Mexico buying something for my car. The price tag read forty dollars in Mexican money. As an American, I am accustomed to paying the ticket price on auto accessories, so I paid the price asked. The man behind the counter looked quite pleased. After the transaction was completed, an American retiree in Mexico came up to me and told me quietly that I could have paid 20 percent less had I bargained. He pointed out that in Mexico almost everything of value is negotiable. As an American, I had trapped myself by the power of legitimacy: the hidden power inherent in a price tag.

3. *The Power of Knowledge.* "Knowledge is power," wrote Sir Francis Bacon. The more a person knows about the seller's cost, organization, business standing, and product, the better he or she can negotiate. The more he or she knows about negotiation, the better off he or she is.

4. *The Power of Taking Risks and Having Courage.* Security is a goal that humans cherish. We share a desire to avoid risk wherever possible. The person who is willing to accept a greater burden of uncertainty with respect to reward or punishment enhances his or her power.

Uncertainty may be based on fear and prejudice rather than rational grounds. For example, two of my friends are lawyers whose incomes have risen over a ten-year period from $100,000 to $300,000 a year. One is always fearful that next year's business will slip back to the $100,000 level. The other has faith in his future growth and generally negotiates higher fees. People assess risk differently even when they have access to the same information. A common stock which looks like a speculation to a person who lived through the Great Depression can appear a sound investment to a young person. By the same token, I know some very intelligent people who lived through the real-estate decline of the 1930s. They are still renting apartments in areas where land values have risen thirtyfold due to population pressures.

Some risks can be foreseen while others cannot. The owner of a machine shop estimates a tight tolerance job on the basis of a 10 percent scrap rate. Past experience with rejections on close-tolerance work permits a rational estimate to be made. On the other hand, one cannot foresee that the internal structure of a particular batch of material will be too porous to hold the necessary dimensions.

Uncertainty can be created by introducing risk at a personal as well as corporate level. Deadlock introduces the possibility that a good negotiator can lose his or her reputation. Risk can be heightened by introducing matters in which the opponent's knowledge or ability to grasp a situation is deficient.

Courage plays a part in the decision to make a concession, to hold one's ground, or to force a deadlock. In personal-injury work, the insurance claims manager can never be sure that his or her low offer will not precipitate costly litigation. Conversely, the claimant can only hope that a final verdict will justify his or her reluctance to accept an earlier offer. It takes courage to tolerate uncertainty, and we differ in our ability to do so.

5. *The Power of Time and Effort.* Time and patience are power. The party most constrained by time limits provides an opponent with a base of strength. It is for this reason that purchasing executives stress the importance of lead time and early-warning inventory systems.

Buying, selling, and negotiation are grueling work, and the willingness to work is power. Perhaps the hardest work of all is imposed on us by the demands of planning and deadlock. Both can be avoided easily: one by not planning and the other by agreement. The party most willing to work hard gains power. Some people are simply lazy and thereby forfeit this important source of strength.

Most of the strategies and tactics in this book are designed to limit the power of the seller who has no competition. The buyer who is committed against being exploited is well on his or her way to keeping the seller from doing so, with courage, persistence, and a lot of negotiating know-how. It also takes common sense. Never let the seller know or think that he or she is the only source unless you have to. The seller who thinks he or she has competition, has competition.

POWER TO THE SELLER: THE LIMITS OF COMPETITION

Salespeople are obsessed with competition. They see a competitor under every buyer's desk. What they forget is that usually buyers are restricted in their ability to use competitive sources. Among these limitations are the following:

1. Personal biases against some sources.
2. Some sources are located too far away.
3. Some sources got the buyer in trouble once.
4. Differing abilities and capacities to produce.
5. Production or engineering people who have preferences.
6. Built-in specification designs that implicitly or explicitly exclude some sources.
7. Some sources have bad track records.
8. Some sources want too much money.
9. Many sources can't deliver on time.
10. Some sources offer a full line of services while others don't.
11. Some sources give ninety days' credit; the others give far less or none.
12. The buyer is used to doing business with some sources and doesn't want to change.
13. Some sources are not known to the buyer.
14. Some sources simply take too long to talk to. The buyer has too much other work to do.

Power to the seller!

PRICE BREAKDOWNS: HOW BUYERS CAN GET THEM

How does a buyer get cost breakdowns when the seller doesn't want to provide them? The suggestions below carry weight:

1. Help the buyer by providing him or her with procedures, policies, and legal regulations that prohibit them from dealing with sellers who won't provide breakdowns.
2. Tie purchase A to purchase B. The seller may decide that his or her best interest lies in providing information.
3. Protest to higher authority.
4. If you can't get full disclosure, settle for partial disclosure. Something is better than nothing.
5. Apply legal or political pressure.
6. Delay giving the order.
7. Point out that the seller's competitors are providing breakdowns.

The buyer should remember that it is not the salesperson who is refusing to provide information. It is the people in the seller's organization. When sellers become convinced that their long-range interests are in jeopardy, cost breakdowns become available.

PRICE BREAKDOWNS: HOW SELLERS CAN AVOID GIVING THEM

Can a seller avoid giving the buyer price and cost breakdowns? It isn't easy, but these policies below have served to frustrate even the most persistent buyers:

1. Written company policies prohibiting breakdowns
2. Unavailability of detailed information
3. Data provided in such a form as to be useless
4. Long delays in developing the data
5. Explanations that data cannot be provided for fear that trade secrets or proprietary information would leak out to the competition
6. High expenses in putting together a breakdown
7. A "we meet competition or we wouldn't be in business" policy expressed by a high officer in the seller's organization.

How little information a seller gives often depends on how resolute he or she is. A firm but tactful no, delivered persistently, goes a long way.

PRICE COMPARISONS: CAN ALL BIDS BE APPLES?

Few things frustrate a buyer as much as comparing apples to pears. Yet this is what they end up doing whenever the purchase is reasonably complex. It takes a genius with an accountant's mentality to wade through the information necessary to make a sensible decision. This state of affairs creates an opportunity for the seller who understands it. He or she can put him or herself into a stronger bargaining position and can get the edge on closing the sale.

As much as a buyer wants all bids to be apples, they hardly ever are. Not only do seller prices vary, but quality, specifications, packaging, and performance characteristics also differ. As if that weren't enough, each seller offers different optional and standard accessories, installation costs, and track records in meeting promises. It's hard to make objective comparisons with so many variables. In the end, the decision is often made on a few shreds of information and a lot of gut feel.

Buyers who know their business understand the problem. They start on the basis that they are in for hard work. They use engineering and cost-analysis specialists to sift the data into somewhat comparable parts. After talking to several sellers, they begin a two- or three-stage purchase cycle. First bids are gotten on what each seller feels the buyer should have. Detailed price breakdowns are secured wherever possible. The experts wade in, sort the data, talk to sellers, and come up with fairly uniform "apples only" requirements. After new bids are received, the job still remains to compare and value accessories that are never identical. Other discussions follow, references are checked, and a final "apples" bid is solicited. The trouble is that most buyers don't have the time or fortitude to go through this jungle of work.

The kind of salespeople who get the order help the buyer find the way out of the jungle. They get involved after the proposal is submitted. They recognize how confused the buyer is and help with comparing apples and pears. I have seen salespeople sitting in the buyer's office with all the bids spread out before them, busily laying out comparison tables item by item. How did they get into this beautiful position? Merely by saying to the buyer that they were calling to help him or her decide in a sensible way. The harassed buyer is thankful for a way out and builds a positive image of the seller that gives him or her the edge—if not the order.

Of course, to close the deal, the seller may have to trim the price, change the product package slightly, and give proof that what he or she recommends makes sense. The important thing is that the seller—not the competition—has the inside track. It takes a hard-hearted buyer not to show his or her gratitude sooner or later.

Yes, all the bids should be apples. Most salespeople I've known work hard to put together a bid. Then they hope for the best while they wait. The high-sales producer knows that the selling job begins after the apples and pears are on the buyer's desk.

PRICE DROPS, TRIAL BALLOONS, AND RUMOR LEAKS

Trial balloons are used frequently in politics. The president, anxious to promote some new policy, allows rumors to leak through the staff that a new tax is being considered. The public reaction is awaited. If it is mild, the president openly announces the new tax program. If the reaction is heavily against the move, the tax approach is either changed or eliminated. The trial balloon gives the president a chance to test the water temperature before jumping in.

Price drops are common in business. Sellers and buyers use them frequently. Buyer price drops are generated to let a seller know (perhaps falsely) how much money is available to be spent on a job. Sellers sometimes use price drops while they are bidding. They wait until most bids are in and then tell the buyer that it looks like their price will be "about" so much. What they are fishing for is an informal reaction to the price drop in order to gauge their next move.

I have used price drops, trial balloons, and rumors to send messages to an opponent that could not be communicated over the table. Sometimes it is best to introduce a new position through the grapevine. If the position is rejected or ignored, little if any face or bargaining leverage is lost. The grapevine has been effective time and again in telling an opponent how my management felt, what my limits were, and whether I was willing to compromise. I have used informal channels to signal new demands, propose possible concessions, and lower the aspirations of an otherwise-stubborn opponent. Rumors are strange things. They tend to gain credibility the more often they are heard—perhaps because so many prove to be true.

Planned leaks may concern matters other than price. Trial balloons and rumors can test the climate for technical surprises, late deliveries, the impact of competition, and potential cost overruns. Reorganizations can be introduced via the rumor mill to see whether problems will arise if the change is actually made later. In fact, I read in a management article recently of a poll that showed that three out of four executives who hear through the grapevine that they have been fired, find that they have been.

A negotiator has to be on guard against this tactic. The trial balloon may reflect a true state of affairs, or it can be totally false. You rarely know for sure. These safety measures are warranted:

1. When the person next to the leader speaks, he or she speaks for the leader.
2. Treat information derived by rumor or trial balloon like any other information. Test it.
3. Be wary of information acquired too easily.
4. Trial balloons may signal divisions within the opponent's organization. They are sometimes the equivalent of a cry for help.
5. Trial balloons and rumors are often used to confuse an opponent, to weaken his or her resolve, or to separate him or her from their organization.

If kept within the bounds of restraint, price drops, trial balloons, and rumor leaks are legitimate tactics of negotiation. They help zero in on a workable agreement.

PRINCIPLE VERSUS PRINCIPAL

I once negotiated for a physician who was asked to make a training film for a studio. At that time the doctor insisted that he would not negotiate two principles:

1. The principle that his name not be used for promotional purposes because this violated medical ethics.
2. The principle that he exercise final authority in editing the film because it might damage his medical reputation if it were handled improperly.

The studio countered that these issues were, in the end, not matters of principle, but of principal. Movie negotiators are tough and persistent. In the end, they made us give up some of our principal for some of our principles.

PRIVATE EYES

Whether or not we like it, private detectives have been used in negotiation and will continue to be used in the future. I prefer not to hire them for this purpose. Private detectives dig up a lot of information, some of which I probably have no right to know.

This is not to be interpreted as an indictment of private investigators. There is nothing wrong with gaining a better understanding of an opponent's financial affairs or personality. Business and social preferences are relevant. Knowing about his or her organization and the people in it is a source of legitimate power.

The trouble is that the zealous private eye goes too far to please a client and earn the $1,000 a day, plus expenses. He or she looks for everything and in so doing is bound to find out things that shouldn't be in any business dossier.

Karrass's Law of Private Information says: "Sensational news drives out nonsensational news." Sordid information takes over. In a world where knowledge is power and communication is instantaneous and widespread, too many people get to look at a file. Sooner or later, someone is tempted to abuse it, and others go along. As General Motors learned with Ralph Nader, private detectives have their limits in business. General Motors made a costly mistake. It could afford to. Can you? Should you?

PRIVATE—NO ADMITTANCE: THIS INFORMATION IS NONE OF YOUR BUSINESS

With respect to information and back-up data, buyers and sellers are on opposing sides. In my opinion, the less the sellers tell the buyer, the better off they are. The more the buyer knows about the seller's costs and profits, the better the negotiating position. With respect to cost data, what is good for one is generally bad for the other.

Sellers should start on the basis that cost and pricing methods are nobody's business but their own. A buyer is well advised to insist that part of the price paid is access to full cost and production visibility. He or she has the right to know what he or she is buying and why the price is right.

The government is quite correct when it insists that sellers reveal full information. It has passed "truth-in-negotiation" statutes to support this position. Few contractors have refused to do business because of this requirement. I remember a remarkable letter from one who did. The supplier was a manufacturer of special technical components. The technical division was part of a much larger consumer-oriented corporation. As buyers, we demanded price breakdowns in accordance with regulations. The contractor refused. The division manager wrote us a letter with a copy to his senator and another to the president. He said that the U.S. government had no right to invade his privacy. He quoted portions of the Declaration of Independence and the Constitution to make his case. He claimed that his profits, costs, and production methods were sacrosanct. The letter closed by stating that no government official, auditor, or elected representative would be permitted to cross his threshold or look at the books.

Oddly enough, we were not angry at getting such an unusual reply. While his position was unheard of, it was nevertheless refreshing. We passed the buck to Uncle Sam, wondering what the government would do. It didn't know what to do either until somebody in Washington finally said, "The hell with it." In this case, the seller made his "no-admittance" position stick. Most sellers capitulate without even trying.

"Private—no admittance" takes courage. The buyer won't like it but will probably respect your position. Down deep, he or she knows that you are protecting his or her own right to privacy, too. Whether that strategy will keep you from losing a valued customer, I don't know. That's the risk that goes with "no admittance." It's a matter of business judgment.

PROBES A SELLER MUST MAKE PRIOR TO NEGOTIATION

To a considerable extent, a seller's bargaining leverage is determined by how much he or she knows about the buyer's attitude toward the product. It is not possible for a salesperson to get as much information as they would like. At the least, he or she should probe for answers to six essential questions *prior* to negotiating. The salesperson who gains an insight into these questions is in a better position to negotiate. Sales management should see that he or she does.

1. What specific objections to the product does the buyer have?
2. What doesn't the buyer like about the seller's competition?
3. What specific benefits offered by the seller's product are most important to the buyer?
4. Does the buyer believe the seller's product statements and proof statements?
5. How does the buyer feel about the seller and the product? What are his or her attitudes?
6. What indications are there that the buyer wants to close and is ready to? Why?

PROMISES AND GOTCHAS

A promise is a concession. It has a discount rate. Some promises aren't worth anything. Others are collectible only if the person who made them is still in a position to carry them out. If you can't get a concession, get a promise.

A large part of business is carried on by unwritten promises: "I'll do this if you do that." Some promises don't even have to be expressed. They are tacitly understood. When you do me a favor, you add one "gotcha" to your account. Gotchas make the world of business go around.

A contract is itself a promissory document in which I say that I will do something and you say you will pay me. It's easy to make a promise but hard to prove it will be kept. A contract defines legal rights and duties. The language may be insufficient to guarantee performance. It may stipulate that you promise to pay me a sum of money on receipt of work. When the work is done, you may run away without paying. All the contract gives me then is the right to sue. The fact is that it may be impractical or impossible to sue because you've gone someplace where you can't be traced.

When contractual language is insufficient to guarantee performance, other steps are necessary. The promised performance must be made credible. For example, funds may be left on deposit or performance bonds posted. Other common ways to assure that promises will be kept include placing friends on the opponent's board of directors, where they can keep an eye on things. When a buyer and seller buy substantial shares in each other's company, they make their promises more credible. Perhaps the most common way of increasing credibility is by making good on small gotchas and thereafter doing so on bigger and bigger ones.

A promise may or may not be enforceable. To be enforceable, it must have a detection and a policing mechanism. There must be a way to tell that the promise has been broken and a way to bring sanctions to bear if it is. A tightly written contract will provide for detection and policing of promises. Some promises are enforceable even without written words or legal backing. People who borrow money at Nevada gambling casinos pay it back.

Promises have a discount rate. I know a contractor who has gotten rich on promises he didn't keep. He breaks them in a subtle way. He has job supervisors at various locations in California and Arizona. In the course of a building project, gotchas arise between the contractor and subcontractors. The subs do extra work in the expectation that it will be settled or made up by the contractor later. But it doesn't happen. Just before the gotchas are paid, the contractor shifts job supervisors. Suddenly the sub faces a new man who knows nothing of the old gotcha and refuses to honor the claim. The subcontractors learn too late that the discount rate on promises made to them was far too great.

Nevertheless, the general principle holds. If you can't get a concession, get a promise. Most people try to live up to what they say.

PUT YOURSELF IN MY SHOES

I like to get other people to put themselves in my position. It gets them involved. They begin to get a picture of my range of alternatives and my limitations.

If I do this with discretion, they become less sure of getting my business and more likely to come up with a better price. It's a nice way to tell them what I want to tell them.

Try it. Just say to them, "Put yourself in my shoes." You will be pleasantly surprised at how often the shoes fit.

QUESTIONS: OBSTACLES TO GOOD QUESTIONS

1. We avoid questions that reveal our ignorance to the other party or to our own people.
2. We are afraid to show that we haven't been paying attention.
3. We have a cultural distaste for prying into another person's business.
4. Some good questions come to mind but are forgotten in the heat of discussion.
5. It is hard enough to follow the other person's reasoning, let alone think of good questions at the same time.
6. Some questions are not asked because we can't formulate them properly.
7. Most of us tend to avoid questions that may embarrass the other party.

8. Some people would rather talk than listen. Questions are designed for listening, not talking.
9. People lack persistence in following up on questions that are answered poorly. They give up too easily.
10. There is rarely enough time to think of good questions. We don't think them through in advance.

Judge for yourself the extent to which these ten common obstacles have impeded your question-asking effectiveness in the past. They can be overcome.

QUESTIONS: SOME SENSIBLE DOS AND DON'TS TO IMPROVE QUESTION-ASKING ABILITY

Questions are mind-openers. They lead both buyer and seller into more active involvement with one another. The most direct route to understanding is a good question. The trouble is that most of us think of our best questions after the negotiation is over, like in the car going home.

There is hope for us. Our question-asking ability can be improved if we follow a number of rather easy "dos and don'ts." First the "don'ts":

1. Don't ask antagonistic questions unless you want a fight.
2. Don't ask questions which impugn the honesty of the other party. It won't make him or her honest.
3. Don't stop listening in your eagerness to ask a question. Write the question down and wait.
4. Don't think you are Perry Mason. A negotiation is not a courtroom trial.
5. Don't pick just any time to ask a question. Wait for the right time.
6. Don't ask a question to show how smart you are.

7. Don't cancel out your teammate's good question by asking yours before his or hers is answered.

The "don'ts" have one thing in common. They are communication barriers. They block information flow.

Now the "dos":

1. Do get your questions ready in advance. Few of us are bright enough to think fast on our feet.
2. Do use every early contact as a fact-finding opportunity. The best answers come months before the negotiation, not at the table.
3. Do have a brainstorming question-asking session among your own people. You'll be surprised at the number of interesting questions they will raise.
4. Do have the courage to ask questions that pry into the other person's affairs. Most of us don't like to.
5. Do have the courage to ask what may appear to be dumb questions.
6. Do ask questions like a "country boy." This attitude encourages good answers.
7. Do ask questions of the buyer's secretary, production person, and engineer.
8. Do have the courage to ask questions that may be evaded. That in itself tells a story.
9. Do take frequent recess periods to think of new questions.
10. Do be quiet after you ask a question.
11. Do be persistent in following up your question if the answer is evasive or poor.
12. Do ask some questions for which you already have the answers. They can help you calibrate the credibility of the other person.

Questions and answers can be looked at as a negotiation in their own right. Every question has the character of a demand. Every answer is a concession. Those who demand better answers properly are more likely to get them.

QUESTIONS: VARIOUS TYPES FOR VARIOUS PURPOSES

Questions serve a variety of purposes and can be phrased in many ways. What follows are *questions and answers about questions.* Many examples of questions will be given. For the most part, they will be sales and purchasing oriented.

Q. *If a buyer is uninterested, apathetic, or undecided, what kind of questions should a salesperson ask?*

A. Directive questions work best when a buyer is uninterested, apathetic, or undecided. For example, if you ask a buyer whether he or she wants the red or blue one, he or she must answer: red, blue, or neither. If he or she says neither, then ask for an explanation. Then work on the objections.

Directive questions are specific. They request answers about a particular point.

Examples of directive questions:

1. What have you been paying?
2. What price must I meet?
3. Have you had trouble with leaks in the braking system?
4. What will this change cost me?
5. Are you in the market for a four-bedroom home?
6. Are you aware that they are going into receivership?
7. What do you think of the consumer-research report on our components?
8. When did you first become unhappy about that feature?

Q. *What are nondirective questions, and when should they be used?*

A. Nondirective questions are general in nature. They permit the answer to be as broad or narrow in scope as the person answering wants. They do not pin down the answerer. Facts, opinions, and evaluations may be incorporated in the answer. Nondirective questions are best used when the other person wants to express himself or herself. The trouble with nondirective questions is that the answers are not predictable or controllable.

Psychiatrists and talk-show interviewers find that nondirective questions elicit more complete answers, perhaps because the subject is more at ease with them than with directive questions.

Examples of nondirective questions:

1. How do you determine a price on spare parts?
2. Would you explain how you manufacture the artificial Christmas tree?
3. What requirements are most important to you as a buyer of toilet paper?
4. What do you look for in a good warranty?
5. How do you feel about using low-priced switches?
6. Do you consider maintenance very important?
7. We have treated you well in the past, haven't we?

Q. *Are there other reasons for asking questions than wanting to get information?*

A. Yes. Most people think that questions are asked only to get information. That is not so. What they forget is that questions also can give information, stimulate thought, or help the other person make a decision. The examples which follow will make this clear.

It should be pointed out that every question has two parts: one that describes the scope, background, or framework of the question and the second, which is the question itself. The preamble may serve one purpose and the question part another.

Examples of questions that get information:

1. What objections do you have to our product?
2. Will you show me how you got to that figure?
3. Will you explain that to me?
4. What are the latest tax rates?
5. What is the vacancy rate?
6. Who owned this car last?
7. Have you been having trouble with maintenance?

Q. *What kinds of questions give information?*

A. Each of the examples below permits the questioner to follow up with further information that he wishes to impart:

1. Have you had a chance to look at our new product?
2. Would it be fair to say that you feel this way . . . ?
3. Did you know that we check each part six ways?
4. Were you aware that our company was rated by *Fortune* as one of the twenty best managed in the United States?
5. Have you compared our warranty? Please do.
6. You're surprised at our low price, aren't you?
7. We did a survey. Do you know what we found?
8. Have you read the latest consumer report on tires?
9. If I understand you correctly, you are afraid our paint will chip, aren't you?
10. Did you know that we have design specialists assigned full time to work with your engineer?

Q. *What kinds of questions stimulate thought?*

A. The examples below share a common quality. They cause the other party to consider another line of reasoning.

1. Would you consider a two-year contract?
2. How does this idea grab you?
3. Are you sure?
4. Would you consider a deal like this?
5. Have you thought about expanding the line?
6. Have you ever arranged a real-estate trade?
7. Can you see yourself driving a Rolls?
8. Inflation is a problem, isn't it?
9. What if we ordered twice as many?

Q. *What questions cause decisions to be made?*

A. These are terminal questions. They lead the other party to make a choice and close the deal.

Examples of terminal questions:

1. Will you take it or leave it?
2. Which one do you want? The red one or the blue one?
3. How many do you want to order?

4. Did you know the price is going up Monday? Better act now.
5. Do you want us to start the repairs right away?
6. Are you prepared to give us the whole order if we reduce the price by 10 percent?
7. Does that model interest you? Why not?
8. What do you think of my offer?

Q. *What's a loaded question?*

A. A loaded question is one that hides within it an assumption that is distasteful or prejudicial to the person answering.

Examples of loaded questions:

1. Do you still beat your spouse?
2. Is your accounting system still bad?
3. Are you asking me loaded questions again?
4. How is your disagreeable boss?
5. Why is your material cost so high?
6. When did you first see the problem?
7. Who is responsible for the mess?

If you are called upon to answer a loaded question, just laugh at it. Get the question clarified and advise that your material costs are not high or that your boss is not disagreeable.

Q. *What is an ambiguous question?*

A. An ambiguous question is one that can be interpreted in more than one way. The person asking such a question may be on a fishing expedition or may be unclear about his or her own objectives.

Examples of ambiguous questions:

1. How did you put this quote together?
2. That doesn't look right, does it?
3. The costs look high, don't they?
4. How do you account for scrap?
5. You can do better than that, can't you?

If you are asked an ambiguous question, get it clarified before answering. Ask the other person to be specific. Don't answer until you understand the question.

Q. *What is a leading question?*

A. A leading question is one that leads to other lines of inquiry or attempts to prove a point by directing the person answering from statement to statement until the logic of the questioner's argument is made. A leading question may also lead to a trap, as when it is raised just to find out if the other party is telling the truth.

Examples of leading questions:

1. Am I getting the most-favored-customer price? Why not? Who is? Why? That's not what your boss said, is it?
2. Is research included in your cost? Where? How is it prorated between jobs? Exactly why do you include it in our charges when you just said that this job requires no new research?
3. How do you handle interest charges and bad debts? Why? Why charge me? I pay my bills.
4. How many did you sell? Oh, that's not what he or she told me.
5. Have you a smaller model? How is that priced? Based on what you say, I can't see how the price on the larger one is justified.
6. What warranty do you offer on the dryer? Oh, I didn't know that. Are there any other differences? Why?
7. Are you sure of that figure? It seems to be different on page 2. Which is right? How do you explain that? Now look at your summary. It's different again. Let's start from my figures in that case.

Q. *What is a rhetorical question?*

A. A rhetorical question is one that is asked not for the purpose of getting an answer but for effect. No answer is expected.

Examples of rhetorical questions:

1. Do you really want me to believe that?
2. Do you always come so well prepared or are we just lucky?
3. Will you get off my back?
4. Would you believe, we just happened to bring it along?

5. Isn't that a coincidence?
6. Now what do you think my boss would say to that?

Q. *What is a question that is answered by a question?*

A. Whenever you are unclear about the point of a question or wish to have more time to think of an answer, it may be well to respond by asking a question of your own. There is the story of the young husband who said to his wife, "I love you but why do you always answer my question with a question?"

Her eyes twinkled and she said, "Do I really?"

Q. *What is a candid question?*

A. A candid question is one that implies or creates an aura of togetherness.

Examples of candid questions:

1. What is the least you'll take? Tell me.
2. You and I both know that's right. Right?
3. Can't you trust me?
4. You can tell me the truth, can't you?
5. That's reasonable, isn't it?
6. It's hard to believe, isn't it? But I lose money on every one I sell. I make it up on volume.

Q. *What is a closure question?*

A. A closure question is one that closes, commits, or freezes the discussion temporarily or permanently. Such questions are raised to force a decision or break off talks.

Examples of closure questions:

1. Can't you see? This is certainly better for you.
2. Is that your final offer?
3. Do you know how good a deal I've offered you?
4. You've seen my costs. Can you ask me to lose money? I won't.
5. Stop. Can't you see that's enough?

QUICK DEALS

Quick negotiations are generally foolish negotiations. However, if one party is prepared for the "quickie" and the other isn't, the advantage lies with the person who is prepared.

My experiments confirmed that quick deals were extreme deals. They were very good for one party and very bad for the other. On balance, it was the skilled person who did well in the "quickies."

The mistakes described on page 225, "Telephone Negotiations," are likely to happen whenever people don't give themselves enough time to think or force themselves into a quick decision. Don't make a quick deal unless you have to or unless you are well prepared to discuss the issues.

RATE OF CONCESSION: ALTERNATIVE PATTERNS

In my experiments, winners had better control of their concession rate than losers throughout negotiations. This was especially so at the crisis stage, when deadlock was imminent. *Successful bargainers made consistently smaller concessions than their opponents. They were less generous and less predictable.* They varied their concession pattern.

Losers had less control. Many gave little through the first half of negotiation but broke with a series of large concessions later. Some losers gave nothing until the last moment, only to concede huge sums as deadlock approached. Winners had better control. Results confirm that winners also had a higher tolerance for uncertainty. They did not crack at deadline.

Assume that a seller decides to consider reducing the initial price by $60. The question is, How shall he or she do so? Eight different patterns to accomplish the purpose are shown. The pros and cons of each will be analyzed.

ALTERNATIVE CONCESSION PATTERNS

PATTERN NUMBER	TOTAL CONCESSION AMOUNT	PERIOD #1 CONCESSION	PERIOD #2 CONCESSION	PERIOD #3 CONCESSION	PERIOD #4 CONCESSION
1	$60	$ 0	$ 0	$ 0	$60
2	$60	$15	$15	$15	$15
3	$60	$ 8	$13	$17	$22
4	$60	$22	$17	$13	$ 8
5	$60	$26	$20	$12	$ 2
6	$60	$49	$10	$ 0	$ 1
7	$60	$50	$10	$(−1)	$(+1)
8	$60	$60	$ 0	$ 0	$ 0

Pattern 1 [0–0–0–60] is firm throughout except at the end. It signals strong obstinacy about the price and offers little hope for compromise. A weak buyer may give up before the last period. A strong one will probably hold fast or make small concessions in response to the seller's stubbornness. He or she will test the situation. The high $60 concession in the fourth period could lead the buyer to try for more even at the risk of deadlock.

Pattern 2 [15–15–15–15] leads nowhere except to encourage the buyer to expect further concessions if he or she has the patience to wait. Of course, if the negotiation could go into overtime (most can) then a [2–2–2–2–1–1] pattern might wear the buyer down.

Pattern 3 [8–13–17–22] would normally be disastrous. It leads the buyer to believe that "happier days are just around the corner." Aspiration level cannot help but rise as time goes on.

Pattern 4 [22–17–13–8] foreshadows a growing toughness about the seller. It signals a willingness to compromise but predicts a strong defense in the offing.

Pattern 5 [26–20–12–2] signals a strong willingness to compromise but shows the buyer that a limit is being reached. It has the danger of raising the opponent's aspiration level during the first half, but diminishes that tendency as the rate of change points to a strong stand. A sensible buyer would conclude that further concessions are not likely.

Pattern 6 [49–10–0–1] is dangerous because a large initial concession may lead the buyer to raise his or her aspiration level a great deal. The subsequent offer does, however, diminish the effect quickly as does the flat rejection in the third quarter and the tiny concession at the end. This is an effective technique for leaving the opponent satisfied that further discussions will be futile. The danger, from the seller's standpoint, is that you will never learn if the buyer would have paid a higher price. The $49 drop in price may have been by much too much.

Pattern 7 [50–10–0–(–1)–(+1)] is a variant of the preceding pattern, with the exception that obstinacy is most strongly indicated by a slight $1 reduction in the offer (due perhaps to a discovered miscalculation). The later restoration of the $1 offer indicates good faith and leaves the opponent more satisfied in the process.

Pattern 8 [60–0–0–0] has a strange effect on the buyer. At first the buyer's aspiration level will be raised and his or her expectations will be aroused. If the buyer transmits this early enthusiasm to members of his or her organization, they will be led to believe that even better news is imminent. The subsequent obstinacy may harden opinion on both sides and thereby cause deadlock. The buyer may be put into an embarrassing position with his or her organization when they expect further concessions but don't get them.

These patterns show that different concession rates can send different messages. How the other person reacts to your concessions may be determined by the amount you concede, the rate at which you concede, and the change of rate. In my opinion, the ideal way to handle concessions if you are a buyer is to start low and give in very slowly over a long period of time. If you are a seller, just turn it around. Start high and give in slowly over a long period of time.

RECIPROCITY

Reciprocity is a dirty word in America. Not so elsewhere in the world. There, one hand washes the other.

A seller should know from whom his or her company buys. A buyer should know the extent to which his or her company markets its products to the seller's organization. Being aware of these things is not the same as violating the laws against reciprocity. Knowing means that you can act with restraint, good taste, propriety, and better business judgment. There isn't an antitrust law in the world that can or ought to keep you from doing just that.

RESIST LIKE WATER

The Chinese have a saying, "It is well to resist like water." When water is put under pressure or made to flow into unfamiliar channels, it falls back. Then, in its own good time, it seeps and creeps back into position, first slowly and then with greater strength reaching its level.

In the face of strong buyer opposition, a salesperson is wise to resist like water; fall back, listen, think, and move forward slowly.

REVERSE AUCTION: HOW TO GET THE SELLER TO OFFER THE MOST WORK FOR THE LEAST MONEY

This is the dream tactic of tough buyers. Its aim is to get competing sellers to outbid one another in offering the most work for the least money. Many a seller has gone broke at a reverse auction. Tough as it is, many a buyer has gotten in trouble using it.

The reverse auction works like this. Suppose you want to buy a pool in Los Angeles. You know that building one can't be too hard because so many people have them. Your needs are simple. It should be 15 × 30 feet, heated, filtered, and ready by June 1. Nothing special about that.

Three contractors bid. Your intention is to give the job to the low bidder. After looking at the bids, you discover that each is different. They offer different heaters, filters, coping, design, plumbing, decking, and financial terms. The choice suddenly becomes complicated. A pool costs $25,000 and you have to live with it for a long time. Mistakes can be costly. What can you do?

Call a reverse auction. After the bids are received, you invite the three competitors to your house: one at 9:00 A.M., the next at 9:15, and the last at 9:30. All three spend the next thirty minutes glaring at one another in the living room. At 10:00 you call the first one into your den to talk business.

Of course, Seller A tells you why his or her pool is best. He or she also sneaks in a few remarks that make you wonder about the competitors. You learn that Seller B is using an obsolete filter and that Seller C has left a lot of empty holes around Los Angeles. The intimation is that Seller C is on the verge of bankruptcy. Seller B then comes in. You then learn that the others use plastic pipe whereas he or she provides copper. You aren't too surprised to learn later from Seller C that the others use inferior heaters, fail to clean up properly, and take no responsibility after the pool is paid for. After investigation of the conflicting claims, you begin to understand the subtleties and risk involved in buying what once appeared to be a simple pool.

Now you are better able to refine the specification as the alternatives become clear. The sellers are then given an opportunity to bid on tighter and tighter requirements. The job is finally given to the seller offering the most product, the most reliability, and the lowest price consistent with those objectives. The reverse auction has achieved two purposes: (1) it has taught you about pools, and (2) it has given you the ability to trade off options you didn't know existed.

There are reasons why the tactic works. For one thing, each seller has sunk a great deal of effort into making the proposal. Each wants his or her investment to pay off. Each feels that with just a little more effort and a few concessions, he or she can close the deal.

Competition for most things in America is fierce. Although we live in a free-enterprise society, it is not often that we see our competitors face to face. The reverse auction recognizes that sellers cannot help becoming anxious when they see their competitors at such close range. Competition then becomes a stark reality instead of a theory.

The reverse auction also puts heat on the seller's management team. Their business judgment is at stake. Should they promise more? Take a lower margin? Throw in extras? Hold the line? Or walk out? Whatever they choose to do, the risk is high that too much will be given away or that the job will be lost. Few people are accustomed to such pressure. They don't like it.

The buyer knows that it takes more courage for a seller to risk losing a contract at negotiation than at an earlier stage. Some companies crack. They make concessions at the auction that under less trying circumstances would be withheld. The buyer also recognizes that the tactic drives a wedge between members of the seller's organization. It forces competition priorities into open conflict. Some of the seller's people want to drop out while others are willing to take almost any profit or technical risks to take the job away from competitors. The buyer is in a position to drive a hard bargain, especially if sellers are hurting for work.

The reverse auction is not without its liabilities. Sellers who crack under pressure often get even later. They resent the auction and make up for the damage done them. Once the contract is gotten, they do not feel badly about charging a fat price for every design change. Many end up delivering late, shading on quality, and breaking promises. Many an advanced defense system, aircraft, or missile has been bought at a reverse auction. On paper the equipment or system looked great, but it could never be made to work right. It turned out to be a bad bargain for the buyer and the seller. That is what can happen at a reverse auction if you don't watch out.

REVERSE-AUCTION COUNTERMEASURES

I've been exposed to reverse auctions many times. There are few tactics as hard for a seller to cope with. The buyer holds most of the trump cards, but a seller can do some things to overcome the buyer's natural advantage:

1. If you have a lemon, make lemonade. Study your weaknesses. The competition will surely bring them up.
2. Don't hurry to make concessions.
3. Sell, sell, sell your strengths and benefits.
4. Know who really makes the decision.
5. Dry-run the auction at home.
6. Limit your authority to a bottom-line figure.
7. Bring experts. The buyer wants to believe somebody.
8. If things look like they are going badly, have an innovative approach in your hat.
9. Use your best, most experienced negotiators.

When the buyer invites you to a reverse auction, it is important that you recognize the problems he or she is getting into. Reverse auctions take a long time. They keep him or her away from the office and behind in daily work. They use up whatever lead time he or she had for making the purchase. People in his or her organization get anxious. They are also kept from carrying out their responsibilities. After a time, the buyer's team doesn't know who or what to believe. They become more afraid to make a mistake. Everyone gets confused, tired, and desirous of getting the mess over with.

All of these factors are to the seller's advantage. It means that the seller who best understands what is important to the buyer, who best convinces the buyer of his or her credibility, and who helps make a rational decision will have the inside track.

The seller who goes into a reverse auction should be sure to use the most skilled negotiators. He or she should give himself or herself lots of time to think and, if possible, be last rather than first in the auction. These measures and the ones mentioned earlier make sense but by no means guarantee success. There are no easy strategies for winning the reverse auction.

RULES OF NEGOTIATION: ONES TO WATCH OUT FOR

One way to control a negotiation is to lay out the rules. Bad rules can stack the deck against you. Here are some that I've seen used against me:

1. Order of speaking
2. Use of experts, and how many
3. Rules of evidence and documentation
4. When questions may be asked
5. Individuals to whom questions may be directed
6. Who may ask questions
7. Outside-interruption rules
8. Tape recording and minutes
9. Mediator rules

10. Security measures
11. Public-announcement rules
12. Eating times
13. Rest and caucus periods
14. Penalty and bluffing rules
15. Telephone calls
16. Where to negotiate
17. Seating arrangements
18. Rules for breaking off discussions
19. Appeal procedures
20. Authority rules
21. Team-change rules.

Whenever your opponent proposes a rule, watch out. Look for the hidden meaning behind it. The best policy is to question why it was made. Feel free to disregard a rule that works against you. A negotiation is not a courtroom. Rules are always negotiable and renegotiable.

SATISFACTION: THE PRESENT VALUE OF FUTURE SATISFACTION

A negotiator is like an investor in the stock market. He or she bargains for profit, but in the case of negotiations, profit is a gain in satisfaction rather than a gain in money.

How do investors make a decision when they have $20,000 to invest? They try to determine what dividends the stock or financial instrument will pay for the next ten years and what the stock or bond will be worth when they sell it. If they are smart, the investors put a probability estimate on the flow of money from the purchase. After all, some stocks don't rise, and some dividends fade away if a company gets into trouble. What the investor finally comes up with consists of two determinations:

whether the flow of money back to them over the next ten years is worth $20,000, and whether there is any other financial instrument that is better than the one they thought of buying. After discounting the future, they either buy the stock, buy a bond or some other instrument, or decide to hold on to the $20,000. In financial terms, they have computed the present value of future profit (or loss) and compared it to their other choices.

Negotiators do the same thing, but on a subjective level. They determine the present value of a flow of future satisfactions (and dissatisfactions) and compare it to making no deal at all or holding out for a better deal.

This puts us in a position to recognize a fundamental but subtle point about negotiation. The flow of plus and minus satisfaction in any deal is in the head of the participant. Some participants are optimists about the future. Others are pessimists. Some are "I-want-my-kicks-right-now" people, and others are prepared to wait a long time.

The banks learned this mind-set long ago, in writing mortgages. People worry a lot more about the down payment than they do about the interest rate, which is spread out monthly over a long period. They hardly worry at all about what will happen when they sell the house.

So an outfit called Home Savings and Loan, the largest in the world, put in a clause that if you sold your house before the mortgage was paid (normally twenty to thirty years) you would have to pay six months' interest on the *original loan.* A lot of people got a rude surprise when they sold their homes in fifteen years after having paid off about half the debt. They still had to pay a penalty even on the part they had paid back. Home Savings and Loan knew that people didn't worry much about the future dissatisfaction of paying an exorbitant penalty for selling a house when they were excited about buying one. It was honest but not quite fair.

From a practical standpoint, what does all this say to the salesperson? It says that the buyer is looking at the deal in terms of the short- and long-term benefits (and losses) he or she may enjoy or suffer. The seller can raise the present value of the offering by getting the buyer to value future satisfaction more than he or she does. The seller can also do the same thing by showing the buyer that future dissatisfactions are unlikely.

Buyers invest in future satisfaction. If they are pessimists, make them optimists. If they want kicks now, show them how much more important kicks will be later. Every negotiator has the same role to perform. The job is to raise the present value of future satisfaction for the other person and thereby help him or her make a decision.

SATISFACTION: THE PRESENT VALUE OF FUTURE DISSATISFACTION

Many years ago, the Russian writer Aleksandr Solzhenitsyn gave an interview to the Western press protesting the treatment of those in Russia who did not agree with Soviet internal policy. What he said about the human spirit is relevant to negotiation. It puts into focus the value people put on present and future dissatisfaction:

> There is one psychological peculiarity in the human being that always strikes you: to shun even the slightest signs of trouble on the outer edge of your existence at times of well-being when you are free of care, to try not to know about the sufferings, to yield in many situations, even important spiritual and central ones—as long as it prolongs one's well-being . . . this would be a good thing . . . to show some endurance and courage somewhat before the critical hour—to sacrifice less, but a bit earlier.

Most people prefer to postpone unpleasant conflicts. They hope the problems will go away. It would be a good thing for them to show more endurance and courage during the negotiation than to suffer the dissatisfactions of a poor agreement later.

The person who understands this quirk in the human spirit and catches it personally can negotiate more effectively because he or she will be willing to face unpleasant matters before they create even greater problems later.

SATISFACTION AND CONCESSION: THE AVAILABLE OPTIONS

The source of all power is the ability to provide satisfaction in one form or another. Every concession benefits the other party and has costs attached to it. The flow of satisfaction between people is not as simple as it looks. Before you start making concessions, think about how you want to do it. These are the options available to you:

1. *The time option:* A concession can provide satisfaction to the receiver now or later, when the receiver chooses to take it all at once or a little at a time.
2. *The benefits option:* A concession can direct its benefits to the organization, specific parts of the organization, third parties, to the opposing negotiator on a personal level, or to all of them at once.
3. *The satisfier option:* The content of a concession may or may not be the source of satisfaction to the one who gets the concession. Satisfaction can accrue from the issue or matter under discussion, from combinations of issues, from matters only slightly related to the issue, or from other satisfiers that are entirely unrelated.
4. *The cost option:* The cost of a concession can be paid for by the organization, by parts of the organization, by outside third parties, or by the negotiator himself or herself.

The flow of satisfaction is more subtle than first appearances warrant. Concessions, if they are to be effective, take into account who will benefit, in what way, when, and from what source.

SCRAMBLED EGGS: HOW DISORDER CAN WORK AGAINST YOU

It is wiser to simplify matters than to confuse them. "Scrambled eggs" does the opposite. It deliberately mixes things up for tactical reasons. Scrambling can be used to forestall a deadlock, make the other person work harder, force through a last-minute demand, or retreat from a prior concession. Sometimes it is used to determine how well the other person keeps his or her wits under pressure. Negotiations should be conducted in an orderly fashion. The scrambler knows that disorder can also work for him or her.

Scrambling may occur early or late in discussions. One person I know likes to mix things up quickly. Shortly after talks begin, she introduces complications by changing the product-price package. New delivery dates, services, quality standards, and quantities are proposed. She does this to see how well prepared the opposition is and whether they are willing to shoot from the hip on unfamiliar issues. Some negotiators use scrambling late at night, when everyone is groggy. They claim that most people would rather agree to anything moderately reasonable than get their minds back into high gear at two in the morning.

The scrambler takes advantage of the mistakes people make when they are confused. Suddenly apples can't be compared to apples, and cost comparisons become impossible to make. Most people tend to say "the hell with it" when things get thoroughly confused, especially when they are tired or have other pressing matters to take care of.

It takes self-confidence to stop the scrambler. These steps help:

1. Have the courage to say "I don't understand."
2. Keep saying "I don't understand" until you do.
3. Insist that matters be discussed one at a time.
4. Recognize that you do not have to talk about things as the scrambler wants you to. Start in your own way and get the scrambler going down your line of reasoning.
5. Remember that he or she is probably almost as confused as you are.
6. Watch for the mistakes you are sure to make.

The key defense is never to negotiate an issue until you understand it. Practice and courage help unscramble the scrambler.

SEATING ARRANGEMENTS

The parties to a negotiation should sit at opposite sides of the table. The solidarity and communication ability of a team is improved if the leader sits at the head position and members sit around him or her. Leaders should face each other on equal terms and be able to command eye contact with their associates. This type of arrangement makes for better team control and morale.

"You are where you sit." Seating protocol can tell a story. A keen observer will try to interpret seating position in terms of who counts and who doesn't. You can send whatever message you think best through seating arrangements and changes. If your opponent is a body-language fancier, he or she will spend the rest of the session trying to interpret the significance of each seating change even when there isn't any.

SELLING YOUR VIEWPOINT

A salesperson is a negotiator. He or she has a point of view and wants to convince the buyer that it is correct. The buyer has one set of beliefs and the seller another. An exchange of viewpoints is a negotiation—a very tough one, because ideas are like possessions. People don't like to part with them.

There are eight points to remember if your viewpoint is to prevail. They are so easy to follow that you won't want to forget them:

Point 1. Talk less and listen more. The other person wants to express himself or herself. If you keep quiet, they will talk. They will reciprocate by being more attentive when you talk.

Point 2. Don't interrupt. Interruptions get people angry and block communications.

Point 3. Don't be belligerent. There is good reason for respecting the soft-spoken person. It is harder to be firm in a moderate, self-controlled way than to be harsh, loud, or derisive. The soft-spoken person's manner encourages the same treatment from others. An argumentative attitude changes no opinions.

Point 4. Don't be in a hurry to bring up your points. As a general principle, it is best to get the other person's full viewpoint before expressing yours.

Point 5. Restate the other person's position and objectives as soon as you understand them. People like to know that they have been understood. It is an inexpensive concession to make. There is another hidden benefit in forcing yourself to restate an opponent's position. It will make you listen better and help you phrase your points in his or her terms.

Point 6. Identify the key point and stick to it. Avoid the tendency to overwhelm with arguments. Cover one point at a time.

Point 7. Don't digress from the key point and keep the other person from digressing. There are three ways to minimize digressions: (1) agree on some nonessential point temporarily for argument's sake; (2) agree to discuss it later; or (3) try to treat the intrusion as being somewhat off the point.

Point 8. Be "for" a point of view, not "against."

People prefer cooperation to conflict. The ideas above lead in the right direction. When you think about it, selling your viewpoint, selling your product, and winning an argument have much in common.

SETTLEMENT BY ARBITRATION

Many commercial and labor contracts call for arbitration if the parties involved cannot resolve differences by negotiation. Arbitration is becoming more widely used in collective bargaining. For the first time, the steel industry has agreed to use arbitration when talks break down. This is a radical departure from past practices and will probably be followed in other major industries.

When two parties submit a dispute to arbitration, both agree to comply with the decision of the arbitrator. Customarily, the parties are permitted to choose one arbitrator each. The two so chosen agree on an impartial third person. The American Arbitration Association has a set of rules by which proceedings take place and become legally operable. The association also provides a stable of mature, experienced people from whom to choose.

Arbitration serves valuable functions. An arbitrator can find face-saving ways to satisfy not only the negotiators but their organizations. The disputants may act as tough as they want in front of the arbitrator. In doing so, they fulfill the expectations of those in the home office who want aggressive representation. Arbitration also contributes to cooperative problem-solving by serving as a catalyst for new ideas. Arbitration is usually less costly to the parties than deadlock or work stoppages.

Despite its advantages there are serious drawbacks to arbitration:

1. Arbitrators are sometimes incapable of understanding the real issues.
2. They may be outdated in their thinking.
3. They may be unconsciously biased for a variety of reasons.
4. They can be swayed by oratory.
5. They may, in resolving a dispute, create difficult future problems and unhealthy precedents.

Arbitration can create a serious negotiating problem. Buyers who want to use it for their advantage do it this way. Knowing that arbitration is available, they drive the seller's asking price from $150,000 to $110,000 by hard bargaining. Then they call for arbitration. The seller is thrown off balance for two reasons: First, because he or she and their organization begin to rationalize that $110,000 is not a bad settlement. Second, because the arbitrator tends to compromise at less than $110,000. From his practical viewpoint, the seller has already reduced his demand to $110,000. What counts is the $110,000 figure, not the $150,000 originally asked for. The buyer who abuses arbitration in this way stands to gain from it—at least in the short run.

Arbitration is a legitimate alternative in the negotiating kit of tools. When you want a decision based on equity rather than power, arbitration may be called for. It is also appropriate when the facts of a particular case are more important than precedent. There are certain kinds of commercial disputes in every industry that might best be settled by arbitration. I would like to see more of it than less. It is, however, not a panacea. And, as pointed out earlier, it may, in fact, be used against you.

SETTLEMENT RANGE: WHAT IT IS AND ISN'T

The settlement range is usually defined as the difference between the least a seller will take and the most a buyer will pay. That makes sense, of course, but it isn't quite right.

The trouble is that there are really three settlement ranges in a negotiation:

1. The one in the buyer's head
2. The one in the seller's head
3. The one that would exist if both told a neutral third party everything that was in their heads.

I believe that it pays to look at the settlement range in a more realistic way. It's a little more difficult to see it in this new way, but you will find it more useful.

The settlement range should be redefined as the difference between the "buyer's estimate of the seller's minimum" and the "seller's estimate of the buyer's maximum." The important point is simply this: The range is based on each person's estimate of the situation, not the real situation itself. Estimates not only tend to be wrong, but can be altered as new information comes in.

The buyer has the ability to change the seller's estimate of the most the buyer is willing to pay. The seller has the ability to change the buyer's estimate of the least the seller is willing to take. That is why every tactic and countermeasure you use is so important. How you make a demand, how much you demand, how you concede, and where you draw the line are important, affecting your opponent's estimates of what is possible and realistic and changing the picture of settlement range that he or she had in their head.

SEX IN NEGOTIATION

It happens.

SHILL

Years ago, if you looked around at an auction, there was a good chance that you would have noticed several people who kept bidding up the price. You could spot them if you got there early because they worked for the management. Their job was to stimulate the bidding. They were shills.

Shill tactics are as old as time. Buyers and sellers use them in business often without realizing it. Real-estate brokers employ shills to stimulate the prospective buyer's interest in a home. A friend of the realtor just happens to drop into the house at the same moment the buyer arrives. Land developments use shills to show that lot 34 near the lake was just sold to Mr. Jones. If you looked into it, you would find that Mr. Jones is on the developer's payroll. This is unethical, and in many states illegal, of course, but not all shill situations are unethical or illegal.

The shill has three functions: *to establish a market price, to stimulate interest in a product, and to create competition.* Buyers use shills, and so do sellers. In my opinion, the examples of buyer and seller shills which follow are ethical.

First we will look at some examples of buyer shills:

1. Letting sales competitors bunch up in the reception room.
2. Having the buyer's secretary let slip the names of competitors who are scheduled to visit the buyer later in the day.

3. Sending requests for proposals to many sellers even when only a few are qualified, and making sure all competitors know about the others.
4. Suggesting that the order will be split between sellers if the price is not right.
5. Negotiating with two companies in different rooms at the same time.
6. Letting the seller know that he or she will have to do "better than that." In that case, the shill is competition.

And now, the seller shills:

1. Showing a prospective buyer that other buyers are touring the plant ready to buy up open capacity.
2. Pointing out that the inventory is in short supply and is subject to prior sale.
3. Saying, "We've got only one left, and it will take a month to get new ones in."
4. Letting the buyer know that management is thinking of closing out the product because it is unprofitable.
5. Advising the buyer that he or she had better order before the strike.
6. Telling the buyer that prices are likely to rise as soon as shortages develop.
7. Showing the buyer that other buyers have already placed orders.
8. Allowing the buyer to see for himself or herself that production facilities are operating at full capacity.

Shills are often used to test a low offer. I know a boat dealer who employs a shill to test the seller's reaction to a low price. The shill makes a low offer in order to reduce the seller's expectations. Later the dealer himself offers a slightly higher price, which by comparison doesn't look nearly as bad.

Antique dealers utilize shills to establish a market price. It works this way. A buyer browses through the store, showing special interest in, let us say, an antique desk priced at $3,500. Two little old people just happen by at that moment. One says to the other, "What a lovely piece. It's really worth a lot more than $3,500. That desk is 150 years old or more. I wish I had the money. I'd grab it." The next thing you know, you own a desk for $3,500 that is probably worth $2,000. You've been shilled by an unethical antique dealer.

The best countermeasure against the shill is a healthy skepticism that says, "Things are not what they appear to be." Look around carefully before you do business. Shills succeed so often that even they become careless.

SHYSTER TACTICS: THE SOMETHING-FOR-NOTHING TRAP

In the dictionary, a shyster is defined as a person who obscures the purposes by never-ending pettiness through verbal or legal smokescreens. The term originated with an unscrupulous lawyer named Scheuster who practiced in Philadelphia in 1843. The shyster tactic is unethical. It is used by people who are so twisted that they have no hesitancy about bilking others.

The maneuver consists of a negotiation that never ends. The shyster's idea is to lure the opponent into a deal by making an especially attractive offer. Once the opponent is mentally committed to reaching agreement, the process begins in earnest.

The shyster makes and breaks verbal agreements with impunity. The methods vary, but often include disapproval by higher authority, inability to clarify items, misunderstanding, transcription problems, errors in figures, legal delays, and missing-person tricks.

The shyster is careful to maintain cordial relations until a contract is signed. Words and figures undergo a subtle transformation at contract time. The shyster's opponent, upon signing, breathes a sigh of relief despite the fact that he or she is not nearly as well off as he or she thought. Poor fool. His or her troubles have barely begun; they include the despair of breach, legal delay, insults, endless debate, double bookkeeping, and costs for judgments not likely to be collected.

What has been described above happens every day to people who are foolish, greedy, and unlucky. Shyster tactics work because people like a bargain and don't want to work very hard. They get lured into the "something-for-nothing" trap. Instead of asking why a person as obviously intelligent as the shyster should be offering such a marvelous deal, they tend to accept the reasons at face value.

Few have the wealth or fortitude to fight the shyster. The best advice in dealing with these exploiters is to run the other way at the *first* sign of bad faith. If running is impossible, the only alternative is to get a very big deposit and lots of help from the best lawyer in town.

SIT-IN PSYCHOLOGISTS: CAN THEY CONTRIBUTE?

Should a psychologist be part of the team? One company has a good many on its staff and uses some of them in negotiation. These people are not "body-language" faddists who believe in instant perception. They are serious, professional psychologists, most with Ph.D. degrees and years of experience.

Sit-in psychologists may play two roles in negotiations involving high stakes. They can serve as trained observers to help recognize subtleties of behavior that the average person might not notice. In addition, and perhaps of greater importance, they can contribute to better team performance by helping resolve internal tension.

At many large American corporations, a group of organization specialists with expertise in psychology participate directly in the day-to-day assignment of line and staff executives. Their role is to help reduce group conflict, facilitate communications, and assist in better utilizing human resources in solving real-life management problems.

The same concept applied to negotiation could return high dividends. Members of the bargaining team typically come from diverse functional areas. Their priorities, decision processes, and risk-taking attitudes differ markedly. In their work as salespeople, engineers, production people, and controllers, they have little opportunity to cooperate together on a daily basis. A sit-in psychologist could contribute to resolving conflict between groups and to opening a flow of communication unhampered by status differences.

The trouble with sit-in psychologists is that good ones are hard to find. A company that uses them regularly found that some were poor observers while others were harder to understand than the opponents they were asked to observe. Psychologists are like the rest of us. Not all are practical. Not all possess common sense.

SKEPTICISM PAYS

A good negotiator must be skeptical. The approach to evaluating what he or she is told by the other party can be summed up in four principles:

1. Never take anything for granted.
2. Check everything.
3. Put everything into its proper context.
4. Draw a sharp line of demarcation between facts and the interpretation of facts.

SMOKESCREENS: SHORT-RANGE FIREWORKS

There are times when people want to change the subject, delay a decision, or cloud an issue. So they send up a smokescreen.

Here are some smokescreens that slow things down and mix things up:

1. A detailed exploration of some obscure, unimportant procedure or process
2. Talking about spouses
3. Rushing to the bathroom
4. Letting somebody who is inarticulate and a bit irrational handle a complicated explanation
5. Getting hungry suddenly
6. Changing the specifications
7. Suggesting a surprise alternative
8. Reading a complicated regulation out loud
9. Permitting lots of telephone interruptions
10. Introducing a new proposition that starts everything all over again
11. Encouraging and permitting irrelevant cross-talk among your people
12. Giving answers to questions that are not asked

SNOW JOB

The snow job consists of giving opponents so much information that they get bogged down in trivia. It is hoped that by so doing they will overlook the really important data and miss the good questions. I once saw a seller wheel in two full file cabinets to back up a position. Everyone laughed when he said, "I just happened to bring them along." There was so much data available that we never did get to look at any of it carefully.

The snow job works because people tend to equate quantity of information with quality. When confronted with large quantities of back-up data, people act as they do at a smorgasbord. They sample a little of this and a little of that. Before long they are too full to eat the main course.

Don't get trapped by long-winded answers and file cabinets of information. Too much data is almost as bad as none. Hidden in the torrent of words may be deliberate errors, self-serving assumptions, and contradictory material. Have the guts to demand detailed proof and the diligence to check things. Don't allow yourself to be overwhelmed by trivia. The snow job is especially designed to keep you from telling "the forest from the trees."

SOURCES OF GOOD INFORMATION: PUBLIC AND PRIVATE

Everybody agrees that knowledge is power. Why, then, do most business organizations fail to use the public and private sources of information available to them? It is because they make it too hard for their people to gain knowledge. The least-effort principle says that if something is too hard to do, it is not done.

Before people can use information, three essential steps are necessary. First, they must know where the information is; second, they must have access to it; and third, they must be organized to receive it. Your first impulse will be to say that this is just plain common sense. Yes, but like a lot of common sense, it is forgotten easily. Unfortunately, it turns out that knowledge is never free. Executives may pay lip service to knowledge, but they often fail to budget the necessary funds. It takes money to store information and make it available for use.

There is a wealth of public information available to buyers and sellers. In this day of mass communication and computers, much of our business and personal history is an open book. Public records are available to anyone on matters such as mortgages, liens, legal judgments, plant improvements, contract awards, taxes, and trial records. Financial data can be gotten through credit checks, stockholder reports, Dun and Bradstreet, and insider-transaction reports. A company's organization directory, telephone book, and in-house newspaper are easily obtainable. Other sources of information include newspapers, clipping services, government studies, *Who's Who* directories, professional societies, and periodicals. Most of the information is available at a relatively low cost, but companies are not organized to get it. When a company isn't organized the individual buyer or salesperson certainly isn't.

An internal-history file should also be made available to the negotiator. He or she should have ready access to his opponent's track record. Performance history, delivery records, and quality problems encountered previously can be useful in making better judgments. The negotiator should know the status of any other business being done with the opponent's company. People are largely predictable. They tend to repeat tactics. For that reason, a brief description of prior tactics used is valuable. Such a record could provide a preview of coming distractions.

A data bank is no better than the material in it or the people who use it. The file should have one purpose: to build negotiating leverage. It should be able to describe what the other party needs, who the people are, their style of negotiating, and company strengths and weaknesses. If the data bank is good, it will be used. If it is not, there isn't any procedure in the world that will make it be used.

I have participated in multimillion-dollar negotiations in which both parties flew by the seat of their pants. Neither had any really useful information about the other. The negotiators were not the ones responsible. Management was. It never provided the channels by which information could be collected or used. Public and private sources of information are available. It's up to management to assure that they are tapped.

SPLIT THE DIFFERENCE: IF NOT IN THE MIDDLE, WHERE ELSE?

Splitting the difference is a quick way to reach agreement. It seduces us. After all, people are used to giving and getting equal shares at home, at restaurants, and at birthday parties. Splitting in the middle is simple. Not splitting in the middle is full of problems. It brings up a tough question: "If not in the middle, where else?"

The question "Where else?" is interesting. If the law in community-property states did not recognize that husband and wife are entitled to equal shares, divorce in those states would be more complicated than it is. If custom did not dictate that regular players share a World's Series purse equally, they probably would hate each other after the series. Yet, each did not contribute equally to getting into the series, so why share equally? Things that are equal are not necessarily equitable. Splitting the difference is equal, but it may not be equitable or fair.

I know a buyer who does well using the split approach. He makes a low starting offer, raises it only slightly, and then says, "Okay, let's split the difference." The buyer knows that it's hard for a salesperson to say no to such a reasonable request. The salesperson who gets sucked into the split finds he or she is giving too much away. Of course, if the difference is small, the salesperson would have good reason for going along.

The next time somebody says, "Let's split the difference," try saying no. You will be surprised at how often you get more than half.

SPYING AND BUGGING: A GROWING REALITY IN BUSINESS

When I first began giving seminars on negotiation, attendees used to get a skeptical look on their faces when industrial spying was discussed. Since Watergate, they are not so skeptical. At the risk of appearing paranoid, I believe that we are in greater danger of industrial espionage than at any other time in business history.

Some time ago, I ran into a Copley News Service release titled "Industrial Spying on Rise," a portion of which is excerpted below. It gives us a foretaste of what the business person's future was likely to hold:

> GENEVA--In Europe, as in the United States and Japan industrial espionage has become a booming industry in its own right.
>
> According to one authoritative estimate, $800 million a year is being spent on industrial spying. It has all the marks of a growth industry. Risks are, strangely enough, rather low, and the return can be high.
>
> A company could put a few million dollars into a research project with much more risk, and another company could pick up the results for $40,000–$50,000 at no risk at all. . . .
>
> There are basically three main types of industrial spies. At the humblest level is the disloyal employee. . . . The next group of spies is the part-timers . . . and the professional spies.
>
> Not so long ago a leading European counterespionage specialist invited to luncheon by the chairman of the board of a very large company was staggered when he was asked quite blandly for assistance in recruiting a good industrial spy to find about what the competition was up to.
>
> But perhaps the most insidious aspect of industrial espionage is the poaching of specialist employees from other

firms. In order to keep a lead over a rival, a company may employ an agent to buy out its key personnel at higher salaries. This, of course, is a normal business risk against which few firms have found adequate protection.

This form of espionage takes its most dangerous form when a company recruits an employee of a rival and asks him to remain in his job with the first employer, receiving, of course, a supplemental retainer from his new employer. The employee becomes, for practical purposes, a spy, even though he may not literally pass on any information to his new employer until he finally leaves for his new job. He may well lie dormant for a year or so, and then leave when a particular research project reaches its final stage. . . .

During the last decade the means by which infiltration can be achieved and information obtained have developed to a degree that almost belies comprehension.

The "bug," a miniature camera, the directional microphone, the telescopic camera, the tape recorder, the storage and transmission of computerized information—and various combinations of these—have made the task of the industrial spy infinitely easier. In the hands of an expert, these means of obtaining information become a major menace. . . .

A director of one of the firms discovered quite by accident that his table lamp had a couple of spare leads. The wire, followed by his security man, led through walls and ducting until they reached the roof. It would have taken only a matter of minutes to connect a microphone to one end of the wires and a transmitter to the other.

Window cleaners and office cleaners, as well as the lower-paid clerical workers, are often used for such tasks. For the small sum of $50 or its equivalent, a charwoman can be persuaded to slip a bugging device under the table. Wastepaper baskets have also proven to be fertile grounds for the industrial spy, enabling him to piece together a vast amount of vital information.

All the items cited in the Copley item are much worse today, with voicemail, computer hackers, instantaneous transfers of information and funds, and high technology devices.

The lure of industrial espionage in negotiation is great. Perhaps nowhere else are the stakes so high and the payoff so quick. Just think what it would be worth for a buyer to know the lowest price a seller will take. On major deals this information might be worth millions. The investment in gaining the information is only a few dollars. The technology is already available to bright high school graduates.

From a negotiation standpoint, I favor a tight, no-nonsense security policy. Such a policy begins with attitudes that highlight the need for guarding information. There can be no security unless sufficient money and enforcement authority are given those in charge. A good program screens employees before they are assigned to major negotiations. It sets up tight procedures by which information is collected, analyzed, and stored for safekeeping. Access to data is given on a strict need-to-know basis. Access to work areas is also controlled stringently. A no-nonsense security policy takes a tough stand against conflict of interest. It prohibits side payments in any form whatever.

Security is a state of mind. The process begins with people who care about what they are doing and are not naïve about the dangers of industrial espionage. It starts at the top of the company. When those on top have no respect for these matters, nobody else will.

These rules will help minimize the risk of industrial espionage. They will not eliminate it.

1. Select closemouthed people with stable dispositions.
2. Emphasize the need for silence.
3. Exclude anyone from data who does not have a need to know.
4. Let those who have a need to know share only what is necessary and nothing more.
5. Determine, if possible, existing conflicts of interest. Be imaginative.
6. See that bribes are reported instantly. Allow no exceptions for any reason whatsoever.
7. Provide your opponent with as little data as you can unless there are tactical reasons for being more generous.
8. Maintain a communications network within the organiza-

tion to know what the other party is digging into and why.

9. Handle all back-up material on a private basis. See that it is stored, locked, and never left unattended.
10. Shift caucus and hotel rooms in which team business is discussed. The rooms may be bugged.
11. Isolate groups who work on major proposal efforts. I know of one company that quarantined thirty people at a seaside resort while they worked for a month on a billion-dollar proposal.
12. Let very few people know the final bid figures.
13. Discipline security violations promptly.
14. Sometimes the easiest access to secured information is through janitorial or other service people. Be on guard against such infiltration.

If it appears that I am overly cautious about security, I am—deliberately so. Most buyers and salespeople, especially those in big companies, live in a dreamworld. They dismiss the possibility of spying and bugging in negotiation, probably because most of them wouldn't dream of doing it themselves. I believe that industrial espionage in negotiation is a growing reality. The stakes are so high and the cost so low that it is inevitable.

SQUEAKY WHEELS

The squeaky wheel gets the most grease. When a buyer is trying to get service from a seller, the more people who ask for the service and the more noise they make about it, the more likely they are to get it. After a while, the seller will give in just to get rid of the nuisance.

This means that sellers who want to collect an unpaid bill might well consider having many people at many levels call about the bill. It means that buyers who want faster action on their complaints might generate that action by having their engineering and production people complain to their selling counterparts. "Squeaky wheels" means that your demands are more likely to be met if lots of people on your side join in the chorus.

"STARBOARD": WHEN KNOWING THE RULES DOESN'T HELP

When I first learned to sail, it was hard enough to control the boat—let alone worry about rules. Marina del Rey in Los Angeles is a tribute to the ability of people to conceive a great idea. There the Pacific Ocean has been tamed and now berths 8,000 boats. The trouble is that they all go out to sea on Sunday. A traffic jam of mammoth proportions results. What makes it worse is that no license is needed for boating. All that is necessary is a boat and some courage. Knowledge is not a prerequisite.

My early Sundays in sailing were full of tension. Tacking this way and that, I managed my way through the channel among far larger boats. One collision and mine would have fallen apart. Boats everywhere, going in every direction—skilled and unskilled sailors, speedboats, and monstrous power yachts all in a helter-skelter mess.

As I sailed along minding my own business, I noticed that people coming at me yelled "Starboard!" at the top of their lungs. Some, less yachtsmanlike, would pass with a mean look. They would say something like, "Look, stupid, I said, 'Starboard.' What the hell's wrong with you?" I didn't know what they were talking about and had enough trouble with my boat, anyway. They got out of my way, and that's what counted.

Later I learned that "starboard" meant that the boat that has the wind coming from its right side has the right of way. The other boat must give way. These people knew the rule. I didn't, yet they—not I—gave ground.

Sometimes knowing the rules doesn't help you. Now I yell "Starboard!" at the top of my lungs. Then I get out of the way because the "idiot" doesn't know what I'm talking about.

STATISTICS: THE BS FACTOR

My attitude toward statistics can be stated simply: "Watch out." Years ago, an artist named Cole used to put Shakespearean sayings under his cartoons. Once he drew a three-breasted woman. The caption read: "Go quickly and take again the count." That's what I do when somebody feeds me statistics.

For over half a century, the Federal Reserve Board has depended on banks to provide financial reports on their dealings in government securities. Important decisions about our money supply have been made on the basis of these statistics. After fifty years a government audit was made to determine their accuracy. It was found that the reports were "virtually meaningless." Until that time everyone had blindly assumed that the data were correct. The thinking was that after all, banks know what they are doing. Do they?

Numbers are a subtle source of power. Those who gather the numbers control the decisions. Even with the best of intentions, gross errors can occur. When a numbers person has larceny in mind, false conclusions are hard to avoid.

I once worked for a wizard named Boyd who was in charge of price estimating. Boyd could come up with any figure he wanted to. He was a cynic about statistics. In spite of this, he maintained the best data bank I have ever seen. He kept price-history cards the way a cook keeps spices. When the occasion arose, he would choose those that best flavored his objectives. Boyd knew that people have trouble separating facts from the assumptions and sources behind those facts. He was a skilled statistical liar.

Statistics have the power to hypnotize the viewer. They are of themselves neither good nor bad. Only by digging deeper do the subtleties emerge. Below the surface can be found a witches' brew of facts, interpretations, assumptions, value judgments, and a few dumb mistakes. What shows is not what is.

Be skeptical of statistics. Go quickly and take again the count.

STATUS AND ITS EFFECTS

Status is part of the price. People exchange status just as they exchange money or goods. When a highly placed person talks to a lowly placed person, he or she confers status in trade for some benefit of a real or psychological nature. A negotiation takes place between them.

People segregate themselves from others much above their own rank. Contact between a salesperson and a division manager is rare. Buyers associate with their counterparts at the table. Those lower in the organization feel awkward with those who are higher. There is a recognized pecking order in business relationships. Woe to the executive who forgets it.

Status intimidates. Those unaccustomed to walking the hallowed halls of corporate headquarters are awed by the silence of "assumed" efficiency. Executives who are part of corporate staff know it isn't so. Within those mahogany offices are people caught in their own status system. Some don't count, some don't know how to count, and some have already been counted out. They are people like the rest of us.

What does all this mean to us in negotiation? It tells us that buyers are uncomfortable with vice-presidents; that ordinary people hesitate to take on experts; that people tend to perceive higher executives as assertive, self-motivated, and independent whether they are or not. Status differences affect the way people act and make decisions. Status is part of the process that makes the deal and part of the deal itself.

My advice to those who face people of higher status is to take them on. You have a better chance with them than with those below. Higher executives are less apt to be prepared, less likely to have time. Take them on in a person-to-person, issue-by-issue basis. The better you prepare, the more knowledgeable you are, the less status matters. Don't be intimidated. Just work harder.

The pity is that status is important in human exchange. People of high status expect to "do to." People of low status expect to be "done to." It is impossible to live in a world of status and be oblivious to it in negotiation. Somebody once said, "Status breeds status." I am convinced that in business "status *breads* status."

STRANGE CASE OF $600 TO $700: WHEN BOTH BUYER AND SELLER HAVE DIFFERENT ASSUMPTIONS

The best way to know whether or not you are getting a good price for services is to get firm bids. However, there are times when nobody is willing to give a firm bid because there are too many unknowns in doing the job. What should the buyer do in a case like that?

I get each seller to give me bids on a minimum and maximum basis with a clear understanding of how they charge for labor and materials and how they keep time records. I also find out what problems they are most worried about.

The strange case of $600 to $700 begins when the contractor says, "It will cost you between six hundred and seven hundred dollars." Two conversations go on at the same time: one in the buyer's head and one in the seller's. The buyer thinks and talks to his or her people in terms of $600. The seller sees a $700 sale in his or her mind's eye. The parties are in a good position to reach agreement on the basis of what is in their own minds. As far as their bosses are concerned, the buyer's boss thinks of $600 while the seller's boss thinks of $700. They are both happy with the deal.

Although hopeful, the buyer tends to budget $700 in order to cover himself or herself. This helps him or her get used to the idea of paying that much. When the bill comes in at $690, he even feels that $10 was saved after all. Acceptance time has had a chance to do its work.

The seller sets his sights on doing the job for $700. It's already in his or her mental bank account. He knows that the buyer has budgeted $700. If the price can be kept to $690, the buyer will be happy. Besides, if the seller can later prove that he or she should have charged $750 in the first place, the buyer will believe he or she got a good deal. Such a buyer may even be generous enough to pay full price on extras later.

The seller who says "$600 to $700" gets *committed to the $700 ceiling*. He or she knows that the customer will be mad as a hornet at $710 and therefore wants to avoid that unpleasant situation. The bottom range of the estimate is usually figured on the low side because the seller doesn't want to lose the sale. These tendencies can prove to be an advantage to an astute buyer.

One approach to dealing with sellers of services that have a range of possible prices is to get each seller to bid on the range. Then try to trim down the high side of the most reliable bidder. At the same time, attempt to nibble for a broad definition of the work and for extra services. These are fairly easy to get at this early stage in the talks. Another effective approach is to discuss the deal with the seller and then give him or her time to think about how nice it would be to clinch the job at between $600 and $700. A few days later, a fixed price can be reached at $650 or so, based on the larger scope of work.

In the strange case of $600 to $700, both seller and buyer march together to drummers that are in their own heads. They make a deal with themselves. Therein lies the problem, and also the opportunity.

STRIKES AND WARS: HIGH-PRICED FORMS OF NEGOTIATION

Dean Acheson once said that negotiation was a form of war. He was wrong. War is a form of negotiation. The difference is important because if you accept Acheson's approach, you must accept a much more exploitive concept of negotiation.

It would be like saying that collective bargaining is a form of strike. Most of us would probably agree that this is patently ridiculous. The strike is certainly a phase of negotiation. We start at the table, move away from it, and then come back again.

The difference between bargaining that takes place before a strike and after is that before it happens both parties incorporate into their strategies and tactics an evaluation of costs and benefits. They intuitively assign probable satisfactions and dissatisfactions with each course of action. In effect, they think about a strike this way: "If we take this stand, there is a chance that the union may strike. If it does, it will cost us about so much in lost business. On the other hand, we might gain this or that." Implicit in the bargaining itself is the possibility of a strike and its associated costs. The threat is always there.

After the strike begins, negotiations continue in a secret or open way. One big difference is that the estimates of probable costs are sharpened by reality. The biggest difference is that both parties convey their resolve by accepting the real costs in preference to a deal they don't like. They test each other's strength and resolve in the marketplace of suffering.

Interestingly, there are still many hidden cards after the strike begins that neither side can evaluate accurately: how long it will last, who will give up, how the suffering itself will be accepted, and how the suffering will change the ultimate settlement when it finally does occur. The strike sharpens some realities but leaves other unknowns in its wake. The negotiation moves from the table to the picket line; from the tactic of lots of words and some actions to lots of action and some words. Power changes its face. What was 80 percent potential power and 20 percent revealed power before the strike becomes 20 percent potential power and 80 percent revealed power afterward. The strike changes decision making because it alters the cost-benefit assessments. But there are still many unknowns and intangibles that can affect the final outcome. One or both parties may even discover that they are not being hurt nearly as badly as they believed they would be.

Strikes and war are high-priced forms of negotiation. It is usually—but not always—cheaper to keep the talks contained at the table.

SUNK COST: THE VALUE OF WASTED EFFORT

The concept of sunk cost works like this: After a person has done a lot of work, he or she doesn't want to waste it by blowing the deal. People would rather take a lower margin than lose their sunk costs. In trying to recover these costs, there is more than money at stake. The more energy they put into getting the deal, the more their egos become part of the price. This applies as much to our present secretary of state as it does to your plumber.

The plumber who has spent time making a detailed estimate, driving crosstown in traffic to your home, writing up a proposal, calling you on the phone four times, preparing for negotiation, and negotiating for two hours, has a great deal of equity in doing the job. He or she would rather take less than have to start all over again with another customer. Sunk costs are part of the price even if the managerial economists don't think they are.

"SUPERKRUNCH": THE HIGH-FINANCE TACTIC

A few big companies are trying something different. It's the "superkrunch" tactic. The buyers call a bidders' conference at which all competitors sit at the table together to discuss a forthcoming proposal. Then it gets rough.

The buyers go through the previous year's purchase agreement and tell the bidders the improvements expected to be made. For example, if last year they got terms of 2 percent—10 days, this year they want 2 percent—15 days; if last year they were permitted to order in minimum lots of $50, this year they want to order in minimum lots of $25; if last year they were willing to accept B-quality merchandise, this year they want B+ quality; if last year they did their own warehousing, this year they want the seller to warehouse; if last year they got no gross-volume discount, this year they want a 5 percent gross discount. Each participant is given a chance to comment on the new demands one at a time.

During the conference, the buyers reiterate how large the order is likely to be. They elicit from one competitor or another a willingness to consider each desired improvement. The competitors go away from the conference with a vague uneasiness that the others are likely to meet the tougher requirements.

When later the bid-request package goes out, it incorporates the changes discussed. The bidders are *afraid not to meet* the new requirements and at the same time *afraid to meet them.* They are afraid to lose money on the big deal and afraid also to lose the deal to a hungry competitor. It is little wonder that the buyer usually comes out well as a result of the superkrunch.

Superkrunch is as tough a tactic as there is, especially in a buyer's market. The best countermeasure is having your salesperson attend and listen without making any commitment. Then proceed to bid as you would ordinarily. This is not easy to do. One seller handles the superkrunch by categorically prohibiting its salespeople from attending the conference. They prefer to be ignorant about the attitudes of competitors in meeting the buyer's stringent terms because those attitudes unduly affect their own pricing strategy.

The tactic is not new. It has been used in the world of high finance for at least a century. A large company decides to float a substantial bond issue. It invites a group of underwriters to the bidder's conference, which turns out to be a superkrunch. All kinds of demands are introduced as part of the bidder's package. If the deal is a big one, the underwriters leave the conference stunned and bewildered—afraid to comply and afraid not to. Needless to say, the company usually turns out to be the beneficiary of the intense pressure created by the superkrunch.

SUPERSMOKESCREENS: LONG-RANGE ROCKETS

This list of supersmokescreens is guaranteed to mix things up to a point where nobody quite knows what is going on. Unlike the short-range smokescreens discussed previously, these are the big ones, the ones that take time, money, and organization to execute. Those of us who have been executives in larger companies will quickly recognize these tactics.

1. Put a new person in charge.
2. Generate a bigger issue.
3. Broaden the problem.
4. Provide loads of detailed information.
5. Create an equal and opposite issue.
6. Stall for time until interest wanes.
7. Set up a new production system.

8. Get a good press.
9. Start a lawsuit.
10. Change the location. Go cross-country.
11. Start a small war somewhere else.
12. Lose masses of data, then reconstruct them from memory.
13. Set up a study group.
14. Conduct your own investigation. Then another.
15. Set up a committee.
16. Assassinate someone's character.
17. Find a "fall guy" and fire him or her in public.
18. Make impassioned public announcements on other subjects.
19. Conduct a summit meeting with someone.
20. Write new procedures or rules.
21. Deny that a problem exists.
22. Agree to anything, but keep doing what you were doing.
23. Take possession, then talk.
24. Set up a new accounting or estimating system.
25. Change the organization.

SURPRISES

A man came home from work. His smiling wife met him at the door and told him she had a surprise for him. She led him blindfolded into the dining room and then excused herself for a moment while he sat at the head of the table. He waited patiently even though he was suffering mild discomfort from the beans he had eaten at lunch. To relieve himself, he passed wind. A bit later, his wife came back. She asked, "Are you ready for the big surprise?"

"Yes," he said, "I sure am."

She took off the blindfold and, there before him, was a beautiful birthday cake and twelve guests.

The Japanese surprised us at Pearl Harbor but lost the war. First, it got us scared; then it got us mad. Surprise has something going for it in war and perhaps in bargaining. On balance, I believe that it is overrated as a tactic in buy-sell negotiations.

However, there are many negotiators who feel that surprise is a good way to keep the pressure on. I have been caught by surprise many times, and it still shakes me up for at least a short period of time. Before you can defend against surprise, it is well to recognize the kinds of surprises you are likely to come up against.

1. *Issue* surprises, such as new demands, new packages, backing off concessions, escalation tactics, position changes, strong evidence of resolve, risk changes, depth of argument.
2. *Time* surprises, such as deadlines, short sessions, change in pace, patience, all-night sessions, lost weekends.
3. *Move* surprises, such as walkouts, recesses, delays, smokescreens, emotional outbursts, frequent interruptions from retaliatory actions, displays of power.
4. *Information* surprises, such as depth of argument, special rules, new data back-up statistics or new sources of information, tough questions, peculiar answers, media changes.
5. *Ego* surprises, such as bursts of abuse, anger, distrustfulness, one-upmanship, disbelief, attacks on intelligence and integrity.
6. *Expert* surprises, such as the introduction of prominent specialists or consultants.
7. *Authority* and lack-of-authority surprises, such as people who have the authority but are missing or who have authority but only up to a certain limit and not more.
8. *People* surprises, such as changes in buyers, salespeople, new team members, disappearance of people, higher-level executives, status differences, the appearance of the boss, bad or good people, smart or inarticulate or hard-to-understand people. Another people surprise: when nobody at all turns up, or when someone shows up hours late.
9. *Place* surprises, such as beautiful offices, uncomfortable chairs, no air conditioning, freezing rooms, holes in the wall, noisy surroundings, big, long parties.

I don't like surprise because it creates distrust and fear. It acts as a communication block. This is not to say that a negotiator should reveal secrets before he or she needs to. Secrets are important. What worries me is that the introduction of unexpected events can cause the opposing negotiator to lose face and thereby harden his or her position. If this happens, we are both in trouble.

The best thing to do when surprised by a turn of events is to give yourself time to think. Listen, say as little as you can, and take a break. A negotiation is not a courtroom or a war. Don't respond to something new until you are prepared.

TACTICAL FLEXIBILITY: WHAT WORKS FOR ONE MAY NOT WORK FOR ANOTHER

Tactics are not enough. There is no right tactic for the wrong strategy or policy. Strategic objectives and priorities are more important than tactics. Yet history is full of great strategies that were defeated by poor tactics. The two go together but are not the same.

Flexibility in the choice of tactics is imperative. Tactics that are right for one person are wrong for another. Tactics that are appropriate at the start of a negotiation may prove unsuitable later. Tactics that worked yesterday will not work as well with the same person tomorrow. Tactics that worked in a buyers' market may prove to be stupid in a period of short supply.

Continual reassessment is the key to good tactical planning. I ask myself these questions over and over again in every negotiation:

1. Can I combine tactics for better effect?
2. Is this a good time to change tactics?
3. Should penalties be prescribed for unethical tactics?
4. How will the other party react or interpret my tactic?

5. Will it backfire on me?
6. If my tactic is rebuffed, will I lose face or bargaining power? How can I minimize the loss?

The choice of tactics involves ethical questions. Ends do not justify means in business or politics. Whether they like it or not, people in business must also be philosophers when it comes to choosing tactics.

In deciding which tactic to use, one rule should not be forgotten: *Never use a tactic unless you have considered what countermeasures your opponent is likely to take.* Not to do so may put you in the same position as a purchasing agent I knew. He told the salesperson, "Take it or leave it," and got fired because of it. The seller sold the whole inventory to someone else. The key to good tactics is *flexibility and business judgment.*

TACTICS AND ETHICS

The two hundred or so tactics in this book represent means to an end for the people who negotiate. They are not ends in themselves. Ends and means cannot be separated from one another. Unethical tactics for achieving worthwhile goals ultimately destroy the positive value of those goals. Unethical means tend to become ends in themselves.

Most of the tactics discussed in this work are ethical. Those that are not have no place in the business world. Those in the gray area between right and wrong should be looked at with skepticism. The fact remains, however, that there are people whose standard of integrity is so distorted that anything is acceptable. To protect ourselves, it is necessary to understand both ethical and unethical tactics and to recognize when they are being employed by an opponent.

TAKE IT OR LEAVE IT: WHEN DOES IT MAKE SENSE?

"Take it or leave it" is negotiation. There are many bargaining situations in which it is appropriate. The tactic has a legitimate place at the table.

One doesn't usually think of "take it or leave it" in long-term labor negotiations. The classic example of one company that did is General Electric, who used it for more than twenty years. General Electric would always open its bargaining sessions with a final offer. The company was careful to back its offer with a mass of detailed breakdowns, facts, and statistics. The tactic worked from 1947 to 1969. Then it didn't. The electrical workers finally decided to leave it. The costliest strike in General Electric's history followed.

Anyone thinking about using "take it or leave it" can learn from General Electric's experience. The tactic aroused intense hostility. It caused the opposing negotiators to lose face. By backing the membership into an "either-or" position, it deprived them of freedom and self-respect. So affected was the union by this frustration that 1969 brought more than a strike. It was a holy war.

Most American business is conducted on a take-it-or-leave-it basis whether we call it that or not. Prices are marked in stores. Some, like your telephone bill, are fixed by regulation. Many industrial goods and services are sold at the same price to all customers. "Take it or leave it" is not as ominous as it sounds. It often represents good pricing policy for the seller and a better way for the buyer to buy.

"Take it or leave it" makes sense under these conditions:

1. When you don't want to encourage future dickering
2. When a drop in price to one customer will force a drop to all

3. When the other party can't afford to leave it
4. When all customers are accustomed to paying the price
5. When you can't afford to risk a loss because you are selling at rock-bottom.

If you are going to give someone a "take it or leave it," there are ways to minimize hostility. First, never use the expression itself because the words alone are enough to anger a saint. Take-it-or-leave-it positions that are backed by legitimacy are less offensive. When a firm price is backed by Robinson-Patman regulations, published lists, clearly seen price tickets, or trade custom, it tends to be accepted more easily. The same is true when the firm price is accompanied by a good explanation and positive proof statements. People are more apt to accept a "take it or leave it" later in a negotiation than earlier. Timing is important in reducing hostility.

"Take it or leave it" is a legitimate tactic of negotiation. A surprising number of people welcome it because it saves them the trouble of bargaining. If you are going to use it, there are two things that you must do. First, give the other party all the time needed to discuss the matter; and second, be sure to tell your boss you are going to use it. The person who forgets that is in real deep trouble.

TAKE-IT-OR-LEAVE-IT COUNTER-MEASURES

What do you do when the other party gives you a firm but polite "take it or leave it"? There are options available. My advice is to test the price hard. It may not be as firm as it looks.

The best approach to testing a "take it or leave it" is to change the nature of the deal. Broaden the problem to include larger or smaller quantities, different quality levels, more or fewer services, extended or shorter delivery periods. Change the product mix to include new items or spare parts or training. Mix items that are not "take it or leave it" with those that are, and then negotiate the bottom-line figure.

In addition, you might want to try any of the following countermeasures to test the take-it-or-leave-it seller's resolve:

1. Walk out.
2. Protest to higher management.
3. Make the salesperson's boss put the firm and final offer in writing.
4. Talk on as though you never heard it at all.
5. Determine whether or not there are some things you can do for yourself to thereby reduce the price.

Try negotiating with a department store or any appliance store the next time you buy a refrigerator. Here are a few ways that people I know have cracked the apparently firm price. Offer to buy a washer with the refrigerator; change the date of sale; exclude installation or transportation; introduce local competitive factors; show that the price in the catalog is lower; ask when and if it is going on sale and talk about the scratched model on the floor. The firm price is not as firm as it looks.

The key to testing "take it or leave it" is to find a face-saving way by which the other person can retreat from this awkward position. If you can, the problem has a chance to evaporate. Most times you've got nothing to lose by testing the "take it or leave it." It's worth a hard try.

TAKING AWAY WHAT YOU GAVE UP YESTERDAY

It is always hard to take away something that you previously gave up. Usually it's a lot harder than saying no in the first place. Yet the tactic of opening a negotiation with demands that take away concessions granted at a previous time is an old one, one that is used time and again in collective bargaining.

This tactic usually helps reduce the opponent's aspiration level and thereby retards his or her inclination to make larger demands. There is a strong risk built into this approach because it may serve to irritate and solidify the opposition. For that reason, the demand should probably be leaked in advance. That gives acceptance time a chance to do its work and to somewhat reduce the hostility generated by surprise.

When and if the opposing party finally does restore the position it had in the first place, the degree of satisfaction it derives from the hollow victory is greater than it should be.

TELEPHONE NEGOTIATIONS: COMMON MISTAKES PEOPLE MAKE

Don't negotiate over the phone unless you have to. If you must, then be sure that you—not your opponent—are the better prepared. This advice is guaranteed to save you money and anguish. People "screw up" over the phone time and again.

There are occasions when the telephone is more efficient than face-to-face talks. Even at that, it is *imperative* that we be aware of common phone pitfalls:

1. The caller has the advantage of surprise.
2. Important things are easily omitted.
3. There is pressure to be decisive and to close.
4. Simple calculations become difficult under time pressure.
5. Calls cost money (especially long distance) and we tend to be overly aware of it.
6. It's hard to listen. Our minds drift.
7. The person called is disorganized. He or she can't find the file, the pencil, or even the secretary.

8. You can't see the other person's reactions.
9. Proof can't be given or checked.
10. Phone calls usually come when the recipient has other things on his or her mind.
11. It is hard to keep from being interrupted.

To this long list of roadblocks three more should be added. Each, by itself, could spell disaster. First, it is easier to misunderstand your opponent over the phone than in face-to-face talks. Second, there is not enough time to think. Third, it is less difficult for the other party to say no when he or she doesn't see you.

Phone negotiations are not inherently either good or bad. They are often the only sensible way to do business. However, people *do* make expensive mistakes over the phone that they would not ordinarily make. All of us have done so. I suggest that phone negotiations are dangerous. They should never be approached casually. If you can avoid them, all the better. If you can't, the dos and don'ts discussed next will help you handle them properly.

TELEPHONE NEGOTIATIONS: DOS AND DON'TS

What follows is a number of telephone negotiation dos and don'ts that make sense but are often forgotten in the heat of getting things done. We'll start with the dos:

1. If you called, listen. Get the full story. Then call back.
2. Talk less. The less you talk, the more the other party will.
3. Dry-run the phone conversation before you call.
4. Make a checklist to avoid omissions.
5. Have a calculator on your desk.
6. Lay out your work papers on a roomy table.
7. Take notes and file them quickly.
8. Confirm agreements promptly in your own words.

9. Have a ready excuse for breaking off the conversation.
10. If you are afraid that your call will be interpreted as a sign of weakness, set the stage for it beforehand.

Just as there are things that should be done to make your phone negotiations more effective, there are others that *should not be done:*

The don'ts:

1. Don't get into a phone negotiation while in the middle of a staff meeting.
2. Don't negotiate an issue to conclusion unless you understand it and have a prepared position.
3. Don't push yourself into a quick decision because phone charges are mounting.
4. Don't hesitate to call back if you discover a computation error.
5. Don't be afraid to reopen an important issue. If, after thinking about it, the deal you agreed to looks bad, have the courage to call back.

Phone negotiations work best for the person who is best prepared. There are few other occasions in business when the return on invested time is so great.

TELEPHONE NEGOTIATIONS: WHEN TO CONSIDER THEM

Although face-to-face talks are better, there are times when I deliberately choose the phone as my medium of negotiating.

The telephone is a great instrument for capturing the attention of people who might otherwise be hard to talk to. Most people find it close to impossible to let a phone ring without answering. Once they pick it up, they find it hard to put down.

Some time ago, a Chicago radio announcer learned that a bank was being robbed. He called the bank on a two-way radio.

Who do you think answered? The robber. He just couldn't resist a ringing phone. Even more incredible, the robber stayed on the phone and kept answering questions after the police surrounded him. Only when he was caught did the conversation end. Listeners found it hard to believe that a man under such pressure would stay on the phone. Psychologists were not so surprised. The robber was behaving in an ordinary way as far as ringing telephones were concerned.

Quick deals are usually bad deals for one party or the other. The phone negotiation is the ultimate quick-deal maker. Despite this, there are times when it is better to deal in this manner rather than face-to-face. The telephone can help you:

1. Say no more easily
2. Appear unconcerned
3. Sound tough
4. Seem resolute
5. Cut off discussion
6. Minimize status differences
7. Limit the flow of information
8. Talk but not listen
9. Interrupt frequently
10. Keep costs down.

But remember: Phone deals can work for you only if you are better prepared than the other person.

TENSION RELIEVERS

Negotiation is hard work. The tension can become excruciating as matters reach a crisis stage and time runs out. Martinis, tranquilizers, and chewing gum help keep tempers down. In the Middle East, worry beads serve the same purpose. But there is nothing like a funny story to relieve tension. I've known people who had a knack for breaking things up with pet quips at the right time.

I keep a file of funny negotiating stories. Someday I'll publish it as the *Negotiator's Joke Book.* Have you heard the one I call "good news–bad news"? It might come in handy when your opponent is mixing a little bad news with his good news.

There is the story of the big Indian chief whose tribe had been driven hither and yon by the white man. Things were desperate when he called the tribe together. "I've got good news and bad news for you," he said. The men grunted.

"First I'll give you the bad news," said the chief. A murmur went through the crowd. He said, "We have nothing to eat but buffalo manure." A hush fell. Here and there was heard, "Terrible, terrible, terrible."

Suddenly one brave asked, "What's the good news?"

"We've got lots of it," said the chief.

There have been many times in negotiation when I've felt that I was being offered lots of it also.

Then there is the one on good explanations. It's about a Gulf War vet who spent four months there, got shot up, and won a few medals. Finally he got his chance to return home and immediately sent a telegram to his waiting wife. It read: WILL SEE YOU AT THE HOUSE ON SATURDAY AT 2:00. CAN'T WAIT. LOVE.

When he got to the house on Saturday at 1:30, it was quiet. He found an open door in the back and walked in. Then he heard a noise in the bedroom. She must be getting ready, he thought. He rushed in to surprise her. There she was in bed with another man. Shocked, the Gulf War veteran ran from the house directly to his parents' home. He told his father about his months of suffering, the telegram, and the betrayal.

His father was a philosophical man who believed that there is an explanation for everything. So he went to see his daughter-in-law to find out what went wrong. An hour later, the father returned, all smiles.

"What happened?" asked his anguished son.

"I told you," said his father, "there is always a reason. She never got your telegram."

Labor and diplomatic negotiators tell funny stories, of course. But they do one more thing that buyers and sellers ought to follow. As a crisis gets close, they spend shorter periods at the table and longer ones in recess. It gives both parties time to think and cool off.

THIRD-PARTY INSPECTION

If I were a salesperson and you the customer, it might be important for me to prove that the price I am offering is identical to the price charged others. How can I prove this without showing you who my other customers are? If we could agree on a disinterested third party, I would be happy to let that person see the records and report to you. That is the essence of third-party inspection.

The right to verify information is always part of the price. Yet it is usually foolish to permit free access to your business secrets. Government auditors can act as intermediaries between parties. For example, when Boeing gives a contract to Lockheed, it has the legal right to know whether or not Lockheed's cost-estimating system and overhead rates are approved. Lockheed, a competitor of Boeing, doesn't want Boeing's people prowling around the plant. Government personnel bridge the investigative gap. They do the auditing and report their findings to Lockheed. In that way both parties are kept happy.

Third-party inspection is no guarantee of accuracy or impartiality. United Nations observer teams are often ineffective because they are not permitted to see what they need to. In some cases, the third party lacks the insight, experience, or intelligence to interpret what is seen. Some third parties are blinded by their own prejudices.

Despite their limitations, third parties can be used to build credibility in negotiation. You and I may be skeptical about one another. When a disinterested third person speaks, we are more likely to believe that person than each other.

THIRD-PARTY INTERMEDIARIES

Third-party intermediaries have been used to resolve international conflicts for centuries. Their role in collective bargaining is also well established. In buy-sell negotiations, they are used less openly but are part of the process nevertheless. Many times the astute use of third-party intermediaries has helped to avert costly litigation or to forestall impending deadlocks.

Experience with international negotiations indicates that countries prefer to deal with private parties before committing themselves to official channels. Old acquaintances, reporters, businesspeople, and church people have acted as conduits with Washington, even when official avenues of communication are closed.

There are a number of things that third parties can do better than those directly involved in a dispute. They can:

1. Invite the parties to take a step toward one another, which for ego or organizational reasons both might hesitate to take otherwise.
2. Stimulate constructive thinking on how a better deal can be made for both parties or how to avoid an impasse.
3. Produce a change of position by suggesting areas of compromise which, if brought up by either disputant, might damage its bargaining leverage or create organizational problems.
4. Represent absent parties to the conflict who also have an equity in its outcome. Such outsiders might be the public, end users of the product, stockholders, employees, banks, or subcontractors. They are rarely at the table in buy-sell negotiations but are affected by final settlement.

The ideal intermediary is hard to find. The person should be tactful, honest, matter-of-fact, and given to what one famous diplomat called "moral accuracy." His or her biases should not show. And, most of all, he or she should be capable of winning the respect of both parties.

THREAT AND HOW TO HANDLE IT

Threats are a form of concession. In effect, the threatener says, "If you stop doing what you are doing, I will concede by waiving my privilege of punishing you." The threat puts the burden of proper action on the other person. The person is, in a perverse sense, "master of his or her own fate."

Negotiation involves a degree of threat by its nature. The fact that rewards can be withheld or punishment inflicted by deadlock constitutes an ever-present threat. The question that confronts a negotiator is whether he or she will benefit by open threat. The answer depends upon five factors, each of which will be considered in greater detail.

First, threat is a tactic in negotiation, not a strategy. Buyers may win a quick concession from a seller by threatening to cut him or her off. When business conditions get better and shortages develop, buyers will find themselves last in line to fill their needs. Threat is essentially a short-run tactic that can destroy an important relationship.

Second, open threat may be appropriate when both parties know that one has the power to inflict punishment without retaliation on the part of the other. The trouble is that people who are abused tend to retaliate in subtle ways. I have seen sellers who were pushed around get even by reducing quality in ways that could not be measured. What's worse, they took a special pleasure in fooling the buyer.

Third, threats can be made more credible by escalation. When someone is exposed to small threats that are carried out, he or she is likely to believe that larger ones will also be executed.

There is little sense in using a threat unless you are reasonably sure that your opponent believes you. That isn't always as easy as it looks.

Fourth, the size of a threat has to be scaled to the size of the problem. The buyer who threatens to cut off a valued supplier and blackball him or her for one delinquent delivery is out of line. Not only does he or she create unnecessary hostility, but he or she looks foolish as well.

Fifth, uncontrolled threat is a dangerous but effective weapon. If we were to retaliate for acts of terrorism by using nuclear bombs, the earth might today look like a moonscape. The world can ill afford the simple but foolish logic of Dr. Strangelove who, in that great film, would "destroy the world to save it." Yet there is awesome power in a threat that must run its course. That is the power in starting an investigation or serving papers in a lawsuit. The wheels begin to grind and cannot easily be stopped.

From a countermeasure standpoint, it is easier to stop something from happening initially than to reverse it once it starts. If you think the other person is going to threaten to keep you from doing something you must do, then you may be better off doing it quickly. "Fait accompli" is a countermove against potential threat. Take the action, then talk. In addition, a negotiator might consider these countermeasures when faced with threat:

1. Protest to highest management. Those executives generally profess to dislike threat as a tactic.
2. Make a commitment to act. Threateners may find ways to retreat or otherwise discredit their threats if they believe that you are going to act anyway.
3. Make the price higher for the threatener by joining with others to soften the blow if the threat is executed. For example, the airlines had a joint agreement that if one airline is struck, revenues would be shared among all of them.
4. Prove that the threat can't hurt you.
5. Be obstinate or irrational. Prove that you are prepared to suffer no matter what the price. Iraq reduced the effectiveness of the world embargo and sanctions when the Iraqis demonstrated their willingness to undergo whatever hardships were thrown at them.

6. Be ignorant. Cut off communications so that the threatener is unsure whether his threatening message has been received.
7. Show the threatener that he or she has more to lose than appearances warrant.

Recent research indicates that the dangers inherent in a threat may be reduced if the threat is implied rather than spoken, mild rather than massive, and rational rather than emotional. People who have the means to threaten tend to use it. Experiments show that when two parties threaten each other, they learn to work together more quickly. But other competent investigators have concluded that when a threat is used by two parties, they stand a good chance of tearing one another apart.

I am against threat. It can create an out-of-control situation. Threat leaves a trail of hostility that does not erase easily. It may work, but the price is too high. There are better ways to make your point.

TIME TALKS

Time talks, and few know it better than lawyers and insurance companies in personal-injury cases. There are times of the year when people need money. Claims agents know they can be successful with low offers at tax time, before vacations, after Christmas, or when college tuition payments are due. Attorneys know that insurance companies settle best after a suit is initiated or a jury selected. The hour before a jury verdict is the birth pang of a negotiated settlement.

Time can convey a message of urgency by subtle means. The mention of a plane schedule, a vacation date, a national holiday, possible organization changes, or a person's retirement party has a way of softly nudging an indecisive opponent into accepting an offer. An acquaintance of mine was once trapped by clever timing into revealing his hand too early. The insurance company made a generous offer. At the same time, the claims adjuster indicated that he was going on a four-week vacation the following Monday. He suggested that it would be a good idea if the plaintiff brought all his records in on Friday. A check would be prepared immediately, and the case would be closed. My friend worked feverishly and got everything together by Friday afternoon. The claims adjuster gave him a happy smile, put the records away, and excused himself to consult with higher authority. He returned shortly and offered half of the earlier amount. The plaintiff was caught off balance. In his haste to meet the Friday deadline, he had put together a package that revealed his entire negotiating position. The claims adjuster never did go on vacation on Friday. It was just a time tactic for zeroing in on the plaintiff's top demand. A phony high offer was tied to a phony time limit.

There is a right and wrong time for everything in negotiation. April 15, Christmas, and the end of the fiscal year have caused many a piece of real estate to be bought and sold. Cost overruns, organization changes, and schedule slippages can be introduced at such a point that their impact is lessened or enhanced. Great decisions are often made because the clock says so.

The timing of a final offer contributes to its credibility. A good offer made early may look like a bluff, but one made after days of discussion can appear to be the bottom line. A well-timed long-distance call can heighten tension during the last minutes of a negotiation. The sudden replacement of a negotiator after a concession can signal that future concessions are not to be expected.

Time talks. It is the hidden language of negotiation.

TREASON WAS PREFERABLE TO DISCOMFORT

Most of us believe that the Declaration of Independence was signed by our Founding Fathers in a burst of patriotism. Not so, said Thomas Jefferson in his letters. Independence Hall was located next to a stable. The heat in July was oppressive and the flies numerous. They bit through the silk stockings of the delegates. Jefferson reported in later years, "Treason was preferable to discomfort."

There have been times in negotiation when I have found myself subjected to unpleasant conditions. They were probably designed by the opponent to lower my resistance. Here are a few that harassed me particularly:

1. Being positioned in a chair facing the sun
2. Sitting in a wobbly chair
3. Doing business in a noisy room
4. Negotiating without air conditioning in July
5. Working through the night without sleep
6. Constantly changing meeting rooms
7. Bitter coffee and soggy sandwiches
8. Third-rate hotel accommodations
9. Working with a hangover
10. Interruptions that never stop
11. Being subjected to bitter personal attack.

If you find yourself treated badly, have the courage to protest. Feel free to go over the head of the person you are dealing with. *Never accept poor treatment. It will only lead to worse abuse later.* This is true in negotiation and true in life.

I don't think you should ever make the other person uncomfortable. It's a stupid tactic. Only a fool assumes that the other person is a fool. A person facing the sun or sitting in a wobbly chair knows what is going on and resents it. He or she will try to get even given the slightest chance to do so.

TRUTH IN NEGOTIATION: A GOOD PLACE TO START

There is a belief among some buyers that if both parties could agree to the facts, the outcome of a negotiation would be better arrived at. These people reason that truth invariably leads to "light" in negotiation. Perhaps so.

Since 1950 Congress has tried to put the lid on a recurring problem: large cost overruns on defense contracts. Congress passed a "truth-in-negotiation" law designed to encourage bargaining based on facts. The Senate prescribed several penalties to discourage misrepresentation and thereby prevent windfall profits. The law required that a seller make available to the buyer current cost facts. It assumed that matters of fact and matters of judgment can be separated for negotiation purposes.

Can facts and judgments really be separated? I think not. Behind all facts are judgments and biases. Among the variables in gathering facts are such matters as who gathers them, where they come from, the methods used to accumulate them, and the assumptions behind them. It is naïve to assume that judgments and motives are absent from facts. Facts never exist in a social or business vacuum.

Truth in negotiation leaves plenty of room to negotiate. Facts are negotiable because there is always a story behind them. Honorable people can differ greatly on the assumptions and interpretations surrounding facts. If, in a perfect world, we could filter out the story and be left with "pure" facts, there would still be a vast area of uncertainty. *Facts are always past oriented. Negotiations are future oriented.* Perceptions and judgments about the future are also subject to hard bargaining.

Buyers are on the right track in demanding truth in negotiation. The more a buyer knows, the better his or her position. That is just common sense. What is dangerous is a naïve overreliance on the word "truth." Truth and facts are a good place to start. They do not determine the outcome of a negotiation. If you don't understand the story, you can't understand the price.

VALUE: THE HIDDEN VALUE OF THINGS WE MIGHT NEED SOMEDAY

Every person should have a dog because dogs don't care if you are successful or not. Once I bought a little poodle for $150. Pierre was a nice dog, but he wasn't worth $150 nohow. Why did I pay the price?

He had more royalty than the king of England. His forebears included champions of champions as far back as dog time went. I paid the $125 premium to put him in dog shows of my mind. Shows he never entered. I gave up the idea halfway through the first brushing. The premium was for something I never used. There is a high hidden value in things we might need someday.

People in negotiation pay for the privilege of using things they may never choose to use. They put a value on accessories to do something that will never come up; on services they will never call for; on performance characteristics they will never need; on manuals and magazines they will never read; on *Encyclopaedia Britannica* for free questions they will never ask; on computer runs they will not have time to understand, and on warranties for things that will never happen.

Satisfaction is in our heads. The value of choices we will rarely if ever take is higher than it should be. Free delivery charges on ice purchased in the winter is the kind of concession you might consider giving. Every business deal has a little ice in the winter buried in its price.

WAYS TO GIVE YOURSELF TIME TO THINK

History provides an excellent example of how a world leader gave himself time to think. When Soviet Premier Nikita Khrushchev met President Dwight D. Eisenhower at the summit meeting in 1956 he came away with less respect for Eisenhower. Khrushchev was wrong. This is what happened.

Khrushchev reported in his book *Khrushchev Remembers* that when he asked Ike a question, the president looked to Secretary of State John Foster Dulles for an answer. Dulles would write a note and pass it to Eisenhower. Only then did the president respond. Khrushchev recalled that he, the head of the Soviet Union, knew the answers. He didn't need somebody to tell him what to say. "Who," he asked, "was really the top man, Dulles or Eisenhower?"

Khrushchev missed the point. What he saw as a weakness was probably a hidden strength. President Eisenhower had a sufficient self-confidence to do two things: to get advice and to give himself time to think.

Never go into a negotiation without considering how to give yourself time to think. Build a thinking buffer to keep yourself from being pushed into a decision. It is remarkable what we humans see in hindsight. Giving yourself time to think changes hindsight to foresight.

The thirteen suggestions that follow are effective. They work as well in negotiating with the Internal Revenue Service as they do with buyers, heads of state, or your spouse.

1. Get the other party to present his position before breaking for the evening.
2. Arrange to get an important surprise visitor or phone call at some crucial point.

3. Go to the toilet. Diarrhea is not all that bad as an excuse.
4. Get hungry or thirsty.
5. Change a member of the team.
6. Don't have the back-up evidence available.
7. Plead ignorance. Ask for time to learn more about it.
8. Have your expert unavailable.
9. Load the other party down with documents.
10. Use an interpreter or third party. Interpreters can be technical people, lawyers, your boss, or translators. In any case, they slow things down.
11. Develop rules among your own people on how questions will be fielded. Sometimes it is best to have all questions directed only to the chief to give others time to answer.
12. Recess and caucus frequently.
13. Have a "dancer" on your team. A dancer is a person who can say much about very little.

Diplomats conduct negotiations with short sessions and long recesses. A question raised one week may sometimes be answered a full week later. Demands and offers are usually made in writing to give both parties time to respond in a sensible way. Quick deals are rare.

On the other hand, American businesspeople conduct negotiations like a Ping-Pong tournament. Buyer and seller are in a big hurry. A few quick slashes and returns, and it's over. Asians and Europeans are not nearly so hasty. They recognize the obvious: *The person who has time to think thinks better!*

WHAT IS SOMETHING WORTH?

What is a loaf of bread worth to a hungry person? There is a world of difference between what something is worth and what it costs. Things that cost little to produce can carry high price tags, and vice versa. Cost is subordinate to worth from a negotiating standpoint. It is just one of many ways to look at the broader question of value.

Different answers are possible depending on how we approach the value problem. Fourteen ways of looking at worth are shown, no two of which yield the same result:

1. Worth may be related to the buyer's ability to pass increased cost on to a third party. A product may actually be worth more to a buyer if he or she pays more for it. This happens when a percentage is added by the buyer and passed on to the customer.
2. Sellers who can build a mousetrap faster because they automate their plant can charge the same price that less efficient producers do. Their costs are irrelevant with respect to price.
3. A part that does the same work as three other parts can be worth the three it replaces.
4. Worth may be related to a buyer's gain. If a seller knows that a buyer will make a windfall gain in reselling the product, the seller may raise his or her price in order to make a claim on part of the windfall.
5. A seller may be content to merely cover direct costs if in so doing he or she can keep employees working during a slow period.
6. The worth of a service may be established by a standard or custom. When I visited a lawyer about making a will, he quoted me the published rate. Later I learned that the going rate was less.
7. Worth can be based on ability to pay. I know surgeons who have mastered rare techniques and unabashedly charge rich patients more for operations than poor patients.
8. When a publicity agent takes on an important client at a low fee, he or she is doing so in the hope that other big-name clients will be attracted.
9. Conspicuous consumption can carry a premium. Membership in an exclusive country club may permit a person to exhibit his or her importance and financial worth in a socially acceptable manner.
10. Worth and special knowledge are related. The tax accoun-

tant with experience on a specific problem may charge on the basis of what he or she knows rather than on a time basis.

11. Worth may be related to matters irrelevant to the economics of a specific transaction. In the age of mergers, small companies may be worth a lot if stock is exchanged and much less if cash is used.
12. Worth and risk go together. If I had $100,000 to my name and was given a raffle ticket that provided a fifty-fifty chance to win $1,000,000 or lose $100,000, I would sell the ticket. Although it is worth $450,000, I would take a great deal less. I could not afford to lose everything on a single wager. A billionaire might well buy this ticket for $400,000. What would you be willing to sell the ticket for if you had only $100,000 to your name?
13. Worth can be related to what might happen if the deal falls through.
14. Worth may be related to cost. In a free competitive market, it sometimes is.

Recognize that an exchange has different values to each participant. The buyer, his organization, the salesperson, and the salesperson's organization do not see the product or price the same way. The salesperson may view the sale in terms of a free trip to Hawaii while the buyer may perceive it as just another requisition to be disposed of. Neither may be deeply concerned with profit, cost, or use. The exchange is worth something different to every person involved.

Worth analysis can shed more light on an opponent's needs than volumes of cost data. Accountants and cost specialists have avoided worth because it is difficult to analyze and defend. Their avoidance is unfortunate because the key to setting sensible targets lies more in what a thing is worth than what it costs.

"WHAT-IF" AND "WOULD-YOU-CONSIDER" TACTICS: HOW TO HANDLE THEM

"What if" is a tactic for getting information from a seller that ordinarily might not be given. A buyer who knows more about the cost and price structure of a seller is bound to make better decisions concerning the choices available.

It works like this. Let us assume that a department-store buyer wants to purchase 2,000 dresses for distribution to his stores around the country. He asks the seller to quote on 200, 2,000, 10,000, and 25,000 dresses. Once the bids are in, a sharp buyer with a good cost analyst can gain a great deal of information. He or she can estimate the seller's production costs, learning experience, setup charges, capacity to produce, and marginal pricing policy. The buyer can also get a better price on the 2,000 dresses by introducing the higher quantities. Few sellers dare lose a big order bidding high on a small one.

You may well ask if it is ethical for a buyer to ask for prices on options the person does not need. The buyer's role is to make sensible business decisions based on the best information he or she can get legitimately. "What if" is a good way to get pricing data as well as other information.

I have used a good many "what ifs" as a buyer. The ones that follow usually opened up new alternatives and generated valuable answers. Their logic is self-evident.

1. What if we double the order (or halve it)?
2. What if we give you a one-year contract?
3. What if we drop the warranty (or increase it)?
4. What if we supply the material?
5. What if we own the tooling?

6. What if we buy apples and pears instead of just apples?
7. What if we let you do the job during the slow season?
8. What if we buy your total production?
9. What if we supply technical assistance?
10. What if we change the type of contract?
11. What if we change the specification like this?
12. What if we give you progress payments?

Any of these "what ifs" provide insights into the seller's business practices and motivations that would not otherwise be available.

"What if" is a little diabolical. It can drive a salesperson and his or her organization up a tree. With every "what if," the salesperson becomes an even greater pest in the eyes of his or her engineering, production, and pricing people. When a buyer says, "What if . . . " sellers jump. They find it hard to say no to the buyer's innocuous-sounding request. Many a salesperson has lowered the price rather than go through the tedious routine of repricing.

The next time the buyer asks for this type of information, the smart salesperson will make sure that he or she doesn't shoot from the hip. A well-considered answer can pay big dividends. The tips that follow will help you give better answers:

1. Probe to find out what the buyer intends to buy. He or she does not have as many options as he or she pretends to. Visit the production people. They'll tell you.
2. Never price a "what if" on the spot.
3. If a concession is offered, make it contingent on getting an order immediately.
4. Not every question deserves an answer. Explain that the warranty is part of the price package and can't be eliminated without government approval or something like that.
5. Some "what ifs" should take a very long time to answer—perhaps more time than the buyer's deadline allows.
6. Ask the buyer if he or she is prepared to order what is priced. When he or she realizes the cost, he or she may be willing to accept a ballpark estimate.

The alert salesperson can turn "what if" into an opportunity instead of a problem if it is handled right. He or she can respond to the buyer's request for information by proving that a three-year order is best for him or her. The salesperson can introduce what I call "would you consider" questions. Would you consider taking grade-B products, a larger delivery, spare parts, a change in specifications, or last year's model?

"What if" and its counterpart "would you consider" open up new avenues of thought for seller and buyer. They can lead to a better deal for both parties at the same time.

WHERE TO NEGOTIATE

In most cases, negotiate at home. In *The Territorial Imperative,* Robert Ardrey found that animals are best able to defend themselves on their own territory. So are the Los Angeles Dodgers. They win more games at home.

Men and women are territorial animals. They form a close attachment to their things. His or her chair, office, and property take on special significance. It is said that a person's home is his or her castle—perhaps because the greatest strength is likely to be there.

People who do business at home are more likely to eat and sleep regularly. They have greater resources at their fingertips, including access to specialists and higher authority. In *Future Shock,* Alvin Toffler showed that people who are exposed to change suffer physical and mental shock. Even going to the bathroom becomes a problem when you are in the other fellow's factory. We waste a good deal of physical and psychic energy just getting to a destination.

Nevertheless, under certain circumstances, a negotiator is better off negotiating away from home. I prefer it when I want to see things and check them for myself. Occasionally it is because I want to delay a decision or because I have so poor a case that fewer problems will occur out of town. When out of town it is easier to explain that the data proving your position was forgotten in the rush to leave your office.

If a negotiation must take place out of town, these precautions help:

1. Consider a neutral location.
2. Get somebody else to handle your day-to-day work.
3. Bring enough help.
4. Bring a calculator.
5. Check your reservation in advance.

Negotiation is probably the hardest work a person can do. Negotiators deserve high per-diem allowances, first-class accommodations, and at least twenty-four hours to recuperate after reaching a destination. They should be comfortable and unhurried.

On balance, given a choice, it's home for me—but there is a danger. Too many interruptions by your associates or family can turn the advantage to the other side.

WHO TALKS TOO MUCH?

Common sense says that the less the other person knows about you, the better off you are. Salespeople and buyers forget this occasionally, but the people who really mess up are others in your organization. These are the people who do not think of themselves as negotiators but as engineers, production, inspectors, accountants, and operations people. They are the ones who talk too much more often than not.

WORD COMMITMENTS: AN IMPORTANT SOURCE OF BARGAINING POWER

Thought precedes action. Words also precede action. When we say or write something, we are disposed to stand up for our statements and act accordingly.

Words are commitments. Once said, they are defended. Try a little experiment. Get a friend to give you a bit of casual advice about something. Then say that you don't see how it will help. Watch him or her begin to build argument after argument to support the advice. Try changing the subject for awhile. In a short time, he or she will bring it up again with more supporting proof. I've tried it and am convinced that people do this as much to defend their own egos as anything else. They become committed to their own words.

This behavior is of profound importance in negotiation. From a seller's standpoint, once engineers or production people in the buyer's organization state their preference for a seller's concept or product, they will defend it. It says that a seller should strive to get expressions of satisfaction from as many people in the buyer's organization as possible. It says that people who give verbal acceptance to the value of a seller's services will find it hard to back off. It says that if you get the buyers or their associates to admit that a problem exists in a competitor's proposal, it becomes difficult for them to play it down later. It says that if buyers or their people express agreement with a seller's line of reasoning, they are likely to defend it to others in the organization.

The buyer should also be getting as many commitments from the salesperson and his or her organization as possible. The seller's verbal commitments give the buyer added bargaining leverage. The buyer should get the seller's proposal and cost breakdowns in as much detail as possible. He or she should let the seller's team explain itself at length. Should get them to prove assertions. Should get higher levels of authority to commit themselves to performance. Should tie progress and cost milestones to detailed schedules. Should talk directly to the seller's engineering, production, and quality people and get them to commit themselves to satisfactory performance. Should take good notes and keep good records. Should get the seller to make one-year and five-year price forecasts. All these kinds of commitments help a buyer to negotiate.

The spoken word is a good commitment. Still better is the written word supporting the spoken word. Best yet are verbal statements accompanied by written words and word-directed actions. Get verbal commitments from the other party. They are an important source of your bargaining power.

YELLING, BITCHING, AND SCREAMING

Some people try to get their own way by deliberately yelling, bitching, and screaming. They know from experience that most people find such tactics uncomfortable to cope with. This is especially so if others are around to witness the scene. The victim cringes at the thought of having to deal with an obnoxious character. So he or she gives in. The loudmouth is accustomed to winning these battles and uses the tactic time and again to get his or her own way or to gain a better place in line than other more reasonable people.

In the days of the British Empire, the British used to insist on speaking English to the natives though few natives understood it. A British quip at that time was, "If they don't understand, speak louder. Somebody is bound to get the point." People who yell, bitch, and scream do so because they have learned like children that it is easier to scream than to take the time to persuade by rational means. In fact, the weaker their position, the more they resort to loudmouth tactics. Their plan is to intimidate the other party into submission. They know it works most of the time because they have used the same tactics since childhood.

As parents, we have a responsibility not to let our children get their own way by yelling, bitching, and screaming. If we let their tactics succeed, as adults they will be unable to cope with the normal frustrations of life. When they rant and rave, we have to call their bluff by proving calmly that the approach will not work. This takes a good deal of parental courage, patience, and self-confidence.

How can we handle the adult who uses such tactics? The question is important because many of us have to deal with people who yell, bitch, and scream in our daily work. The key defense is not to be intimidated. If you remain rational, refuse to take abuse, deal in terms of fact—not emotion, and act with quiet dignity and firmness, the loudmouth will soon stop. If not, then it is wise to bring him or her to someone at a higher level who is trained to handle the screamer with calm authority. The loudmouth has won a lot of easy victories since childhood. Don't let him or her win another one at your expense.

ZERO IN: WAYS TO FIND OUT WHAT A BUYER WILL PAY AND WHAT A SELLER WILL TAKE

Are there any ways to zero in on what a buyer will pay or a seller take? People who negotiate would love to know what the other person wants, but even if they did know, they wouldn't quite believe it anyway. Luckily, there are tactics for finding out.

The approaches that follow work—but not every time or with everybody:

1. The "what-if" approach to zeroing in: A buyer zeros in on the seller's $1-each proposal by offering to consider buying something extra if the price is reduced to 92 cents. He or she then goes for the 92 cents without the extra purchases.
2. The "would-you-consider" approach. A seller finds out whether a buyer would consider paying $250,000 for a house if the furniture were included. If the buyer bites, the seller can tell how much the buyer has in mind or has budgeted.
3. The "hot-spring-land-developer" approach: The developer tells the buyer about a deal somebody else got last year at $50,000 a lot. If the buyer says "I'd sure take that lot at that price today," the developer knows this is a live one at over $50,000.
4. The "I-think-I-can-get-it-for-you" approach. The seller finds out what a buyer is willing to pay by offering something that isn't available. He or she then switches to what is available at a higher price.
5. The "I'll-take-the-whole-lot" or "big-order" approach: The buyer is offered cloth at $30 a yard in 100-yard lots, then offers the salesperson $15 a yard for the entire lot. This can tell what the seller paid for it.
6. The "lost-sale" approach: The seller bids $1 each, then holds out as long as possible in order to get the buyer to state what price he or she is willing to pay. It is usually very low. The seller expresses surprise at the price and says that it is obvious that he or she is out of the running. The seller then asks the buyer to give an idea what the low bid really is for future reference. The buyer relaxes and talks about it. The seller then says that he or she will talk to management, returning the next day with a better last-ditch bid.
7. The "make-him-an-offer-he-must-refuse" approach: In this case the buyer makes the seller a very low offer on a boat. The seller refuses it. The buyer says that he or she obviously can't afford this boat but is curious as to what a boat like it is worth. The relaxed seller talks, never dreaming that the buyer is still in the market. The buyer then comes back with another offer.

8. The "shill" approach: A shill makes a lower offer to test the seller's reaction to it. The real buyer then negotiates from what the shill learned.
9. The "crazy" approach: The seller of a piece of property is offered cars, boats, desert land, and a lot of other nonsense for this good property. The seller laughs at the buyer because the offer is absurd. He or she then tells the buyer more than he or she should about what he or she will take because the buyer is "obviously" out of the picture. Real-estate brokers use this approach to zero in on what a seller of land really wants.
10. The "reaction-to-a-comparable-sale" approach: The seller tests the buyer's reaction to a high price by showing or telling about another sale made at that price. Buyers can test sellers' reactions to a low offer by telling them about a comparable purchase at the low price.
11. The "mistake" approach: The seller offers to sell something to the buyer at a low price to get interest. Later the offer is withdrawn because a mistake was "found."
12. The "better-product" approach: The seller finds out how much money the buyer has available by testing to see whether he or she is interested in the Oldsmobile on the Chevy lot.
13. The "worse-product" approach: The buyer finds out what the seller will take by offering to consider a somewhat lower quality, then tries to buy the higher quality for the lower price.
14. The "escalation" approach: The seller makes a deal with the buyer and then raises the price after "thinking about it."
15. The "bogey" approach: The buyer expresses great interest in the seller's product but professes to show that he or she is limited by funds from buying it. They then get an insight into the trade-offs available and are better able to zero in.
16. The "arbitration" approach: Negotiations are allowed to proceed at full pace. As many concessions as possible are extracted from the opponent. Then talks are allowed to break down. Arbitration is then used to extract further concessions.

17. The "take-it-or-leave-it" approach: The buyer gives the seller a "take-it-or-leave-it" offer to test his or her reaction.
18. The "if-I-do-this-will-you-do-that?" approach: The buyer zeros in by proposing a possible concession tied to a seller's concession. If the buyer succeeds in getting the seller to concede, he or she then tries to negotiate from that lower plateau.
19. The "what's-the-price-of-both-of-them?" approach: The buyer gets the price of two paintings. He or she then asks what the price of only one would be. The artist is usually high in quoting one only. The buyer then negotiates for the other painting based on the lower remaining price. For example, if the artist wants $800 for both paintings and wants $500 for one only, the negotiator proceeds on the basis of $300 for the second.

When all else fails, try asking a direct question. I am amazed at how often a seller will tell a buyer the least he or she will take and the frequency with which a buyer tells the seller how much he or she is willing to pay. A lot of people just want to get the whole thing over with. They come right down to their bottom line immediately.

DUMB MISTAKES I'VE MADE AT LEAST ONCE

I keep a file of dumb mistakes. More often than not, it is my own error that finds its way into the file. Some years ago, my wife contributed a gem.

We bought a new dining-room set and decided to sell our old one, which was in excellent condition. The price in the classified ad was $280. The old set was put into the living room as we eagerly awaited results from the ad. A few people called the first week but the set was either too big, too small, or too old for them. With every passing day the old set in the living room became an ever-growing nuisance. We ran another ad, this time with better results.

A woman called and graciously volunteered a lot of information she shouldn't have. She told me how long she had been looking for a set and how high priced the sets were. When told what color our set was, she volunteered that it matched her dining-room wallpaper perfectly. She expressed great satisfaction with what she termed "my reasonable price." When that conversation ended, I was sure we had a live one. I passed the good news on to my wife.

On Sunday morning the woman called and said she would be over to our house in an hour. It was an arduous thirty-mile trip for her. My wife, having read my book, *The Negotiating Game,* suggested she take over the negotiation. We laughed about it. Before the woman came, we talked about the importance of setting our targets high and making concessions carefully. We set a target of $250, which my wife agreed to reluctantly. She wanted the "thing" out of the house and expressed a willingness to take $200. I firmed up her resolve to the $250 figure. It wasn't easy.

Within ten minutes after the woman and her husband arrived, my wife returned in triumph. She had closed the deal at $250. I helped load the table and chairs onto their station wagon. After they left, I asked her, "How much did they offer?"

With a chagrined look on her face, she said, "I was hoping you wouldn't ask me that. They offered $250 and I blurted out, 'I'll take it,' just like that."

When I asked her why, the reasons were interesting. The woman was a nice person. She loved the set. There was the money and transportation all ready to go. It seemed unfair to dicker about price especially when the price paid was our target anyway. Besides, there was always a chance that the set would not be sold and would have to remain where it was forever. To this day I would guess that those nice people are kicking themselves for not offering $200 instead of $250. My wife's dumb mistake was in saying yes too soon. Their dumb mistake was in not testing her resolve better with a low offer. If they had known what a pain the "thing" was, they would have.

The mistakes discussed in this section are real. I've made them myself more than once. In most cases, nobody—including my boss—seemed to know the difference, except me. Perhaps the examples that follow will help you negotiate more effectively. I dedicate them to my wife (with her permission, of course). I wonder if this is fair. After all, she did read the book. But, my own mistakes were still rolling into the dumb-mistake folder and I was close to fifty then. Even today, there are still a lot of dumb mistakes to make.

DUMB POWER MISTAKES

The worst kind of mistakes I've made are in the area of power perception. These mistakes are serious because they recur despite intentions to do otherwise. They also tend to rob me of the bargaining leverage so necessary for effective negotiation.

Below are a few of the dumb mistakes I've made that you may be able to avoid:

1. *Do not underestimate your power*. Most people tend to have more power than they think. Only by making a systematic analysis of power can your own strength be understood. The base of power rests on firmer stuff than competition or the ability to provide financial rewards or punishment. Commitment, knowledge, risk taking, hard work, and bargaining skill are also real sources of power.

2. *Do not assume that your opponent knows your weaknesses.* Assume that he does not and test that assumption. You may be better off than you think.

3. *Don't be intimidated by status.* We are so accustomed to showing deference to rank and class differences that we carry our attitudes to the table. It is well to remember that some experts are superficial; that some people with Ph.D.s quit learning years ago; that some people in authority are incompetent; that a specialist may be excellent in his or her field but without skill in other areas; that learned people, despite high positions of power, lack the courage to pursue their convictions or have none. There is as much danger from having a "little-shot" complex as a "big-shot" complex.

4. *Don't be intimidated by statistics, precedents, principles, or regulations.* Some decisions are made on the basis of premises and principles long dead or irrelevant. Be skeptical. Challenge them.

5. *Don't be intimidated by irrationality or boorishness.* If you permit your opponent to invalidate or berate you as a person, he or she will. He or she is probably "crazy like a fox." Denounce irrationality loudly. There are members of the opponent's organization who are as disturbed about this irrationality as you are.

6. *Do not reveal your total power early.* I have found that a slow development of my power position is more effective than laying my leverage on the line immediately. Perhaps it is because the introduction of slowly developed strength reinforces comprehension by my opponent and thereby improves the probability of opinion change. The slow tempo provides time to accept ideas.

7. *Do not emphasize your own problems or the possible losses* to *yourself if deadlock occurs.* In all likelihood, there are constraints on your opponent's action as severe as those on yourself. Concentrate on his or her problems. They are your opportunities.

8. *Do not forget that your opponent is at the table because he or she believes there is something to gain by being there.* You may discover that this negotiation, no matter how small it is, is part of a larger framework in your opponent's objectives. This alone may provide you greater bargaining power than is apparent from the situation. Be positive in your approach. Assume that your opponent wants agreement as much as you do. If he or she doesn't, learn why.

DUMB CONCESSION MISTAKES

These are mistakes almost everybody makes. The reasons are many. For the most part, errors in concession occur because people forget what they are doing. I'm sorry to say that I've made every one of the mistakes below and will again if I don't discipline myself. It's been pretty expensive.

1. *Do not set the initial demand near your final objective.* An important government contract manager, Gordon W. Rule, said, perhaps too strongly:

> In every negotiation it must be assumed—unless you are dealing with juveniles—that your opposite numbers will always table maximum positions first. Equally important it must be assumed—unless you are dealing with fools—that your opposite numbers have not disclosed their minimum positions in any matter.

There is sufficient evidence to conclude that it pays to start high. Don't be shy about asking for everything you might want and more.

2. *Do not assume you know what your opponent wants*. It is far more prudent to assume that you do not know and then proceed to discover the realities of the situation by patient testing. If you proceed to negotiate a deal on the basis of your own untested estimates, you are making a serious mistake.

3. *Do not assume that your aspiration level is high enough*. It is possible that your demands are too modest, or too easy to achieve. Your opponent may not know what he or she wants or may have a set of values quite different from your own.

4. *Never accept the first offer*. Many people do if the offer is as high as they expected or hoped to get. There are two good reasons not to: First, your opponent is probably willing to make some concessions. Second, your opponent will be left with the feeling that he or she was a bit foolish for starting too high. In either case, the negotiator who takes the first offer too fast makes a mistake.

5. *Never give a concession without obtaining one in return*. Don't give concessions away free or without serious discussion. A concession granted too easily does not contribute to your opponent's satisfaction nearly as much as one that he struggles to obtain.

6. *Do not agree with an opponent who claims that an issue is beyond compromise on the basis of principle or some other criterion. Every issue may be negotiable*. Not long ago, a famous football player is rumored to have said, when asked about a conflict between his outside interests and football responsibilities, "I'm quitting football because of principle." O. J. Simpson, the ex-USC star turned

actor, who refused to play for awhile, said, "There's no principle involved in my holdout. Just money." The extent to which an opponent will exchange principle for principal must be tested.

7. *Don't make the first concession on important issues.* My experiments indicate that losers make the first concessions on major issues.

8. *Concessions that are poorly made can serve to further separate the parties rather than bring them together.* A concession may serve to raise the aspiration level of an opponent if it is interpreted as a signal of success and strength. How a concession is made is as important as the amount.

9. *When your opponent makes a concession, don't feel shy or guilty about accepting it.* Resist the impulse to tell your opponent how wise he or she is to make the concession. Be matter-of-fact about the logic of the decision.

10. *Never lose track of how many concessions you have made.* The overall number is an important matter that can provide bargaining leverage. Keep a record.

11. *Do not go into a negotiation without listing every issue beforehand. Establish an aspiration level, a minimum, and an initial asking price for each issue.* Gordon Rule suggests that the issues be classified in terms of "must" and "give" categories. He further recommends that "give" issues be combined with "must" issues in order to preserve an "aura of flexibility" at all times. His suggestions make good sense.

12. *Do not dissipate your "bank account of flexibility." Flexibility is like money in a checking account.* Every concession should bring you closer to some goal. If all concessions have been used up, then deadlock is harder to avoid.

13. *Do not telegraph your concession pattern too clearly.* Each concession should point to a possible settlement. However, your opponent should not be certain as to where it will be or whether it will be.

14. *The buyers should not honor a high demand by making a counteroffer.* They should insist that the seller reduce the initial demand before a counteroffer is made. If the buyers cannot do this, they should respond with a supportable but low offer.

15. *Don't make concessions until you know all the demands.*

16. *Do not feel constrained to stick with a concession on a specific issue.* The whole agreement is more important than individual issues. Indicate to your opponent that all concessions on issues are tentative and based on a satisfactory overall agreement. Some people tend to stick to interim concessions when they should not. They fear that their integrity may be impugned if they retreat from a tentative agreement. Such rigidity can be costly, especially if your opponent shows no such scruples.

17. *Don't concede on a "quid-pro-quo" basis.* Concessions do not have to be matched in kind. Exchange little for much, later for now, little issues for bigger issues, obscure items for clear items, unmeasurable issues for measurable issues.

CRISIS AND CLOSURE MISTAKES

The mistakes made at the end of a negotiation happen so fast that they are not recognized until after the session is over. One of American's most important negotiators, a man accustomed to billion-dollar deals, told me recently about a case in which the tension got so great that he and his opponent overshot each other by making simultaneous concessions. Both were so concerned with what they were going to say that nobody in the room besides the two of them had any idea that each had conceded more than was necessary. Needless to say, they quickly split the difference and explained the unexplainable on the basis of arithmetical errors.

The mistakes below happen to anybody under pressure:

1. *Never make the error of assuming that an impasse on an issue will result in deadlock in the overall negotiation.* If an impasse develops, go on to the next issue.

2. *Do not be intimidated by your opponent's last and final offer.* He or she will probably be back (perhaps with hat in hand). Help to save face when he or she returns.

3. *Deadlock is unpleasant for both parties, not only for yourself.*

4. *Do not be afraid to admit that you have made an error in coming to an agreement.* If some error in fact, judgment, or statistics has

been made that affects the final agreement, it should be dealt with promptly. Admitting such mistakes takes courage. Some people prefer to bury these errors because they are usually not seen by outside observers.

5. *Do not make a last and final offer until you have evaluated precisely how the statement will be made and how discussions will be continued if it is not honored.* Never bluff unless you know what you will do if your bluff is called.

6. *Do not fail to prepare members of the home organization for deadlock or threat tactics by the opponent.* If deadlock occurs or threats are executed and those at home are unprepared, then your opponent will have the psychological advantage.

7. *Never get panicked into a final agreement by a time deadline.* It is easy to fall into the time trap. Be skeptical about deadlines. Most of them are negotiable.

8. *A final agreement is not necessarily fair or reasonable.* It is the one that occurred when each party believed that further concessions were either unimportant, unobtainable, or available only at great risk of loss. There is no point in worrying whether your opponent has been given a fair deal. It is hard enough to determine if the outcome was fair to yourself. Both parties believe they have gained satisfaction from the negotiation, or they would not have signed the agreement. Would you?

9. *Don't be afraid to break an oncoming impasse by changing the time shape of money.* It is an excellent way to keep talking and be sure you are heard. Everybody tends to put different values on present and future flows of money or satisfactions—accountants in particular.

10. *You will not succeed in winning objectives if you try to be liked in this final phase of negotiation.* The crisis stage is a severe test of each party's intentions and motives. It is not a social tea, nor is it fun. The person who wants to be liked will give away quite a lot.

On occasion, the difference between the positions of opposing parties is so great that negotiations appear useless. We see this clearly in the international sphere where, for example, the Israeli and Arab viewpoints are, at first glance, irreconcilable. Buyers are reluctant to bargain with a seller whose price is very high, and sellers feel much the same way. This is a mistake most of us make. No matter how far apart people are, they can and should negotiate if a matter is important enough.

OTHER DUMB MISTAKES

The ten dumb mistakes below are of a general nature. They happen more often than people like to admit.

1. *Negotiation is not a contest.* With a little effort, a better deal can be found for both parties at the same time.

2. *Don't start a negotiation with a chip on your shoulder, or on a discourteous note.* President John F. Kennedy once said, "Civility is not a sign of weakness." There is no point to abusing an opponent. An attack on a person's ego serves only to heighten resistance. He or she will harness energies to protect not only assets, rights, and privileges but his or her self-importance. A negotiator jeopardizes his or her objectives by attacking an opponent's dignity or invalidating his or her self-worth. If you are angry, write your opponent a long letter, then tear it up. The longer the letter, the better you will feel.

3. *Never let an issue be discussed unless you are prepared for it.* The temptation to play it by ear must be resisted. Nobody is smart enough to know what to do unless he or she thinks about it first.

4. *Never fear to negotiate, no matter how great the differences are.* It is impossible for both parties to recognize where and how a deal can be made. The final outcome may become apparent only after extended discussions. President Kennedy said, "Let us never negotiate out of fear. But let us never fear to negotiate." An agreement is possible even when its structure is not the least bit apparent.

5. *Don't negotiate with a second-rate team.* Too much is at stake to use mediocre assistance. A team leader must select people whom he or she respects. It is more important to have tough-minded experts at your side than "nice guys."

6. *As a manager, don't let complaints about your negotiators cause you to overreact.* Complaints by your opponent are probably a sign that all is going well for your side.

7. *Never go into an important negotiation without inoculating your team*. No plan is complete without considering how you will defend yourself against arguments. Inoculation may be achieved in a variety of ways, one of which is the devil's-advocate approach. Despite the importance of running through your opponent's arguments beforehand, I have seen this tactic only rarely. Discipline yourself to do it. You'll be glad you did.

8. *Don't concentrate exclusively on cost analysis*. Worth analysis is even more important. The more you demand from your people in terms of quality analysis and preparation, the more they will deliver.

9. *Don't assume that your opponent knows what he or she has to gain from a settlement*. Take the time to spell out each of the short- and long-run benefits as clearly as possible. You may be making it easier for him or her to sell the deal to his or her own people.

10. *Don't talk. Listen!*

CONCLUSION

Dumb mistakes are easier to recognize when somebody else makes them than when we do. They are also easier to view in hindsight than to avoid beforehand. Knowledge *does* improve bargaining skill, but theoretical knowledge alone is not good enough. The best way to deepen your knowledge is by doing a postmortem after every negotiation. Put your mistakes (and those of others) on a 3 × 5 card. Go through the "dumb-mistake" file once in a while, especially before a big negotiation. You will find it worth the effort.

By the way, don't ever show the file to your boss. That would be a really dumb mistake.

RATE YOURSELF AS A NEGOTIATOR

1. Do you generally go into negotiation well prepared?
   (a) Very frequently
   (b) Often
   (c) Sometimes
   (d) Not very often
   (e) Play it by ear

2. How uncomfortable do you feel when facing direct conflict?
   (a) Very uncomfortable
   (b) Quite uncomfortable
   (c) Don't like it but face it
   (d) Enjoy the challenge somewhat
   (e) Welcome the opportunity

3. Do you tend to believe what you are told in negotiations?
   (a) No, I'm very skeptical
   (b) Moderately skeptical
   (c) Sometimes unbelieving
   (d) Generally trusting
   (e) Almost always believing

4. To what extent is it important to you to be liked?
   (a) Very important
   (b) Quite important
   (c) Important
   (d) Not too important
   (e) Doesn't make any difference

5. Are you an optimizer in your business dealings?
   (a) Almost always concerned with optimizing
   (b) Quite often concerned
   (c) Moderately concerned
   (d) Not very concerned
   (e) It doesn't matter much at all

6. How do you look at negotiation?
   (a) Highly competitive
   (b) Mostly competitive but a good part cooperative
   (c) Mostly cooperative but a good part competitive
   (d) Very cooperative
   (e) About half cooperative and half competitive

7. What kind of deal do you go for?
   (a) A good deal for both parties
   (b) A better deal for you
   (c) A better deal for him or her
   (d) A very good deal for you and better than no deal for them
   (e) Every person for himself/herself

8. Do you like to negotiate with merchants (furniture, cars, major appliances)?
   (a) Love it
   (b) Like it
   (c) Neither like nor dislike it
   (d) Rather dislike it
   (e) Hate it

9. When a deal you made turns out to be quite bad for the other party, do you let him or her negotiate a better deal?
   (a) Willingly
   (b) Sometimes
   (c) Reluctantly
   (d) Hardly ever
   (e) It's his or her problem

10. Do you have a tendency to threaten?
   (a) Very often
   (b) Quite often
   (c) Occasionally
   (d) Infrequently
   (e) Very rarely

11. Do you express your viewpoint well?
   (a) Very good
   (b) Above average
   (c) Average
   (d) Below average
   (e) Pretty badly

12. Are you a good listener?
   (a) Very good
   (b) Better than most
   (c) Average
   (d) Below average
   (e) Poor listener

13. How do you feel about ambiguous situations—those which have a good many pros and cons?
   (a) Very uncomfortable—like things one way or another
   (b) Fairly uncomfortable
   (c) Don't like it but can live with it
   (d) Undisturbed—find it easy to live with
   (e) Like it that way—things are hardly ever one way or another

14. When people express ideas you don't agree with, how do you listen?
   (a) Turn them off
   (b) Listen a little but find it very hard
   (c) Listen a little but don't mind it too much
   (d) Listen reasonably well
   (e) Listen attentively and well

15. How thoroughly do you negotiate with people in your own organization in setting priorities and goals (before the session)?
   (a) Moderately often and moderately well
   (b) Not very often and not well
   (c) Negotiate hard, often and well
   (d) Negotiate pretty often and reasonably hard with them
   (e) Generally do what is required and expected without negotiating with them

16. How would you feel about negotiating a 10 percent raise with your boss if the average raise in the department is 5 percent?
   (a) Don't like it at all—would avoid it
   (b) Don't like it but would make a pass at it reluctantly
   (c) Would do it with little apprehension
   (d) Make a good case and not afraid to try it
   (e) Enjoy the experience and look forward to it

17. Do you like to use experts in negotiations?
   (a) Very much
   (b) Quite a lot
   (c) Occasionally
   (d) If I have to
   (e) Rarely

18. Are you a good team leader?
   (a) Very good
   (b) Quite good
   (c) Fair leader
   (d) Not very good
   (e) Lousy leader

19. Do you think clearly under pressure?
   (a) Yes, very well
   (b) Better than most people
   (c) About average
   (d) Below average
   (e) Not well at all

20. How good is your business judgment?
    (a) Experience shows that it's very good
    (b) Good
    (c) As good as most other executives
    (d) Not too good
    (e) I hate to say it, but I guess I'm not quite with it when it comes to business matters

21. What do you think of yourself?
    (a) High self-esteem
    (b) Moderate self-esteem
    (c) Mixed feelings
    (d) Not too good
    (e) Not much

22. Do you get respect from others?
    (a) Easily
    (b) Most of the time
    (c) Occasionally
    (d) Not usually
    (e) Rarely

23. Do you consider yourself a tactful, discreet person?
    (a) Very much so
    (b) Pretty much so
    (c) Reasonably
    (d) I slip fairly often
    (e) I seem to talk first and think later

24. Are you an open-minded person?
    (a) Yes—very much so
    (b) Moderately
    (c) Most of the time
    (d) Somewhat closed-minded
    (e) Pretty fixed in my ideas

25. How important do you consider integrity in yourself?
   (a) Highly important
   (b) Quite important
   (c) Moderately important
   (d) Somewhat important
   (e) It's a tough world

26. How important do you consider integrity in others?
   (a) Highly
   (b) Quite
   (c) Moderately
   (d) Somewhat
   (e) Every person has to care for himself/herself

27. When you have the power, do you use it?
   (a) I use it to the extent I can
   (b) I use it moderately without any guilt feelings
   (c) I use it in behalf of justice as I see justice
   (d) I don't like to use it
   (e) I take it easy on the other person

28. How sensitive to body language are you?
   (a) Highly sensitive
   (b) Quite sensitive
   (c) About average
   (d) Less observant than most
   (e) Not very observant

29. How sensitive are you to the other person's motivations and wants?
   (a) Highly sensitive
   (b) Quite sensitive
   (c) Moderately
   (d) Less sensitive than most people
   (e) Not sensitive

30. How do you feel about getting personally involved with the other parties?
   (a) I avoid it
   (b) I'm quite uncomfortable
   (c) Not bad—not good
   (d) I'm attracted to getting close to them
   (e) I go out of my way to get close—I like it that way

31. How well do you penetrate the real issues of negotiation?
   (a) I generally know what counts
   (b) I get it right most of the time
   (c) I can guess at it fairly well
   (d) I get a lot of surprises
   (e) I find it hard to know what the real bottom-line issue is

32. What kind of targets do you tend to set in negotiations?
   (a) Very hard to reach targets
   (b) Quite hard to reach
   (c) Not too hard—not too easy
   (d) Fairly modest targets
   (e) Not too hard—relatively easy targets

33. Are you a patient negotiator?
   (a) Almost always
   (b) More than average
   (c) Average
   (d) Below average
   (e) I get it over with—what's the point of fooling around?

34. How committed are you to your goals in negotiation?
   (a) Very strong commitment
   (b) Quite
   (c) Somewhat
   (d) Not too committed
   (e) Pretty flexible—no sense driving too hard

35. Are you persistent in negotiations?
(a) Very, very persistent
(b) Quite persistent
(c) Fairly persistent
(d) Not very persistent
(e) Not persistent

36. How sensitive are you to the personal issues facing the opponent in negotiation? (The nonbusiness issues like job security, workload, vacation, getting along with the boss, not rocking the boat.)
(a) Very sensitive
(b) Quite sensitive
(c) Moderately
(d) Not too sensitive
(e) Hardly sensitive at all

37. How committed are you to your opponents' satisfaction?
(a) Very committed—I try to see that they don't get hurt
(b) Somewhat committed
(c) Neutral, but I hope they don't get hurt
(d) I'm a bit concerned
(e) It's every person for himself/herself

38. Do you tend to emphasize the limits of your power?
(a) Yes, very much so
(b) Usually more than I like to
(c) I weigh them moderately
(d) I don't dwell on them
(e) I am a positive thinker most of the time.

39. Do you study the limits of the other person's power?
(a) Very much so
(b) Quite a bit
(c) I weigh them
(d) It's hard to do because I'm not him or her
(e) I let things develop at the session

40. How do you feel about making a very low offer when you buy?
   (a) Terrible
   (b) Not too good, but I do it sometimes
   (c) Only occasionally do I do it
   (d) I try it often and don't mind doing it
   (e) I make it a regular practice and feel quite comfortable

41. How do you usually give in?
   (a) Very slowly if at all
   (b) Moderately slowly
   (c) About at the same pace my opponent does
   (d) I try to move it along a little faster by giving more
   (e) I don't mind giving hefty chunks and getting to the point

42. How do you feel about taking risks that affect your career?
   (a) Take considerably larger risks than most people
   (b) Somewhat more risk than most
   (c) Somewhat less risk than most people
   (d) Take slight risks on occasion, but not much
   (e) Rarely take career risks

43. How do you feel about taking financial risks?
   (a) Take considerably larger risks than most people
   (b) Somewhat more risk than most
   (c) Rarely take any risk
   (d) Take slight risk on occasion but not much
   (e) Considerably less risk than most people

44. How do you feel with those of higher status?
   (a) Very comfortable
   (b) Quite comfortable
   (c) Mixed feelings
   (d) Somewhat uncomfortable
   (e) Very uncomfortable

45. How well did you prepare for the negotiation of the last house or car you bought?
(a) Thoroughly
(b) Quite well
(c) Moderately
(d) Not well
(e) Played it by ear

46. To what extent do you check into what the other person tells you?
(a) I check it out well
(b) I check most of it
(c) I check some
(d) I know I should check, but don't enough
(e) I don't check

47. Are you resourceful in coming up with creative solutions to problems?
(a) Very much so
(b) Quite
(c) Sometimes
(d) Not too much
(e) Hardly ever

48. Do you have "charisma"? Do people tend to look up to you and follow your lead?
(a) Very much so
(b) Quite a bit
(c) About average
(d) Not too much
(e) Definitely not

49. How experienced are you as a negotiator compared to others?
(a) Very experienced
(b) More than average
(c) Average
(d) Less than average
(e) A novice

50. How do you feel about leading people in a team?
   (a) Comfortable and natural
   (b) Fairly comfortable
   (c) Mixed feelings
   (d) Somewhat self-conscious
   (e) Quite anxious

51. Compared to your peers, how well do you think when not under pressure?
   (a) Very well
   (b) Better than most
   (c) Average
   (d) A little worse than most
   (e) Not too good

52. Do you have a short fuse when it comes to getting excited?
   (a) I'm calm
   (b) I'm basically calm but do get riled up
   (c) About like most people
   (d) I'm somewhat hot tempered
   (e) I have a short fuse

53. Do people tend to like you socially?
   (a) Very much
   (b) Quite a lot
   (c) Average
   (d) Not much
   (e) I think they don't like me

54. How secure are you in your job?
   (a) Very secure
   (b) Quite secure
   (c) Moderately secure
   (d) Rather insecure
   (e) Very insecure

55. How would you feel if you had to say "I don't understand that" four times after four good explanations?
   (a) Terrible—wouldn't do it
   (b) Quite embarrassed
   (c) Would feel awkward
   (d) Would do it without feeling too badly
   (e) Wouldn't hesitate

56. How well do you handle tough questions in negotiation?
   (a) Very well
   (b) Above average
   (c) Average
   (d) Below average
   (e) Poorly

57. Do you ask probing questions?
   (a) Very good at it
   (b) Quite good
   (c) Average
   (d) Not very good
   (e) Pretty bad at it

58. Are you closemouthed about your business?
   (a) Very secretive
   (b) Quite secretive
   (c) Secretive
   (d) Tend to say more than I should
   (e) Talk too much

59. Compared to your peers, how confident are you about your knowledge in your own field or profession?
   (a) Much more confident than most
   (b) Somewhat more confident
   (c) Average
   (d) Somewhat less confident
   (e) Not very confident, frankly

60. You are the buyer of some construction services. The design is changed because your spouse wants something different. The contractor now asks for more money for the change. You need him or her badly because he or she is well into the job. How do you feel about negotiating the added price?
   (a) Jump in with both feet
   (b) Ready to work it out but not anxious to
   (c) Don't like it but will do it
   (d) Dislike it very much
   (e) Hate the confrontation

61. Do you wear your heart on your sleeve? Do you tend to telegraph your feelings easily?
   (a) Very much so
   (b) More than most people
   (c) About average
   (d) Not very often
   (e) Hardly ever

SCORE SHEET

Add your positive and negative scores separately, according to the table below. Subtract them from each other. This will give you a total point score from –668 to +724. (For example, if you selected answer (b) to question 1, your score would be +15. Selection of answer (a) to question 2 gives you a score of –10, selection (d) to question 3 gives you a score of –4, and so on.)

Question	*(a)*	*(b)*	*(c)*	*(d)*	*(e)*
1	*+20*	*+15*	*+ 5*	*–10*	*–20*
2	*–10*	*– 5*	*+10*	*+10*	*– 5*
3	*+10*	*+ 8*	*+ 4*	*– 4*	*–10*
4	*–14*	*– 8*	*0*	*+14*	*+10*
5	*–10*	*+10*	*+10*	*–5*	*–10*
6	*–15*	*+15*	*+10*	*–15*	*+ 5*
7	*0*	*+10*	*–10*	*+ 5*	*– 5*
8	*+ 3*	*+ 6*	*+ 6*	*– 3*	*– 5*
9	*+ 6*	*+ 6*	*0*	*– 5*	*–10*
10	*–15*	*–10*	*0*	*+ 5*	*+10*

Question	(a)	(b)	(c)	(d)	(e)
11	+ 8	+ 4	0	– 4	– 6
12	+15	+10	0	–10	–15
13	–10	– 5	+ 5	+10	+10
14	–10	– 5	+ 5	+10	+15
15	+ 8	–10	+20	+15	–20
16	–10	+ 5	+10	+13	+10
17	+12	+10	+ 4	– 4	–12
18	+12	+10	+ 5	– 5	–10
19	+10	+ 5	+ 3	0	– 5
20	+20	+15	+ 5	–10	–20
21	+15	+10	0	– 5	–15
22	+12	+ 8	+ 3	– 5	– 8
23	+ 6	+ 4	0	– 2	– 4
24	+10	+ 3	+ 5	– 5	–10
25	+15	+10	+ 5	0	–10
26	+15	+10	+ 5	0	–10
27	+ 5	+15	+10	– 5	0
28	+ 2	+ 1	0	– 1	– 2
29	+15	+10	+ 5	–10	–15
30	–15	–10	0	+10	+15
31	+10	+ 5	+ 2	– 2	–10
32	+10	+15	+ 5	0	–10
33	+15	+10	+ 5	– 5	–15
34	+12	+12	+ 5	– 5	–15
35	+10	+12	+ 3	– 3	–10
36	+16	+12	+ 4	– 5	–15
37	+12	+ 6	0	– 2	–10
38	–10	– 8	0	+ 8	+12
39	+15	+10	+ 5	– 5	–10
40	–10	– 5	+ 5	+15	+15
41	+15	+10	– 3	–10	–15
42	+ 5	+10	0	– 3	–10
43	+ 5	+10	– 5	+ 5	– 8
44	+10	+ 8	+ 3	– 3	–10
45	+15	+10	+ 5	– 5	–15
46	+10	+10	+ 3	– 5	–12
47	+12	+10	+ 3	0	– 5

Question	*(a)*	*(b)*	*(c)*	*(d)*	*(e)*
48	*+10*	*+ 8*	*+ 3*	*0*	*– 3*
49	*+ 5*	*+ 3*	*0*	*– 1*	*– 3*
50	*+ 8*	*+ 5*	*+ 3*	*0*	*–12*
51	*+15*	*+10*	*+ 5*	*0*	*– 5*
52	*+10*	*+ 6*	*0*	*– 3*	*–10*
53	*+10*	*+ 8*	*+ 4*	*– 2*	*– 6*
54	*+12*	*+10*	*+ 5*	*– 5*	*–12*
55	*– 8*	*– 3*	*+ 3*	*+ 8*	*+12*
56	*+10*	*+ 8*	*+ 2*	*– 3*	*–10*
57	*+10*	*+ 8*	*+ 3*	*0*	*– 5*
58	*+10*	*+10*	*+ 8*	*– 8*	*–15*
59	*+12*	*+ 8*	*+ 4*	*– 5*	*–10*
60	*+15*	*+10*	*0*	*–10*	*–15*
61	*– 8*	*– 6*	*0*	*+ 5*	*+ 8*

After you have computed the total point score, you can determine whether you fall into the highest, lowest, or intermediate range.

Highest Quarter Ranking	+376 to +724
Second Quarter Ranking	+28 to +375
Third Quarter Ranking	–320 to +27
Lowest Quarter Ranking	–668 to –321

Take the test again six months from now and compare results. If you want another viewpoint, let your boss rate you. Then compare his or her thinking to yours.

INDEX